'Dove Cottage'. A painting by Dora Wordsworth. Here William and Dorothy lived together. Dora lived here as a small child.

By the same author:

Columba: Hermit Volume II 1994

Chedworth and Other Sites (Poems)
Arbor Vitae Press 1995

DOROTHY WORDSWORTH
On A Wander By Ourselves

by

ANNABEL THOMAS

NEW MILLENNIUM
292 KENNINGTON ROAD, LONDON SE11 4LD

Printed and bound by B. W. D. Ltd. Northolt, Middx.
Issued by New Millennium*
ISBN 1 85845 063 2
*An imprint of The Professional Authors' & Publishers' Association

For my mother

In living with her brother William, Dorothy Wordsworth had, to some degree escaped the servitude of women in those days when there was no extensive education for women and very few careers open to them. She had escaped being subservient to an uncongenial husband, or to stupid relations. She was an exceptional woman remarkable in her character, a great writer and she was sister soul and an inspiration and a great friend to her brother William. In their life alone together she found immense fulfilment in inspiring him and writing herself.

Dorothy and William's life together was one of harmony and love, often she directly inspired him by writing of, and seeing, beauties before him - 'Daffodils' 'Westminster Bridge'.

In her journal there are many evidences and entries of their tender friendship and love. Dorothy was very upset when William went away - to Yorkshire, or anywhere - and once even slept in his bed when he was absent; she felt so lonely once when, on expecting his return, she heard that he'd been seen on the road, she writes: 'I believe I screamed'. William wrote many beautiful tributes to her: *Among all lovely things my love had been* and many more.

Dorothy was admired by her friend Coleridge, Hazlitte was enchanted by her. Thomas de Quincy the writer, author of *Confessions of an English Opium Eater* and *Recollections of the Lakes and the Lake Poets* was a friend and admirer of both William and Dorothy. De Quincy, who lived in Dove cottage after the Wordsworths, wrote describing Dorothy 'Her face was of Egyptian brown; rarely in a woman of English birth had I seen a more determinate gypsy tan. Her eyes were not soft, as Mrs. Wordsworth's, nor were they fierce or bold; but they were wild and startling, and hurried in their motion. Her manner was warm and even ardent; her sensibility seemed constitutionally deep; and some subtle fire of impassioned intellect apparently burned within her, which, being alternately pushed forward into a conspicuous expression by the irresistible instincts of her temperament, and then immediately checked in obedience to the decorum of her sex and age and her maidenly condition (for she had rejected all offers of marriage out of pure sisterly regard to her brother and his children) gave to her whole demeanour and to her conversation, an air of embarrassment and even of self-conflict, that was sometimes distressing to witness. Even her very utterance and enunciation often, or rather generally,   suffered in point of clearness and steadiness from the agitation of her excessive organic sensibility and, perhaps, from some morbid irritability of the nerves. At times the self-counteraction and self-bafflement of her feelings caused her even to stammer. But, on the other hand, she was a person of very remarkable endowments intellectually; and, in addition to the other great services which she rendered her brother, this I may mention as greater than all the rest and it was one which equally operated to the benefit of every casual companion in a walk, viz the exceeding sympathy, always ready and always profound, by which she made all that one could tell her, all that one could describe, all that one could quote from a foreign   author, reverberate as it were, *à plusieurs reprises*, to ones own feelings, by the manifest impression it made upon her. The pulses of light are not more quick or more inevitable in their flow and undulation than were the answering and echoing movements of her sympathising attention. Her knowledge of literature was irregular, and not systematically built up. She was content to be ignorant of many things; but what she knew and had really mastered, lay where it could not be disturbed - in the temple of her own most fervid heart'.

In 1802 William brought an old friend of theirs to live with them - he married Mary Hutchinson.

Dorothy's beautiful journal at Grasmere begins in May 1800 and continues until January 16th. 1803. Did she need the intimate friendship of just herself and William living alone together to write so beautifully?

William and Mary's first child, John, was born in June 1803. Dorothy wrote happily of this in a letter to her friend Mrs. Clarkson. The Coleridges' also had a new baby, their only daughter Sara, born in December 1802. The Coleridges' children, who lived with their parents in nearby Greta Hall, were frequent visitors to the

Wordsworths staying weeks at a time. Dorothy was very fond of the Coleridge children Hartley, Derwent and Sara.

Soon after the birth of the baby John, William, Dorothy and Coleridge set of in a jaunting car for a tour of Scotland, leaving Joanna Hutchinson to keep Mary and John company. Dorothy wrote her recollections of this tour which are almost all happiness. William also found it inspiring and wrote *To a Highland Girl* and *The Solitary Reaper*, Coleridge, however, left them after a fortnight to go off on his own.

Once on his own Coleridge cheered up and did a walking tour of the highlands. He saw more of Scotland than the Wordsworths, going to Fort William and Inverness and returning to Edinburgh two days before the Wordsworths arrived there.

Though he had a breakdown at an inn in Fort William due to opium withdrawal the highlanders looked after him kindly and he recovered. He was shocked awake by the news of the death of Southeys only daughter, Margaret, which he got at Perth, and that Southey grieving, was coming to Greta Hall for comfort.

Dorothy and William stuck mainly to the Trossachs. At the border country they called on Walter Scott. Scott had much in common with Wordsworth; he was the son of a lawyer - he had only published a collection of Border ballads at that time - he enjoyed nature walking, he and his wife invited Dorothy and William in to breakfast and he helped and guided Dorothy and William, took them to Melrose Abbey and read them *The lay of the last minstrel*, his latest poem, he also found them inns.

On their return to Grasmere Coleridge planned to go to Malta, hoping to improve his health, and Dorothy set to work to copy out all William's poems for Coleridge to take with him. She wrote her lovely *Recollections of a tour made in Scotland* (AD 1803), this I have included.

CHAPTER 1

Dorothy was happy as a little girl with her friend Jane, who lived opposite her Aunt in Halifax and was the same age; both girls running wild in the fields and in and out of each other's houses.

Dorothy, who later walked everywhere like a Gypsy, often walked with William and his wife Mary, whose unladylike ambition was to walk the Alps on foot.

Dorothy was sent to a little boarding-school for a year or so, which she enjoyed, and there she learnt much in accomplishments and basic subjects.

However, upon the death of her father, there was less money as his employer, the Earl of Lowther, refused to pay the debts he owed him (her father having spent much on the Earl of Lowther's behalf out of his own pocket, by way of a loan). As the children were unable to receive what was owing them, and as their guardian uncles - Richard Wordsworth on their father's side and Christopher Cookson on their mother's side - only inherited a small estate from Dorothy's father, they were forced to remove her from the boarding-school.

So she returned to the home of her beloved Aunt Elizabeth Threlkeld, in whose good care her dying mother had wisely left her and who Dorothy thought a perfect woman. She went to day-school with her dear friend Jane Pollard. In this intelligent, cultivated and religious community to which her Aunt belonged, she was surrounded by care, and was supremely happy. There in Halifax in Aunt Threlkeld's guardianship and in the friendship of her schoolfriends, Dorothy thrived and grew in those qualities of clear honesty, sensitivity, and cheerfulness. She had a deeply generous spirit and an affectionate nature, seeing the best in ordinary people, loving both children and nature, and most especially those dear to her.

Dorothy read deeply and widely in the French and English classics; indeed all her life she continued to educate herself through reading. She was also skilled and capable in household tasks as well as being careful in household budgeting.

On a Continental tour with William and Mary, Dorothy's extreme sensitivity made her exclaim when visiting the battlefield of Waterloo, 'where heaps of our countrymen lay buried beneath our feet - There was little to be seen, but something like horror breathed out of the ground.'

In Milan she and William and Mary saw Leonardo's Last Supper, 'and were sad that its fading and vanishing must go on year after year'. They then saw a firework display 'The Burning of Troy', which Dorothy loved, saying 'the rockets twisting, eddying, shooting, spreading,' sent her into an ecstasy - 'I had never before seen fireworks better than we sometimes exhibit to children.'

It was because of the love and happiness of her years in Halifax with her Aunt Elizabeth (of whom she said, 'indeed you know she has been my mother') that Dorothy grew in strength of character and intellect, and all their lives she and Elizabeth loved each other.

But sadly in May 1787, owing to the lack of money provided for their ward and the legal expenses of trying to make Lord Lonsdale pay his debts to the Wordsworth orphans, her guardians economised still further by forcing Dorothy to leave her dear and beloved Aunt, her best friend Jane, her other friends and her school and sending her to live with her Cookson grandparents above their drapers' shop in Penrith.

Elizabeth Threlkeld was a cousin who had been a witness at the marriage of Ann Wordsworth (Dorothy's mother). As Ann lay dying she had begged Elizabeth to care for little Dorothy, then aged 6 years.

Elizabeth for some payment from Grandpa Cookson gave Dorothy a happy home in Halifax. Her Aunt's brother, William Threlkeld, lived nearby with his wife and children. Elizabeth took care of her dead older sister's children Samuel, Martha, Edward, Ann, and Elizabeth Fergusson, aged between 10 and 17. Dorothy became the much-loved baby of this big family; and when her brother-in-law died, Elizabeth took over his haberdashery business too. This splendid woman was a good mother to all these children.

They belonged to a good Unitarian community led by John Ralph, who taught people to work out their own salvation, gave simple services and founded a library 'to promote religious knowledge, and for the benefit of the poor'. This was the open-minded, civilised and cultured society in which Dorothy grew up.

In Halifax Dorothy went with her friend Jane to Miss Mellin's Day School. Miss Mellins and her sister Hanna were, like Elizabeth Threlkeld, attenders of the Northgate End Chapel of Ralph Taylor. The lessons at Miss Mellin's school were sensible and without frills. Dorothy stayed there from the age of 12 - 15, and was known for her lively cheerfulness.

Dorothy had many friends. As well as Jane Pollard, one of the six daughters of the wool merchant William Pollard, there was also Patty Taylor (of whom Jane was jealous, but with no cause), and Jane's sisters, Harriet Branchen - tall and fine-looking, Mary Grimshaw, Dorothy's Fergusson cousins, Betsy Fergusson and the studious Molly Waterhouse, who had read *Lock On Human Understanding, Euclid* and other books. Dorothy proudly announced that she herself reached 8 stones, for to be fat was the fashion in those days. Her friends were all the daughters of Halifax businessmen and tradesmen - hence the sensible education.

It was only when she moved to her Cookson grandparents, that she felt terribly the loss of her kind Aunt. Her grandfather, who was ill, continually scolded, and her grandmother insisted that she, as a poor relation, must earn her keep by continual housework - all this to the tune of endless, boring small-town gossip, which was her grandmother's only interest. She thought Dorothy a strange, wild girl:

She said, 'I would give anything to go to Halifax instead, to that dear place which I shall ever consider as my home, the loss of a mother can only be made up by such a dear friend as my Aunt.'

She remembered Elizabeth Threlkeld's home in the Southgate as 'the place where I passed the happy hours of my childhood'. She was terribly homesick.

All this was the reason of her extreme fixation on and love for William - her need to remember and remain a valued member of

3

his household all her life.

As no horses were sent for her beloved brothers at the end of term, William hired a horse and rode over to see if anyone was ill. Only Dorothy wanted to see him, himself and John and Christopher. So often the orphans wept together because they had no parents. Dorothy's brothers were very dear to her: 'William and Christopher clever - at least so they appear to the partial eyes of a sister, and John silent and shy - they are just the boys I would wish them, and kind and loving to their sister.'

On August 5th, the three youngest went back to Hawkeshead, and William returned to lodge till he went up to Cambridge. Next year 'our poor John, called a dunce,' was to go off to sea. John himself was delighted to be a sailor in the first East India Company's fleet - and Richard, shrewd and slow, 'diligent and far from dull', was already an articled clerk to his lawyer cousin Richard Wordsworth in Braithwait.

Dorothy was left once more alone with the cold silence of her grandparents and to pour out her heart to Jane Pollard in a letter; grieving and sitting up writing in the night by candlelight.

She was always hurt and wounded by the failure of her father to have her home after her mother's death, she said. She wrote on her 34th birthday, which was, as always, on Christmas Day: 'I was never once at home, never for a single moment under my father's roof after her death, which I cannot think of without regret.'

The sorrow of all this, coupled with the sorrow of losing her second home which had been so happy with her aunt in Halifax, all this was indeed a trauma from which she never recovered. She did however heal herself somewhat by being in William's home and loving him and all his and also by her love for her other brothers.

Dorothy was dependent upon the charity of her relatives: she and her brothers had from their father's estate £600, and this put on deposit at Carlisle Bank would give an interest of £24 a year for each child. This would only cover some of Dorothy's keep, and she was not allowed to spend Christmas at Whitehaven, to which she was invited by Uncle Richard, her other guardian, because of the travel expenses. She was bitterly disappointed because there she would have seen her brothers John and Christopher. William and Christopher's expenses had to be paid at university over and above their £24 - Uncle Christopher complained that William was very extravagant and overspent £300 in two years - he left Cambridge owing £400. It is unlikely that Dorothy ever had what was due to her. She was never actually given money, merely a loan in 1793, and that was in response to her asking for her 'allowance'.

But in Penrith, as Dorothy told Jane in a letter, she had beloved girlfriends of her own: Mary and Peggy Hutchinson, also orphans, living with their Aunt Elizabeth Monkhouse and a severe great-aunt Gamage, so they were in a similar situation to herself, 'at the mercy of illiberal and ill-natured relatives.'

'Mary and her sister Margaret and I used to steal to each other's houses, and when we had had our talk over the kitchen fire, to delay the moment of parting, paced up one street and down another, in moon and starlight'. So her friendship with Mary Hutchinson, later her sister-in-law, was early and deep.

The three girls walked in the woods and meadows together. They would walk on Sunday evenings through the vast Lowther woods, entering below a mill, and would walk along the woodland path between the trees, in sunlight and shadow as far as the stone quarry - the boundary. Dorothy wrote of these walks as being 'some of the happiest in my youth'.

She was short and slight, active, and passionately affectionate. Mary was older by two years. She was tall and dark-haired and had a calm and radiant nature. She had a slight cast in one eye, but this did not spoil her sweetness of countenance. Peggy, seeming bright-cheeked, was deceptively healthy-looking, as she was sadly to die young. These three young women had a strong friendship and were supportive of each other. Each one had a unique and striking character, and for long afterwards Dorothy looked affectionately back on their loving companionship.

Dorothy sent Jane Pollard a catalogue of the very pretty collection of books she had from her brothers: 'I have The Iliad, The Odyssey, Fielding's works, Hayley's poems, Gil Blas (in French), Gregory's legacy to his daughters, and my brother Richard intends sending me Shakespear's plays and The Spectator - I have also Milton's works, Dr. Goldsmith's poems, and other trifling things - I think I hear you say 'how will you have time to read all these?' I am determined to read a great deal now both in French and English. My Grandmother sits in the shop in the afternoon and by working particularly hard for one hour I think I may read the next, without being discovered, and I rise pretty early in the morning. So I hope in time to have perused them all! I am at present reading The Iliad and like it very much - my brother William read a part of it to me.

So you have got high-heeled shoes, I do not think of having them yet a while. I am so little and wish to appear as girlish as possible - I wear my hair curled about my face in light curls frizzed at the bottom, how have you yours?'

Dorothy always wanted to appear girlish, not to grow up too much, to be cared for by her brothers, in order to make up for the deprivation of her father, to be a child in her father's house.

Dorothy had left school at 15, and was used as a household drudge by her narrow-minded grandmother. She therefore depended on the loving kindness and understanding and respect for her intellect from her intelligent brothers, who gave her a little library. Her brothers were sent out into the world - to university, to sea (adventures and travel), and to be an articled clerk to lawyer relatives.

Luckily then an angel arrived in Dorothy's life in the shape of her kindly and cultured Uncle William Cookson, her grandparent's younger son, who was living some time in the house and offered to tutor her, perceiving her intelligence and misery. He taught her from 9-11 each morning to read and write French, some Arithmetic and promised Geography.

Uncle William had become a member of the Church of England and so had qualified for St. John's Cambridge. He did well in his BA degree and had tutored the sons of George III. He had taken holy orders, and was now awaiting a living. Dorothy adored him, he was 'the Uncle I so much love, every day gives me new proofs of his affection and every day I like him better than I did before'. He let her sit beside him in his room by firelight, and write to Jane, instead of scribbling her letters in her cold room, during any time she could snatch from her endless housework.

He took her to visit the master of Penrith Grammar School, the Reverend John Cowper and his kindly daughter Dorothy, whom Dorothy Wordsworth hoped he would marry. Then her Penrith grandfather died. William came for a holiday visit and joined the three girls in their country walks. Dorothy and William were delighted to be together, and William also continued his quiet friendship with Mary Hutchinson.

In October 1788 Uncle William and Miss Cowper told Dorothy they were to be married and would move into a new living in Norfolk and they invited her to live with them. 'I was almost mad with joy,' said Dorothy, 'to live in the country with such kind friends.' She was witness at their wedding, and accompanied them on their honeymoon. Having visited William at Cambridge on their way - which amazed and delighted Dorothy, she went with them to their new home at Forncett St. Peter.

Monday evening, January 25th (and 26th 1790):
Dorothy wrote to Jane Pollard from Forncette:

'The two kind friends with whom I live in that retirement which before I enjoyed I knew I should relish. I have leisure to read; work; walk and do what I please, in short I have every cause to be contented and happy. We look forward to the coming of our little relation with anxious expectation; I hope to be a good nurse, though by the by I must make considerable improvement before I arrive at any degree of excellence. I verily believe I never took an infant in my arms that did not the moment it was there by its cries beg to be removed. My brother John I imagine sailed for India on Saturday or Sunday in the Earl of Abergavenny; he wrote to me the other day while on board her in excellent spirits - William is at Cambridge, Richard in London, and Kitt at Hawkeshead, how we are squandered abroad.'

Dorothy writes to Jane with her usual felicity of expression:

'Did I ever tell you that I had got a little school; indeed

when I recollect, it is not possible that I should have told you, as I have only kept it six months. I will give you my plan. I have nine scholars, I had at first ten but I dismissed one and during the winter I did not think it prudent to supply her place. Our hours in winter are on Sunday mornings from nine till church time; at noon from half past one till three; and at night from four till half past five; those who live near us come to me every Wednesday and Saturday evening.

I only instruct them in reading and spelling and they get off prayers, hymns and catechisms. I have one very bright scholar, some very tolerable, and one or two very bad. We distribute rewards such as books, caps, aprons, etc. We intend in a little time to have a school on a more extensive plan - so that this of mine is only a temporary thing. We are to have a mistress who is to teach them spinning, knitting, etc. on the weekdays, and I am to assist her on Sundays when they are to be taught to read. Mr. Wilberforce' (a friend of the Cooksons, an abolitionist and politician) 'has been with us rather better than a month, tell your father I hope he will give him his vote in the next general election. I believe him to be the best of men.

He allows me ten guineas a year to distribute in what manner I think best to the poor, it is a very nice sum by which I am enabled to do more good than perhaps might ever have been in my power - remember all this is between ourselves, therefore don't mention it.'

Dorothy says, 'oh Jane, you are very dear to me. I love you if possible better than ever since your last arrived and I would not leave a scrap of paper unfilled if I had time to say more but I every moment expect to have my letter called for - adieu my dear girl,
     D. Wordsworth'

'Tuesday morning - I find I have a little more time, therefore I will not omit telling you that I have seized the first opportunity I have of getting a letter conveyed to the office. Be very particular in telling me how you go on. What are you *reading? Do you walk much? Are your relations all well? Do you often see our family? What does my Aunt say of me? In short, tell me everything and continue to love me - my dearest Jane.'*

As with her Uncle William Cookson and his family and friends, so later with her brother William Wordsworth and his - all her talented and original writing came from this love, this involvement. For her it was only a branch of her central work, her mission of loving service.
Writing to Jane, she tells her:

'I fear not poverty in youth and why should I expect it in age, when I have four brothers all of whom have received a good education and suitable to their station in life, and who are all sincerely attached to me; while I am young I thank God I am not destitute of means of supporting myself, then I bear the rest with fortitude and put myself into a situation by which I may procure a livelihood till my brothers are able to assist me - I confess you are right in supposing me partial to William. I hope when you see him you will think my regard not misplaced - William has a great attachment to poetry; indeed so had Kitt, but William particularly, which is not likely to procure his advancement in the world; his pleasures are chiefly of the imagination, he is never so happy as when in a beautiful country. Do not think from what I have said that he reads not all - and not only poetry and those languages he is acquainted with, but history, etc. etc.'

She tells of the pleasant Miss Burroughs who lives nearby:

'But I cannot help regretting that I have not a more intimate friend near me; but I am convinced that I will never form a friendship that will not appear trifling indeed with what I feel for you. You are the friend of my childhood and how endearing a thought is that. You shared all my little distresses and were partner to all my pleasures. It gives me great concern when I

9

*think that I ever gave you pain by my attachment to Peggy
Taylor; surely I never appeared to give her the preference. I
am well convinced that she never held so large a share of my
affection as you, by many degrees - I am indeed greatly mortified
on hearing of Mr. Wilberforce's bad success - every friend to
humanity must applaud his zeal and lament that it failed in its
effect - I beg my dear friend that you will write as soon as
possible - a long letter*
  Yours unalterably,
  D W

Dorothy was happy with the Cooksons at Forncett. Indeed
she disliked going into Norwich for plays, dances, concerts; aside
from that she went there to the dentists also.

She loved the quiet, rural life at Forncett, the routine, the
good works, the reading, the walks, she tamed robin redbreasts to
come into her room and fly around. She fed them, and this she did
all her life until her old age.

In the summer of 1789 the Cooksons invited her dear Aunt
Elizabeth Threlkeld to stay, the first time Dorothy had seen her aunt
since she left Halifax. Great was Dorothy's delight and interest
when Elizabeth Threlkeld at 45 became engaged to be married to
William Rawson, a Halifax merchant. She married him on 7th of
March 1791 in Halifax parish church. Dorothy bombarded Jane
with enquiries about the gown and a description of the bridegroom.

When Jane teased her about possible lovers and suitors,
Dorothy replied firmly and clearly, 'no man I have ever seen has
appeared to regard me with any degree of partiality; nor has anyone
gained my attention, of this you need not doubt.'

She later repeated to Jane firmly, on her enquiry about lovers,
'I cannot suppose you entertain any such improbable suspicions as
you are pleased to hint. I shall think you unkind if you say anything
more to me upon the subject.' Jane wisely did not do so. Dorothy
only ever mentioned marriage in her letters once more, at the age of
30 saying, 'It would be absurd at my age to talk of marriage.'

Dorothy loved children and nature and her family, household

skills and craft. She adored her friends and was endlessly imaginative and generous in helping and giving to those she loved. Wordsworth's 'exquisite sister' had an asexual quality and a gift for perfect friendship. She was herself someone apart, real, individual. Jane Pollard eventually in 1795 - and to Dorothy's delight - married John Marshall, a rich linen manufacturer of Leeds. The couples' fathers were old friends. Jane had 12 children, and her husband became an MP.

Dorothy writes to Jane of seeing her beloved brother Kitt, who was shy and resembled William in some ways, and of looking forward to living with William in a little parsonage, 'when he has taken holy orders'. She gave a beautiful description of William as having, 'a sort of violence of affection - if I may so term it - which demonstrates itself every moment of the day when objects of his affection are present with him, in a thousand almost imperceptible attentions to their wishes - in a sort of restless watchfulness which I know not how to describe; a tenderness that never sleeps, and at the same time such a delicacy of manners as I have observed in few men'.

She invites her friend Jane to spend a year with herself and William in their future parsonage, describing with delight their life there: 'I have laid a particular scheme of happiness for each season. When I think of winter I hasten to furnish our little parlour, I close the shutters, set out the tea-table, brighten the fire. When our refreshment is ended, I produce our work, and William brings his book to our table and contributes at once to our instruction and amusement, and at intervals we lay aside the book and each hazard our observations upon what has been read without fear of ridicule or censure. We talk over past days, we do not sigh for any pleasure beyond our humble habitation. The central point of all our joys.'

She is very proud indeed of William's book of poems just published *Evening Walk*, and *Descriptive Sketches* and gives some delicate criticisms of his use of the word 'moveless' and his meaning of this applied to a swan, meaning the sort of movement which is smooth, without agitation, and 'viewless'. She wishes to know Jane's frank opinion of the poems, says she and Kitt have read them and given careful criticism.

She tells Jane of their little people, the Cookson's children, 'I wish I could introduce them to you. they are the sweetest children I ever saw. Healthy and strong to a remarkable degree and of course very lively. Believe me unalterably yours Dorothy Wordsworth. Pray write immediately'.

Dorothy worked hard in the Cookson household. She helped with her Aunt's lying in, cared for the children, made linen and shared her Aunt's bed so as to be near to help. She said, 'lying in is not half so tremendous a business as is generally thought'. For the birth of George in 1793 she was up all night, and she nursed the children through smallpox, which put her in danger. She looked after the four children, Nancy, Christopher, William and George, when their mother was away, and had to 'literally steal the moments I employ in letter writing'.

She slept in a garret and did all this hard work very cheerfully, as she loved her Uncle and Aunt. Writing to Jane, she referred to them as 'two kind friends', and she would do the same in her brother William's house later on; it was expected of a single woman to help in these ways living with her family - and also she was very intelligent and loved reading and wrote beautifully - like some other very erudite and intelligent women writers of that time, who worked hard for their families and households.

Indeed to have a drapers shop, or a haberdashery shop, as her grandmother and Aunt Threlkeld had had - admirable and independent trade as this now seems to us - was considered in those days less ladylike and acceptable than to help with and live in a relative's family; there one could have an honourable home in exchange for one's labour, as Dorothy was doing, and in fact did all her life.

In 1793 they had a holiday. William Cookson was installed as Canon of Windsor where he had taught the Princes, and they all went to spend three months at Windsor in August that year. London, visited on the way, Dorothy did not enjoy, except for the view from the top of St. Pauls.

But she was truly enchanted by Windsor and said it was like being on fairy ground. She was delighted by the kind old King George

III and his love of children, his talking to their little Mary about her new hat - Dorothy gives a glittering, fairy picture of it all. She says, 'When I first set foot upon the terrace - I fancied myself treading on Fairy Ground and that the gay company about me were brought there by enchantment'. Of Queen Charlotte driving with four white ponies in a phaeton in the park below the terrace she says, 'her equipage and her train of horses looked so diminutive that it was impossible to avoid comparing them with the descriptions one has read of fairies travelling on Fairy Ground - '

They had several good excursions with two young ladies and her young male cousin whom she liked, to Egam Races, and to see the views. She went to a ball - her first - in fear and trembling: 'I had the most severe tremblings and palpitations during the first dance that can be conceived by any trembling female - my partner was a wretched one and I had not danced for five years!' Then she luckily danced with Mr. Heberden, 'a young man with whom I was very well acquainted. I felt myself quite at ease,' and so the rest of the ball was a pleasure to her.

Dorothy was William's touchstone to his childhood, his love of nature and poetry, and he was hers. When he stayed at Forncett at Christmas 1790 for six weeks, she used to walk with him in the twilight each evening talking for a very long time.

But she truly and sadly wrote to Jane Pollard, 'kind as are my Uncle and Aunt and much as I love my sweet little cousins, I cannot help heaving many a sigh at the reflection that I have passed one and twenty years of my life, and that the first six years only of this time was spent in the enjoyment of the same pleasures that were enjoyed by my brothers, and that I was then too young to be sensible of the blessing: We have been endeared to each other by early misfortune. We in the same moment lost a father, a mother, a home, we have been equally deprived of our patrimony by the cruel hand of Lordly Tyranny. These afflictions have all contributed to unite us closest by the bonds of affection notwithstanding we have been compelled to spend our youth far asunder, "we drag at each remove a lengthening chain", this idea often strikes me forcibly. Neither absence nor distance nor time can ever break the chain that links me to my brothers. - But why do I talk to you thus? Because these are the thoughts that are uppermost in my breast at the moment, and when I write to the companion of my childish days I must write the Dictates of my heart. In our conversations so full of tenderness I have never constrained my sentiments; I have laid open the inmost recesses of my heart; ... '

Many were the plans and castles in the air Dorothy built for her future with William. William Cookson said he could make possible a curacy for her brother at Forncett, but not hold it open indefinitely. William Wordsworth did not sound very enthusiastic, however, he said he would return to Cambridge to fill in the 18 months before he was old enough to take holy orders, and would study oriental languages. This he transformed into a long visit to France to improve his French. He returned seven months later, in December 1792 with two poems. These poems were addressed to Dorothy and she - with some criticism - described their beauties, 'beauties which could only have been created by the imagination of a poet'.

But on William's return he wrote a letter from London telling of his lover Annette and their little daughter Caroline. Dorothy, true and real as always and loving her brother, wrote at once to her 'chère soeur' Annette and hoped that Annette, William, Caroline and herself could share 'un petit ménage' together. This was truly Dorothy - with her love for her brother William, and so her brother's lover, her love for children, her generosity and unconventionality. Indeed Dorothy later lived with William and Mary in just such a ménage à trois; her love for William and his for her was tender and dependent and erotically platonic, so he was living between two women, his beloved sister and his wife, all sharing in the care of the children. Mary also had been before the marriage a much-loved friend of both Dorothy and William; her sister Sara Hutchinson also. The Sara whom Coleridge loved, and who had lived with Dorothy and William, so they were living in new and changing patterns of love and community.

Poor Annette had had to return to her home at Blois, her beloved child Caroline had been put out to nurse, and she was separated from her. In her grief she cherished Dorothy's letters -

'cet intéret si touchant que vous prenez à mes peines'. She so hoped William would return to marry her, but France declared war on England in February 1793, and gradually the mail boats ceased sailing from England to France, though Dorothy wrote consoling letters to Annette until March, when they stopped sailing to France altogether. And within six months any Englishman found in France was arrested.

Annette hoped that Caroline would be like her dear, kind aunt Dorothy.

That it was left up to Dorothy to break the news about Annette and Caroline to her uncle, was found out in a letter from Annette to William compassionately saying, 'l'engage de ne rien dire à ton oncle; ce sera un combat pénible qu'elle aura à soutenir. Mais tu le juges le néccessaire.'

This letter with Annette's reply to Dorothy was confiscated by police at Blois and was kept in the department archives, where they were found 130 years later. So was discovered the wonderful story of Annette and Caroline.

Uncle William Cookson was furious and withdrew his offer of a curacy for William and forbade him to visit his sister at Forncett. Then Dorothy rebelled and took her life into her own hands. Instead of doing the bidding of her relatives, however fond she was of them, she was courageous and individualistic, subtle but determined, realising she would never see her beloved brother, with whom she hoped to live, she hatched a plan of her own, to see him in Halifax.

William had an open invitation to visit their kind Aunt Rawson (Dorothy's dear Aunt Elizabeth, now married), and indeed her hospitable new husband William Rawson. William Cookson would allow Dorothy to visit the Rawsons, but might not if he knew William was going to be there - so their plan to meet had to be kept secret.

Dorothy wrote to Jane and invited her there too, 'and find me united with my dear William'.

She wrote, very depressed, 'I cannot foresee the day of my Felicity, the day in which I am once more to find a home under the same roof as my brother, all is still obscure and dark and there is much ground to fear my scheme may prove a shadow, a mere vision of Happiness ...'

Dorothy did not explain to Jane why William Cookson did not want her to meet William, she said only, 'The subject is an unpleasant one for a letter, though I must confess he has been somewhat to blame.'

She said nothing even to Aunt Rawson of William's hope of coming to Halifax while she was there, and Jane she implored to keep all this secret, 'do not mention I entreat you my plan of meeting William or Uncle William would know that the plan was a premeditated one'.

Dorothy had to wait six months at the Cooksons for the arrival of Mr. Griffiths, Aunt Rawson's cousin who would be on a business trip first to London, and then to the north, taking Dorothy to the Rawsons.

Aunt Cookson generously gave her £5 for her forthcoming visit to Halifax. But it was a sad and difficult and heavy six months waiting for Dorothy at the parsonage, in the atmosphere of the Cooksons' disapproval of William. Dorothy subsequently lost her £5 and her purse, and had to write to her brother Richard, the lawyer, for money. She wrote, 'It hurts me to apply to you in this distress but I have not a farthing in the world.'

Dorothy was very worried about William - no curacy, the hoped-for post as tutor fallen through. Instead of going to stay with his friend William Calvert, William set off across Salisbury Plain to Bristol and the Wye Valley; then into north Wales. Writing a poem, he seemed to his friends to have been on the edge of a nervous breakdown.

William wrote of himself as being,

'More like a man flying from something that he dreads than one who sought the thing he loved.'

In the autumn and winter he wandered about among his friends in Cumberland. 'I have been doing nothing, and still continue to be doing nothing, what is to become of me I do not know,' he wrote. His guilt and sorrow were not realised at the time by Dorothy, who imagined him with his friend Jones in Wales.

Eventually Dorothy took matters into her own hands, and travelled by herself by coach, and miraculously on her very little

16

money, to Halifax to the Rawsons, to her Aunt's new home by the banks of a river, Mill House, with its spaces and freedom and welcome, its beloved garden, and her dear friend Jane Pollard, whom she had been so longing to hold in her arms. Her Aunt and Uncle William, a Unitarian and Halifax textile merchant, were kind and gentle to her, and by 7th February 1794 William had arrived there and Dorothy was reunited with him under the same roof, and very happy because of it. There they stayed for 6 weeks, and Dorothy then realised how troubled and disorientated William was, and how much he needed her for his sanity and his rehabilitation. The Rawsons were liberal, gentle and generous and merely thought him eccentric; Dorothy hoped they would like him, he seeming 'rather plain than otherwise', and awkward in conversation with strangers.

William Wordsworth was still as radical, however, and this was dangerous while The Terror reigned in France. His brother Richard warned him about his radical ideas.

In May 1794 the Habeus Corpus Act was suspended, and the Radical Society members were arrested for treasonable practices. William was very sympathetic to their cause - Richard asked his brother to burn the letter of warning he sent, as 'Lord Lowther has spies all over the country'. Dorothy was unafraid in the face of her brother's danger. She accepted his radical ideas as she accepted the ideas and enthusiasms of all those she loved. She knew that he hated The Terror in France and that he did not believe in bloody revolution, and though she regretted him styling himself on 'that odious class of men called democrats', she accepted his rebellion against Church and State, which was a new, revolutionary step for her.

Then on a night more glorious and freer yet, she set out on a walking tour with William, to celebrate their reunion. She was delighted with this. It was as if it were a walk into their future. They were 'two glad foot-travellers through sun and showers'. The early April was stormy, yet Dorothy adored the muddy tramp to Windermere 'with my brother at my side', and saw 'the most delightful country that ever was seen'. She said later, 'I am always glad to see Stavely. It is a place I dearly love to think of, the first mountain village I came to with William, when we first began our pilgrimage together. Here we drank a basin of milk at a public house and here I washed my feet in the brook, and put on a pair of silk stockings at William's advice.' They came to Grasmere at sunset and 'there was a rich yellow light on the waters and the islands reflected there'.

Next morning they walked the last 15 miles to a stone farmhouse, lonely 'Windy Brow' on Latrigg above Keswick. This farm belonged to William's schoolfriend William Calvert, who lived there with his younger brother Raisley. The Calverts moved into a cottage next door to provide houseroom for William and Dorothy.

Dorothy wrote from Windy Brow, 'We are now in a farmhouse about a mile from Keswick. When I came, I intended to stay only a few days, but the country is so delightful and, above all, I have full enjoyment of my brother's company, that I have determined to stay a few weeks longer. After I leave Windy Brow I shall proceed to Whitehaven.'

There were, however, criticisms and rumblings from the Penrith relatives at Dorothy rambling freely about the countryside and staying in a remote farmhouse with William and two of his friends. This was from Mrs. Christopher Crackenthorp - Mrs. Christopher Cookson (they had changed their name to Crackenthorp on Uncle Kit inheriting the Crackenthorp estate).

Dorothy Wordsworth wrote,

'I am much obliged to you for the frankness with which you have expressed your sentiments upon my conduct and am at the same time extremely sorry that you should think so severely to be condemned. As you have not sufficiently developed the reasons for your censure, I have endeavoured to discover them; and I suggest no other possible objections to my continuing here a few weeks longer suggest themselves, except the expense and that you may suppose me to be in an unprotected situation. As to the former of these objections I reply that I drink no tea, and that my supper and breakfast are of bread and milk and my dinner chiefly of potatoes from choice. In answer to the

second of these suggestions, namely that I may be supposed to be in an exposed situation, I affirm that I consider the character and virtues of my brother as sufficient protection, and besides I am convinced that there is no place in the world in which a good and virtuous young woman would be more likely to continue good and virtuous than under the roof of these honest, worthy, and uncorrupted people, so that any guardianship beyond theirs I should think altogether unnecessary.

I cannot pass unnoticed that part of your letter in which you speak of my "rambling about the countryside on foot". So far from considering this a matter of condemnation, I rather thought it would have given my friends pleasure to hear that I had courage to make use of the strength with which nature has endowed me, when it not only provided me with infinitely more pleasure than I would have received from sitting in a post chaise – but also the means of saving me at least 30 shillings.

In mentioning the inducements which I have to stay at Windy Brow a few weeks longer, it will be unnecessary to speak of the beauty of the countryside or the pleasantness of the season. To these are added the society of several of my brother's friends from whom I have received the most friendly attentions and above all the society of my brother. I am now 22 years of age and such have been the circumstances of my life that I may be said to have enjoyed his company only for a very few months. An opportunity now presents itself of obtaining this satisfaction, an opportunity which I could not see pass from me without unspeakable pain. Besides I not only derive much pleasure, but much improvement from my brother's society - I have regained all knowledge I had of the French language some years ago, and have added considerably to it, and now I have begun reading Italian, of which I expect to have soon gained a sufficient knowledge to receive much entertainment and advantage from it.'

From this letter it is clear that Dorothy had grown up, found her own independence and place in the world, as well as her identity, and could say so calmly and clearly if criticised.

Dorothy was indeed very happy at Windy Brow, the tenant farmer and his wife she considered 'happier than anybody I know'. She adored the beautiful scenery, the view up Borrowdale. They rambled Gypsy-like all day, exploring among meadows, rocks and streams, and also studied together.

The next fifteen months were for Dorothy a period of visiting relatives and friends. First she went with William to visit their guardian Uncle Richard at Braithwaite near Whitehaven, at his son's house. On the way through Cockermouth they stopped to look at the house of their birth. Dorothy had not seen it since she was six. She said, 'it is a spot which I remember as vividly as if I had been there the other day, though I have never seen it in its neatness, as my Father and Mother used to keep it since I was just six years old'. Now it was empty and desolate, 'all was in ruin, the terrace walk buried and choked up with the old privet hedge - the same hedge where the sparrows were used to build their nests'.

These things upset them, especially Dorothy, who wrote very sorrowfully about their feeling orphaned and homeless to her lawyer brother Richard, begging him to work hard at the Lonsdale suit and for the settlement of her brothers' and her own rightful estate, 'daily more distressing and intricate - these things make me feel very uneasy'. Richard replied to another, a letter from William, 'allow me to assure you that I have always my sister's, yours, and my younger brother's interests at heart'. He was trying all he could, but the law was going its own slow way.

At Braithwaite Dorothy was given leisure and freedom by her sweet, kind aunt; but in mid-June her uncle, already ailing with jaundice and dropsy, died. His respectful obituary appeared in The Gentlemen's Gazette of July 1794.

Dorothy and William left the grieving house, and as they had no money William had to return to the Calverts at Keswick; and Dorothy rode off on her uncle's horse, first to another cousin Mrs. Barker at Rampside, on the coast near Furness Abbey, then after a fortnight she went on to stay with the Speddings of Armthwait. This was the family of William's Hawkeshead Grammar School friends.

Dorothy found them, 'in every respect charming women who have read much and are amiable and engaging in their manners. They live in the most beautiful place that was ever beheld.'

In August Dorothy moved on to her duty visit to Aunt and Uncle Crackanthorpe at Newbiggen Hall. To her great surprise Uncle Kit was very affectionate to her. She says, 'I could not resist and in any case I am very glad we had a meeting'. He continued affectionate and kind and gave her 'ten guineas generously, and the manner of giving it made it doubly so'. Dorothy decided he would always have loved her but for his proud and selfish wife. She stayed some months with them, then spent the bitter cold winter with the Griffith family at Newcastle. In spite of the intense cold she found 'our good friends very cheerful, pleasant companions', and she delighted in 'all the Newcastle adventures'. She stayed there until early April 1795.

Dorothy meant to go in a chaise with her cousin Elizabeth Threlkeld back to the Rawsons in Halifax. Suddenly she remembered her dear friends Mary and Peggy Hutchinson, with whom she had 'compared grievances and lamented the misfortune of losing our parents at an early age'; the days of their youth in Penrith, when they used to walk together in the woods to the quarry, and sit late over the fires in each other's houses talking, and walked back home with each other in the moonlight and lamplight in the streets of Penrith. They kept house now for their brother Tom on his farm at Sockburn near Darlington. Dorothy wrote to suggest a meeting and they asked her and she agreed to stay. Their farm was 'washed round by the Tees, a noble river. We spend our time very pleasantly in walking, reading, working, and playing at ball in the meadow in which the house stands, which is scattered over with sheep and green as emerald'. They were very happy, 'exactly as our imagination and wishes used to represent'. She so wished she and William had such a home, 'but these are airy dreams'. She felt sadly as she left that she would never see the Hutchinsons again. A very unprophetic feeling!

She returned by heavy coach to Halifax, and the Rawsons made her lovingly welcome; there were dinner and tea-drinking meetings, visits at the Threlkelds - cousin Patty now managing the haberdashery.

They rebelled in that liberal family against the guinea a head tax on hair-powder and Dorothy was against the war with the French Republic. Her cousin Edward Ferguson had shorn his hair very close rather than pay the tax. At Mill House one could have radical opinions openly; and Uncle Rawson gave Dorothy two beautifully bound books, Akenside's *Pleasures of Imagination* and Roger's *Pleasures of Memory*, edited by Mrs. Barbauld, a Unitarian verse writer and pamphleteer on the rights of Man. That summer Dorothy was present at her friend Jane's marriage to John Marshall of Leeds and could congratulate her friend 'with the most heartfelt pleasure'.

She so loved being at Mill House with its large garden bright with flowers, with her dear Uncle and Aunt Rawson, that she felt sad at the thought of leaving it: 'Mr and Mrs R', she wrote, 'have been so very very kind to me.'

In August 1785 she had the great pleasure of her brother Kit coming to stay for a week. Kit was studying hard at Cambridge, and graduated as tenth Wrangler. He was 'delightful - and to tell you he is very like me will make you smile, as it is a little like vanity; it is, however, allowed by everyone, and I myself think I never saw a stronger likeness'. Christopher had a strong face, high forehead, aquiline nose, and firm mouth. So had Dorothy and her Aunt Rawson. All this shows in a silhouette of Dorothy made when she was young. They all three had deep set eyes. Dorothy's were dark grey, and very expressive of her intense emotions and extreme sensitivity; she was small, and swift in her movements, very active, deeply feeling and affectionate and very loyal, like a flashing, many-faceted jewel, spontaneous and utterly genuine in her response to people and nature and the world.

All through this time she was longing to begin her life with William, but they yet lacked money.

Then Raisley Calvert, William's friend, who while dying was nursed by William, left him some money because he believed in William as a poet. This legacy of £600 - later £900 - William supplemented with help from his lawyer friend Basil Montague with whom he lodged in London. Montague, a widower, would pay William and Dorothy to bring up his little two year old son Basil in the country, offering them a home given by two of his pupils, the Pinny brothers. These were the sons of a West Indian merchant of Bristol. One of the Pinney brothers, John Frederick, offered William a home in the West Country, Racedown Lodge, on the Dorset-Devon border. Pinney's father had bought this property in case anything went wrong with his West Indian business because of the American war. The place was empty except for a poor relation caretaker, Gill.

Dorothy was very pleased indeed. 'It will be a very great change for me,' she wrote to Jane (now married and called Marshall), 'but it is of a nature well suited to my inclinations. You know I am active, not averse to household employments and fond of children.' She was anxious and sometimes fearful, but knew she would do her best. Her Uncle William approved, her brother Kit was pleased that he and John would 'have a place to draw to'. Her dear Aunt Elizabeth also approved. Dorothy said, 'my Aunt says she has no doubt of me and Mr. Rawson is of the same opinion. He thinks I am equal to the charge'. And it would be a 'permanent establishment after much wandering. It will greatly contribute to my happiness and place me in such a situation where I shall be doing something.'

Silhouette of Dorothy Wordsworth, black paper on Chinese white, oval
portrait circa 1806. It is anonymous, only recently discovered this century.
It is inscribed on the reverse 'Miss Wordsworth' in the hand of Elizabeth
Cookson. It was found among the Cookson family papers.

CHAPTER 2

So Dorothy went to live with William, and care for the child at Racedown Lodge. After that Dorothy always lived with William and did not leave him again, and their lives ran harmoniously and creatively together.

There is a poem Dorothy wrote later for the child, 'Edward':

The Wind

What way does the Wind come? What way does he go?
He rides over the water, and over the snow,
Through wood and through dale; and o'er rocky height
Which the goat cannot climb, takes his sounding flight;
He tosses about in every bare tree,
As, if you look up, you plainly may see;
But how he will come, and whither he goes,
There's never a scholar in England knows.

He will suddenly stop in a cunning nook,
And ring a sharp 'larum; but, if you should look,
There's nothing to see but a cushion of snow,
Round as a pillow, and whiter than milk,
And softer than if it were covered with silk.
Sometimes he'll hide in the cave of a rock,
Then whistle as shrill as the buzzard cock;
But seek him - and what shall you find in the place?
Nothing but silence and empty space;
Save, in a corner, a heap of dry leaves,
That he's left, for a bed, to beggars and thieves!

As soon as 'tis daylight tomorrow, with me
You shall go to the orchard, and then you will see
That he has been there, and made a great rout,
And cracked the branches, and strewn them about;

Heaven grant that he spare but that one upright twig
That looked up at the sky so proud and so big
All last summer, as well you know,
Studded with apples, a beautiful show!
Hark! Over the roof he makes a pause,
And growls as if he would fix his claws
Right in the slates, and with a huge rattle
Drive them down, like men in a battle.

But let him range round; he does us no harm,
We build up the fire, we're snug and warm;
Untouched by his breath see the candle shines bright,
And burns with a clear and steady light;
Books have we to read, but that half-stifled knell,
Alas! Tis the sound of the eight o'clock bell.

Come now we'll to bed! And when we are there
He may work his own will, and what shall we care?
He may knock at the door, we'll not let him in;
May drive at the windows, we'll laugh at his din;
Let him seek his own home wherever it may be;
Here's a cosy warm house for Edward and me.

* * * * * * *

Dorothy's poem was full of her love and minutely observed
appreciation for wild wayward nature, her sympathy with beggars
and tramps, was full of her love and trust in her brother's house, in
spite of her fear of deprivation, of her feelings of safety in her
brother's house, of the safety of the child in her care.

To Jane Marshall she writes from Racedown Lodge:

'We are now surrounded by winter prospects without
doors, and within have only winter occupations, books, solitude
and the fireside, yet I may safely say we are never dull. Basil is
a charming boy, he affords us perpetual entertainment. Do not

26

suppose from this that we make him our perpetual plaything, far otherwise. I think that is one of the modes of treatment most likely to ruin a child's temper and character. But I do not think there is any pleasure more delightful than that of marking the development of a child's faculties and observing his little occupations. We found everything at Racedown much more complete with respect to household conveniences than I could have expected. You may judge of this when I tell you we have not had to lay out ten shillings for the use of the house. We were a whole month without servant, but now we have one of the nicest girls I ever saw; she suits me exactly, and I have all my domestic concerns so arranged that everything goes on with the utmost regularity. We wash once a month. I hire a woman to whom I give ninepence for one day, to wash, on the next we have got the clothes dried and on the third have finished ironing. It is the only time in which I have anything to do in the house, but then I am very active and very busy as you will suppose. I have been making Basil coloured frocks, shirts, slips, etc. and have a good deal of employment in repairing his clothes and putting my brother's in order. We walk about two hours every morning - we have many pleasant walks about us and what is a great advantage, the roads are of a very sandy kind and are almost always dry. We can see the sea 150 or 200 yards from the door, and at a little distance have a very extensive view terminated by the sea seen through different openings of unequal hills. We have not the warmth and luxuriance of Devonshire, though there is no want either of wood or cultivation, but the trees appear to suffer from sea-blasts. We have hills which seen from a distance almost take the character of mountains, some cultivated nearly to their summits, others in their wild state covered with furze and broom. These delight me the most as they remind me of our native wilds. Our common parlour is the prettiest little room that can be; with very neat furniture, a large book (case?) on each side of the fire, a marble chimneypiece, bath stove, and an oil cloth for the floor. The other parlour is rather larger, has a good carpet, sideboards in the recesses on each side of the fire, and has upon the whole a smart appearance, but we do not like it half so well as our little breakfast room. I have only one great disappointment since I came, and that was about the little girl. I lament it the more as I am sure if her father knew all the circumstances he would wish her to be placed under our care. Mr. Montague had intended being with us a month ago, but we have not seen him yet; we hope however that he will be with us before Christmas. I have the satisfaction of thinking that he will see great improvements in Basil. Our nearest neighbours have called upon us; I do not think we shall be much benefited by their society, as they do not seem much inclined either to go out or see their friends; nor indeed if they were would they be any great advantage to us, as though they are very good kind of people, and seem desirous of doing everything in their power, they have not much conversation. William has a letter from France since we came here. Annette mentions having despatched half a dozen, none of which he has received. My Aunt Cookson was brought to bed of a girl nearly three weeks ago. She has now five children. She was doing very well when my Uncle wrote to me.

The greatest inconvenience we suffer here is in being so far from the post office; with respect to household conveniences we do very well, as the butcher coming from Cruikern brings us everything we want. With respect to letters we are, however, more independent than most people, as William is so good a walker, and I too have walked over twice to Crewkern (the distance is seven miles) to make purchases, and what is more we turned out of our way three miles, in one of our walks thither to see a house of Lord Powlett's and a very fine view. We were amply repaid for our trouble. If you want to find our situation out, look in your maps for Crewkern, Chard, Axminster, Bridport and Lime; we are nearly equidistant from all those places. A little brook which runs at the distance of one field from us divides us from Devonshire. This country abounds in apples; in some of our walks we go through orchards without any other *enclosure or security than as a common field. When I spoke of the sea I forgot to tell you that my brother saw the West India fleet sailing in all its glory before the storm had made such dreadful ravages. The peasants are miserably poor; their cottages are shapeless structures (I may almost say) of wood and clay - indeed they are not at all beyond what might be expected in savage life. You must not find fault with this small paper, for if I have written it so close that my letter contains more than your large sheet, but if I had had any other I would not have made use of this, for I feel as if I have a great deal more to say - How does your mother's health continue in general? When do you expect to see Harriet? Give my kind love to all at Ovenden. Perhaps you may be there when this letter reaches you. Remember me affectionately to Mrs. Marshall, Mr. M. and Ellen (Jane's older sister). I often think of the happy days I spent with you and of the hospitality and kindness. Excuse miserable writing. William desires his best compliments to you and Mr. M. - adieu - my dear Jane, believe me ever your favourite friend,*

      D. Wordsworth'

Dorothy was very happy: 'I think Racedown is the place dearest in my recollections upon the whole surface of the island,' she wrote, 'it was the first home I had'. She tells of 'the lovely meadows over the tops of the combs', which she could see from all the windows. In the garden William handled the spade with 'great dexterity' and their gardener ground orchard apples for cider. William hewed wood and their gardener planted 'one bed cabbages one bed peas'.

Their coal came by sea from Lyme, and they had a small cartful brought by a local farmer, as it was expensive.

Dorothy studied Italian very hard, and read Pinney's books: *The Fool of Quality* by Henry Brook, Madam Roland's *Memoirs* and *Tristram Shandy*. Her Italian became so good she read Ariosto with William.

Little Basil throve in their care. Having lost his mother at birth he had been passed around his father's friends or lived confined in his father's chambers. He arrived 'extremely petted from indulgence and weakness and perpetually disposed to cry' - Dorothy wrote to Jane (now a mother), who asked about Dorothy's system. 'It is a very simple one - we teach him nothing but what he learns from the evidence of his senses. He has an insatiable curiosity which we are always careful to satisfy to the best of our ability. It is directed to everything he sees, the sky, the fields, trees, shrubs, corn, the making of tools, carts, etc., etc. He knows his letters but we have not attempted any further step in the path of book learning. Our general study has been to make him happy.' She told her Aunt Rawson, who had brought her up from the age of six, 'till a child is four he needs no other company than the flowers, the grass, the cattle, the sheep, that scamper away from him when he makes a vain, unexpected chase after them, the pebbles upon the road, etc.' Basil learned without punishment 'by experience alone' - if he did not get up at the proper time no one came and dressed him, he was just left lying in bed till four. After six months Basil had changed 'from a shivering, half-starved plant to a lusty, blooming, fearless boy' who played outside in all weathers with delight. Dorothy watched his development with absorbed interest. 'He is my perpetual pleasure,' she said. Dorothy truly loved children with a lifelong love.

Dorothy always remembered her lovely walks with William round Racedown and Pilsdon, Lewisdon, Blackdown, and the earthwork called Lambert's castle.

In New Year 1796 the Pinney brothers came to visit. They had only one slight snowfall all the mild winter. Dorothy enjoyed walking with the three men. In the evening the Pinneys, so Dorothy said, 'relished the pleasures of our fireside'. The brothers were 'very agreeable in conversation', cultivated and well-educated. They paid for their board. Old Mr. Pinney in Bristol found that the Wordsworths were paying no rent and kicked up a fuss, but his sons, both enchanted by Dorothy and William, persuaded their father to let their friends live at Racedown rent-free.

When they left, Dorothy wrote to Jane and Aunt Rawson, 'we seem to be quiet'. William and Dorothy were absorbed in each other and little Basil. William wrote of it later, telling of Dorothy:

'She in the midst of all, preserved me still
A poet, made me seek beneath that name
My office upon earth, and nowhere else - '

Dorothy was William's still, gentle centre, his lamp and guide to his true self and guardian of his identity - she with her integrity and reality, and love of and faith in him. She taught him how to look at and write of the world and his experience first hand, by her direct and natural way of description, fired by her sensitivity and love of nature and people; many beautiful phrases in Dorothy's letters and journals are echoed in William's poetry. She spoke with her own voice, and enabled William to find and speak with his.

Inspired by her love for William, Dorothy's fine spiritual and religious gift was now given to early romanticism's idea that every natural sight was full of the spirit.

It is not known how soon she began her beautiful journals. Certainly she bought a diary to note 'lovely things' seen on her walks later that year, 1796.

William was to say of his sister in 'Lines Composed a Few Miles Above Tintern Abbey':

' ... in thy voice I catch
The language of my former heart, and read
My former pleasures in the shooting lights
Of thy wild eyes. Oh! Yet a little while
May I behold in thee what I was once,
My dear, dear Sister!'

With Dorothy the intensity of her feeling was direct and innocent, both in her living and in her writing.

Wordsworth wrote of Dorothy's enabling him to see and hear Nature minutely: 'she gave me eyes, she gave me ears'.

Sadly, in spring 1796 Peggy Hutchinson died. This Dorothy learned from a 'melancholy letter' from Mary, who had nursed her sister of her deathbed from consumption.

In the autumn Mary came to stay with Dorothy and William

at Racedown for 7 months. She was brought by her brother Henry, and the three childhood friends were very happy together. They all had a similar family history, being orphaned and making loving homes together, brothers and sisters. 'My friend Mary Hutchinson is staying with me; she is one of the best girls in the world and we are as happy as human beings can be,' Dorothy wrote to Jane. Mary was quieter than Dorothy, and was, like her brothers and sisters, very loyal. Mary was particularly reserved and self-sacrificing. She sat and wrote letters with Dorothy or sewed, Dorothy making frocks and smocks for Basil. They mended William's clothes, and delighted in each other's company.

Dorothy and Mary heroically sewed shirts for Dorothy's lawyer brother Richard in London, in spite of the fact that he sent them the cloth and demanded the shirts without sending proper instructions and measurements. William bought half the share of the cloth and had to have shirts sewn for himself also. William worked at his tragedy, 'The Borderers'.

Mary and Dorothy were very happy together, 'I am very happy in her society,' Dorothy wrote to Richard. The girls went for long walks through apple orchards, and upon Pilsden in the beautiful countryside, seeing 'distant volumes' of smoke from chimneys 'where every cottage hidden from the eye, pointed out its lurking place by a wreath of white smoke'.

Indeed Dorothy, Mary and William were all very happy together. Dorothy had always hoped for a female friend in her life with William - first had been Jane, but by now Jane was married and was a mother, so Dorothy took Mary as her beloved friend in her life with her dear brother. She probably shared with her their feelings about Annette and William's child Caroline, and copied poems for William full of his feelings, such as 'The Ruined Cottage' and 'The Three Graves'. Mary was a friend of both Dorothy and William from their childhood, and it was into this first world that they all three re-entered in friendship and devotion to one another, linked by William's poetry.

The winter 1796-97 was terribly cold, and lasted until May. The starved birds stripped the countryside of berries. William wrote to Richard, 'poor little Basil has been very ill. Dorothy had a bad cough, and I an awful cold.' Basil was so ill, Dorothy was afraid they would lose him. She had a violent cold, high fever, swollen face and terrible toothache. She seemed to be recovered by June, but was very thin. Three years later she wrote to Jane that she was thinner still. Her teeth gradually broke and had to be taken out: 'They will soon be gone, let it pass', she writes, recording the breaking of another tooth on May 31st 1802 when she was thirty. 'I shall be beloved - I want no more'. The friends of her youth in Halifax were shocked at the change in her, but Dorothy was completely without personal vanity.

There were also financial troubles - debt: William's Uncle Richard died. He had been the second trustee of the family estate and had advanced over £400 for William's education; now his son Robinson was asking for at least some repayment.

The legacy from Raisley Calvert was secured against any debts, and their small incomes were increased by the interest from this. They lived rent-free at Racedown and looked after little Basil Montague, but there was no way they could repay Robinson Wordsworth.

Dorothy honestly admitted that Robinson's claim was so just that 'it is absolutely necessary that something must be done'. However, nothing could be done and they could only just make ends meet. Dorothy's idea of taking on another child came to nothing, and their plight gave them such a bad name that it was 'universally reported in Cumberland that he - William - had used his uncle's children very ill'. William vaguely and hopelessly expected his brother Richard to raise some money for him.

Mary Hutchinson left for Crewkerne on June 5th 1797. Dorothy was very sad to lose her friend. Mary took some of the shirts they had made for Dorothy's brother Richard to leave with him in London on her way home. Dorothy hoped Richard would take Mary sightseeing in London in return.

Next day, Coleridge arrived, along the Chard Road. Seeing Dorothy and William in their orchard, across the angle where the Chard and Crewkerne Roads met, he took a short cut to them, leaping a gate and crossing a field. He jumped the stream which was the county boundary and came to them in the Racedown orchard. There are three descriptions, like three echoing mirrors - Dorothy wrote to Mary almost immediately: 'You had a great loss in not seeing Coleridge. He is a wonderful man. His conversation teems with soul, mind, and spirit. Then he is so benevolent, so good-tempered and cheerful, and, like William, interests himself so much about every little trifle. At first I thought him very plain; that is, for about three minutes: he is pale and thin, has a wide mouth, thick lips, and not very good teeth, longish loose-growing half-curling rough black hair. But if you hear him speak for five minutes, you think no more of them. His eye is large and full, not dark but grey; such an eye as would receive from a heavy soul the dullest expression; but it speaks every motion of his animated mind; it has more of the "poet's eye in fine frenzy rolling" than I ever witnessed. he has fine dark eyebrows, and an overhanging forehead.

'The first thing that was read after he came was William's new poem, 'The Ruined Cottage', with which he was much delighted; and after tea he repeated to us two acts and a half of his tragedy 'Osorio'. The next morning William read his tragedy 'The Borderers'.'

This chimes with William's description of Coleridge in late life as 'Coleridge was the only wonderful man I ever knew'. Wordsworth describes Coleridge about five years later:

'A noticeable man with large grey eyes,
And a pale face that seemed undoubtedly
As if a blooming face it ought to be;
Heavy his low-hung lip did oft appear,
Deprest by weight of musing Phantasy;
Profound his forehead was ...'

And after Coleridge died about two years later, William wrote of him:

'The rapt one of the godlike forehead
The heaven-eyed creature ...' - his beloved friend.

Portrait of Coleridge 1796 by Robert Hancock
Reproduced with the kind permission of
The National Portrait Gallery

William and Coleridge had met in Bristol two years before this, and at Nether Stowey, Somerset where Coleridge lived with his wife and child.

Coleridge was so enthralled with the Wordsworths, and they with him, that he stayed with them twice as long as he had intended to. Then as they could not bear to be parted from each other, he drove them back with him to his cottage in nether Stowey. They met Sara Coleridge, battling valiantly with housekeeping in the damp cottage, and her son Hartley, whom Dorothy immediately adored. They were joined there by Charles Lamb, a friend and schoolfellow of Coleridge's. They all lived close to one another in the small cottage, the servant Nanny included. Charles Lamb was shattered by the tragedy of his much-loved sister Mary suddenly going insane a year before and killing her mother. They were all very sympathetic to him.

Coleridge gave this fine description of Dorothy, writing to Cottle, his poetry publisher: 'Wordsworth and his exquisite sister are with me - She is a woman indeed! In mind, I mean, and heart - for her person is such that if you expected to see a pretty woman, you would think her ordinary - if you expected to find an ordinary woman, you would think her pretty! But her manners are simple, ardent, impressive -

In every motion her most innocent soul
Outbeams so brightly, that who saw would say
Guilt was a thing impossible to her -

Her information various - her eye watchful in minutest observation - and her taste a perfect electrometer - it bends, protrudes, and draws in at the subtlest beauties and most recondite faults.'

William, Dorothy and Coleridge were enchanted with each other. In the first year of their enraptured friendship, Coleridge wrote his three marvellous poems, 'The Ancient Mariner', 'Kubla Kahn' and 'Christabel', and seldom wrote in this imaginative way again. Coleridge wrote to Godwin (the radical philosopher friend of William and Coleridge and Shelley's father-in-law) 'tho we were three persons, it was but one God'. Coleridge also wrote that he and

William and Dorothy 'have formed a deep conviction that all is contemptible that does not spring immediately out of an affectionate heart'.

William wrote 'The Prelude', thinking both of Coleridge and Dorothy:

'The sister of my heart
Who ought by rights the dearest to have been
Conspicuous through this biographic verse.'

William, Dorothy and Coleridge called themselves 'The Concern'. Coleridge and Dorothy had an intangible contact and appreciation of each other - both loved specially the smoke from cottage chimneys curling up from the valleys; the novels of Samuel Richardson; indeed, all three were so mutually inspiring, and happy to have found each other. Yet each was already scarred in life by their own particular suffering: Dorothy in her desolation at their being orphaned and scattered apart, William at the loss of Annette and his child, Coleridge by his opium dependency.

William and Dorothy had only expected to stay at Nether Stowey for a fortnight, but Dorothy never returned to Racedown at all. She was soon copying a list of errata for Coleridge to send to his publisher Cottle in Bristol. Both William and Dorothy were enthralled by Coleridge, his great erudition and brilliant mind - 'he talked on for ever' and they listened as if enchanted. They loved the beautiful Somerset countryside. Sara Coleridge accidentally spilt a skillet of boiled milk on Coleridge and scalded his foot, so he had to sit at home in the garden while William and Dorothy ranged the countryside.

Dorothy wrote to Mary: 'There is everything here: sea, woods wild as fancy ever painted, brooks clear and pebbly as in Cumberland, villages so romantic; and William and I, in a wander by ourselves, found out a sequestered waterfall in a dell formed by steep hills covered with full-grown timber trees. The woods are as fine as those at Lowther, and the country more romantic; it has the character of the less grand parts of the neighbourhood of the lakes.'

And most magically wonderful - like a fairy tale - was the

discovery of Alfoxden Park by William and Dorothy 'in a wander by themselves' come to their fairy tale house, near Coleridge's, in the midst of the dreaming Somerset countryside. Dorothy wrote to Mary Hutchinson on August 14th 1797 from Alfoxen near Nether Stowey, Somerset:

'Here we are in a large mansion, in a large park, with seventy head of deer around us. But I must begin with the day of leaving Racedown to pay Coleridge a visit. You know how much we were delighted with the neighbourhood of Stowey - The evening that I wrote to you, William and I had rambled as far as this house, and pryed into the recesses of our little brook, but without any more fixed thoughts upon it than some dreams of happiness in a little cottage, and passing wishes that such a place might be found out. We spent a fortnight at Coleridge's; in the course of that time we heard that this house was to let, applied for it and took it. Our principal inducement was Coleridge's society. It was a month yesterday since we came to Alfoxton.

The house is a large mansion, with furniture enough for a dozen families like ours. There is a very excellent garden, well stocked with vegetables and fruit. The garden is at the end of the house, and our favourite parlour, as at Racedown, looks that way. In front is a little court, with grass plot, gravel walk, and shrubs; the moss roses were in full beauty a month ago. The front of the house is to the South, but it is screened from the sun by a high hill which rises immediately from it. This hill is beautiful, scattered irregularly and abundantly with trees, and topped with fern, which spreads a considerable way down it. The deer dwell here, and sheep, so that we have a living prospect. From the end of the house we have a view of the sea, over a woody meadow-country; and exactly opposite the window where I sit is an immense wood, whose round top from this point has exactly the appearance of a mighty dome. In some parts of this wood there is an undergrove of hollies which are now very beautiful. In a glen at the bottom of the wood is the waterfall of which I spoke, a quarter of a mile from the house. We are three miles from Stowey and not two miles from the sea. Wherever we turn we have woods, smooth downs, and valleys with small brooks running down them through green meadows, hardly ever intersected with hedgerows, but scattered over with trees. The hills that cradle these valleys are either covered with ferns and bilberries, or oak woods, which are cut out for charcoal - Walks extend for miles over the hill-tops; the great beauty of which is their wild simplicity; they are perfectly smooth, without rocks. The Tor of Glastonbury is before our eyes during more than half of our walk to Stowey; and in the park wherever we go, keeping about 15 yards above the house, it makes part of our prospect.'

This wonderful house was negotiated for them by kind Tom Pool, Coleridge's friend - a tanner at Nether Stowey, who was a reliable countryman, yet book-loving and a Democrat, who had found Coleridge his cottage. So now he made the arrangements about Alfoxden House. It belonged to a minor, Mrs. St. Albyn, had a life-interest in it. Tom Pool strongly recommended William Wordsworth as a tenant, and witnessed the signing of the agreement by William and the agent John Bartholomew; the rent of Alfoxton was £23 a year. So it was much more expensive than rent-free Racedown. But they were driven by their love of Coleridge and their need to be near him. It was less than a fortnight since they came to visit Coleridge, but these were people alive to the leadings of the spirit and destiny. William went back to Racedown to collect little Basil and Peggy and their books and clothes. So suddenly began great exploration in English Romantic poetry and prose.

Dorothy wrote to Mary Hutchinson,

'We have been on another tour. We set out last Monday evening at half past four. The evening was dark and cloudy; we went eight miles, William and Coleridge employed themselves in laying the plan of a ballad (The Rime of the Ancient Mariner) to be finished with some pieces of William's - William's play is

finished, and sent to the managers of the Covent Garden Theatre. We have not the faintest expectation that it will be accepted.'

On July 17th 1797 John Thelwell came to visit Coleridge. Thelwell was a political agitator and a friend of Coleridge's through correspondence, who had been arrested under the Treasonable Publications Act. He now hoped to find a sanctuary for himself and family nearby Stowey, although Coleridge had warned him that it might cause riots if he settled in the district. When he arrived they all had the idea of a party in his honour at Alfoxden House. Pool's old mother provided a forequarter of lamb which she had sent over for Dorothy to cook - otherwise they never could have afforded a party. Fourteen people were to come: Thelwell, Coleridge, Tom Pool and people of his progressive circle of friends. It was a mammoth task for Dorothy, who managed all the cooking, helped only by an old woman who occasionally lent a hand. Thomas Jones, a cottager of Alfoxden acted as waiter. The guests all arrived at 11 am to listen to a reading of Wordsworth's tragedy under the trees. In the afternoon they all sat down to a meal in the big dining room at the back of the house overlooking the sea; and after dinner Thelwell gave an impassioned political speech, which quite frightened Thomas Jones as he waited on everybody. He described Thelwell as a 'short little man with dark cropt hair - who got up after dinner and talked so loud and in such a passion'.

It is doubtful if Dorothy heard any of this as she was cooking in the kitchen during the whole party, and serving the food up with very little help. Thelwell felt that the whole Alfoxden group were 'a most philosophical party'.

Dorothy was extremely happy at Alfoxden, with their beautiful walks there in the park, 'wading almost up to the knees in fern - and the slim fawns that we used to startle from their couching places among the fern at the top of the hill. 'The kindly hill which screened from the sun ...'

William and Dorothy and at that time Coleridge were like one soul; as Dorothy wrote in her diary, William wrote nearly similar poems, close to her thoughts. Coleridge also wrote many poems that echo Dorothy's writings, her sayings; and William echoed

Coleridge, and he William.

About this time they became insecure in their tenancy of Alfoxden. Everybody in England was afraid of French spies and invasion - the idea that the Wordsworths were spies came about because William was very quiet, and never spoke about politics. It was also suspected by a previous Alfoxden servant called Mogg, who in turn recounted it to a previous Alfoxden cook, who told it to her present employer Dr. Lyson at Bath. He wrote to the Home Secretary about an emigrant family who had contrived to get hold of Alfoxden: The man 'with only a woman who passes for his sister' roamed the countryside by day and night - with their visitors carrying campstools and a portfolio. They were 'very attentive to the river near them'. This was actually because Coleridge was writing a poem called 'The Brook' and Dorothy and William were helping him trace the local stream from the Quantock source to the Bristol Channel just beyond Kilve.

The Home Secretary sent a detective called Walsh, who questioned Mogg and was not impressed, saying 'he was by no means the most intelligent man in the world'. Walsh wrote from an inn in Nether Stowey that 'I think this will turn out to be no French affair, but a mischievous gang of disaffected Englishmen'. He questioned Thomas Jones, who had waited at table at the Alfoxden party, and recognised from his description Thelwell, the speaker and honoured guest, as the notorious Radical of that name. Walsh decided that 'the inhabitants of Alfoxden House are a sett of violent radicals'. Walsh also remembered that the name of Wordsworth was known in the Home Office as that of a radical. Although the investigation was dropped, the Wordsworths had in fact been in some danger.

Worse was to come: Mrs. St. Albyn, alarmed at the rumours, tried to turn William and Dorothy out of Alfoxden House - Pool wrote her a diplomatic letter in which he explained that they had entertained Thelwell because he had turned up unexpectedly, and this was only common hospitality. Secondly, Mrs. St. Albyn had heard that Jones had told Mogg that Dorothy was seen 'washing and mending their clothes all Sunday'. Pool then stressed that Dorothy

41

had lived long and happily with her clergyman Uncle William Cookson, and gone to church regularly in those days, though neither William or Dorothy had gone to church while at Alfoxden. Coleridge, William and Dorothy were warned by 'friendly medium' (no doubt Pool) of Mrs. St. Albyn's suspicions, and they realised they could not stay at Alfoxden much longer.

But none of this touched their happiness in Coleridge's company. With him they explored the lovely Somerset countryside. Coleridge with his marvellous poetry of speech transformed their vision. He 'talked above singing', wrote Hazlitt, remembering his echoing voice in the woods of Alfoxden, for everywhere on their walks 'he would go on in the most delightful explanatory way over hill and dale, a summer's day, and convert a landscape into a didactic poem or Pindaric ode'.

Dorothy believed most things he said, and believed that she could see Glastonbury Tor from the Park. This was in fact the hill of Brent Knoll. Coleridge was fascinated by Glastonbury; his notebooks at this time are full of the legends about it. Coleridge, however, had great respect for Dorothy's judgement. He listened to her real sense in countering an overenthusiastic scheme he and Tom Wedgewood had for educating brilliant children, and when she rebuked a sarcastic review he had written and shown her in the hope that it would make her laugh, he never wrote such a review again.

Their walks toward Devon and beyond inspired some of the best poems in English literature. In early October 1797, Coleridge went off on his own and stayed in a farmhouse. There he took two grains of opium to check dysentery, and wrote 'Kubla Kahn', that mysterious dream-vision poem, in the composition of which he was interrupted by 'a person from Porlock' calling at the house - and when he returned to his writing, he had lost track of his idea. There remains only the beautiful, stunning fragment we know. He brought this back to Dorothy and William - 'a fragment composed in a sort of Reverie brought on by two grains of opium'. It was not published until much later; we do not even know if Coleridge himself treated it seriously. Thereafter Dorothy always called any can she used for water in the house by the name of 'Kubla'.

A month later Dorothy, William and Coleridge walked the coastal track between North Exmoor and the Bristol Channel. 'Our road lay through woods, rising almost perpendicularly from the sea, with views of the opposite mountains of Wales.' After climbing out of the trees, to the sugarloaf, 'a barren top like a monk's shaven crown', they retook the road and reached Lynmouth in the early November evening. Next day a guide showed them 'a valley at the top of one of these immense hills which open at one end to the sea, and is from its rocky appearance called "the valley of the stones", west of Linton.'

Coleridge suggested that he and Wordsworth collaborate in a story written in 'a kind of loose poetry', like a popular German work which had been translated, Gessner's *Death of Abel*. Coleridge suggested 'a narrative addressed by Cain to his wife', using the landscape of the Linton Valley. Cain 'hears the screams of women and children surrounded by tigers, sacrificial blood' - Coleridge carried happily on regardless, but Wordsworth could only gaze at an almost blank sheet of paper, which had two stanzas beginning 'away, away' and getting in the tigers and drops of blood, but not much else. Eventually, Coleridge said, 'the whole scheme broke up in a laugh, and the Ancient Mariner was written instead'. Thus casually began one of the most beautiful poems in English literature.

They returned to Alfoxden to find money troubles. Basil Montague arrived saying he had lost a Chancery suit, and as he felt unsure of practising Law, he could no longer pay for little Basil - nor any of the money he owed for him. Dorothy at once said she would continue looking after little Basil whatever happened.

At the same time Aunt Wordsworth, Uncle Richard's widow wrote about the debt owed for William's Cambridge education, and they could not pay this. Coleridge also had many debts. 'As our united funds were very small,' said William, they decided again to try a combined work with the idea of selling it to a periodical The Monthly Magazine. On a cloudy 13th November William, Dorothy and Coleridge set out to walk to Watchet, a little seaport eight miles away. Dorothy wrote to Mary of the two men 'employing themselves in laying out the plan of a ballad' to be published.

The plan was made and the ballad started that same evening while they all three stayed at a little inn in Watchet, with its curved harbour and sailors cottages and the sound of the sea, where the River Wash flows out to the open sea.

William contributed much to the idea, structure and scheme of the Ancient Mariner, though little of the composition. He did, however, remember giving the lines: 'And listens like a three years child

The Mariner hath his will'

And Coleridge remembered William contributed:

'And thou art long and lank and brown

As is the ribbed sea-sand'

It is also possible that Dorothy gave to Coleridge an expression, 'As green as emerald'. Coleridge writes at the beginning of the poem of the 'cold country towards the South Pole' -

'And ice mast high came floating by

As green as emerald'

From a folk song maybe.

From such strange folksongs and childhood sources Coleridge might have been inspired. Perhaps even by the sun and moon clock on his clergyman father's church in Devon:

'The moving moon went up the sky

And nowhere did abide

And softly she was going up

And a star or two beside.'

Dorothy and William in December 1797 had an exciting stay in London, spurred on by Coleridge. Coleridge's own play had been rejected, as he said 'to the kitchen or cloaka'. He praised and offered William's play The Borderers via an actor to Covent Garden management. Dorothy told Mary that she had not the slightest hope of any success, but told her Aunt Elizabeth in Halifax that she dreamed of the play having a prodigious run, and told of 'wildish' schemes for spending all the money from this. She bought herself a new pair of shoes.

The Wordsworths stayed with the Nicolsons, relatives of Halifax friends, at 15 Cateaton Street, London, and William amended his play at the suggestion of various actors. While they awaited the decision of the management, they had free tickets to Covent Garden and Drury Lane. Dorothy loved this, especially the glittering theatre, 'men seen at the extremity of the Opera house, diminished into puppets'. She wrote to her brother Christopher, now a junior fellow at Trinity College, Cambridge that she had twice seen Mrs. Siddons act - on Saturday 2nd December as Portia in The Merchant of Venice, and Monday 4th December as Isabella in an adaptation of The Fatal Marriage by Southern. Dorothy's clear and strong imagination responded to these performances and plays, to the theatre. She loved to read Shakespeare to herself in the evening. A ballet pantomime fire her imagination. Much later, in the Highlands in a hut watching beams of firelight intertwined, she though 'what a feast it would be for a London pantomime maker, could he but transport it to Drury Lane'.

William's play was eventually rejected as well as Coleridge's. Dorothy wrote to Cousin Elizabeth, who commented, 'however they are happy in having very fertile imaginations, which are a constant source of entertainment to them'.

William and Dorothy returned, spent three weeks in Bristol, including Christmas Day - Dorothy's birthday - and returned to Alfoxden in the beginning of January 1798. They sent Basil Montague, who had been looking after his son little Basil, back to London with some more shirts for brother Richard, but all was changed. Coleridge told them he had accepted an invitation to be a Unitarian preacher in Shrewsbury. He had had, but refused, an offer of £100 from Tom and Josia Wedgewood, and told William and Dorothy that they would not be allowed to stay at Alfoxden beyond early summer. Coleridge left on 12th January 1798 for Shrewsbury, and there received the magnificent offer of £150 annuity for his whole life from Tom and Josia Wedgewood. This he accepted in order to pay his debts and for his family. He also wanted to be able to travel to visit Dorothy and William wherever they should be when they left Alfoxden. So that 'wherever your after-residence may be, it is probable that you will be within the reach of my tether'.

CHAPTER 3

As they would be leaving her beloved Alfoxden in a few months' time, Dorothy now began the journal of her life at Alfoxden. She started it on 20th January 1798, of her own inspiration. She begins, 'The green paths down the hillsides are channels for streams. The young wheat is streaked by silver lines of water running between the ridges, the sheep are gathered together on the slopes. After the wet, dark days, the countryside seems more populous. It peoples itself in sunbeams. The garden, mimic of spring, is gay with flowers. The purple-starred hepatica spreads itself in the sun, and the clustering snowdrops put forth their white heads, at first upright ribbed with green, and like a rosebud, then completely opened their heads hanging downwards, but slowly lengthening their slender stems. The slanting woods of an unvarying brown, showing the light through the thin network of their upper boughs. Upon the highest ridge of that round hill covered with planted oaks, the shafts of the trees show in the light like the columns of a ruin.' This is her exact, individual, tender observation, her unerring power of description.

As Dorothy walks and watches she is in a sea-green forest of moss-serpents coiled up the trees. 1st January 1798. 'Walked on the hill tops - a warm day. Sate under the firs in the park. The tops of beeches of a brown-red, or crimson. Those oaks, fanned by the sea-breeze, thick with feathery sea-green moss, as a grove not stripped of its leaves - Moss cups more proper than acorns for fairy goblets.'

'22nd. Walked through the wood to Holford. The ivy twisting round the oaks like bristling serpents. The day cold - a warm shelter in the hollies, capriciously bearing berries. Query: Are the male and female flowers on separate trees?' Dorothy, companion of the trees, their observer, admirer, biological observer also.

The lovely description, Dorothy's entry for 23rd January, 'Bright sunshine went out at 3 o'clock. The sea perfectly calm blue, streaked with deeper colour by the clouds, and tongues or points of sand. The crescent moon, Jupiter and Venus. The sound of the sea distinctly heard on the tops of the hills' - 'the villages marked out by beautiful beds of smoke. The turf fading into the mountain road. The scarlet flowers of moss.' And on 24th her beautiful appreciation of colour and sound: 'Walked between half-past three and half-past five. The evening cold and clear. The sea of sober grey, streaked by the deeper grey clouds. The half-dead sound of the near sheep-bell, in the hollow of the sloping coombe, exquisitely soothing.'

Dorothy was infinitely sensitive and alive to all the moods and weathers of the Quantock countryside near the sea, by day and night. '25th Jan. Went to Pool's after tea. The sky was spread over with one continuous cloud, whitened by the light of the moon, which, though her dim shape was seen, did not throw forth so strong a light as to chequer the earth with shadows. At once the clouds seemed to cleave asunder, and left her in the centre of a blue-black vault. She sailed along, followed by a multitude of stars, small and bright and sharp. Their brightness seemed concentrated, (half moon).'

'4th February, Walked a great part of the way to Stowey with Coleridge - The morning warm and sunny. The young lasses seen on the hill tops, in the villages and roads, in their summer holiday clothes - pink petticoats and blue. Mothers with their children in arms, and the little ones that could just walk, tottering by their side. Midges or small flies spinning in the sunshine; the song of the lark and redbreast; daisies upon the turf; the hazels in blossom; honey-suckles budding. I saw one solitary strawberry flower under a hedge. The furze gay with blossom. The moss rubbed from the palings by the sheep, that leave locks of wool, and the red marks with which they are spotted upon the wood.' Her exact observation building up to early spring atmosphere in careful poetry.

And 26th February (Mr. and Mrs. Crewkshank were the future tenants of Alfoxden), 'Coleridge came in the morning and Mr. and Mrs. Crewkshank; walked with Coleridge nearly to Stowey after dinner. A very clear afternoon we lay sidelong upon the turf, and gazed on the landscape till it melted into more than natural loveliness. The sea was very uniform, of a pale greyish blue, only one distant bay, bright blue as the sky; had there been a vessel sailing upon it, a perfect image of delight. Walked to the top of a

48

high hill to see a fortification. Again sat down to feed upon the prospect; a magnificent scene, curiously spread out for every minute inspection, though so extensive that the mind was afraid to calculate its bounds. A winter prospect shows every cottage every farm, and the forms of distant trees, such as in summer have no distinguishing mark. On our return, Jupiter and Venus before us. While the twilight still overpowered by the light of the moon, we were reminded that she was shining bright above our heads, by our faint shadows going before us. We had seen her on the tops of the hills, melting into the blue sky. Pool called while we were absent.'

They lived happily in the company of day and night; moon stars.

1st February, 'About two hours before dinner set forward to Mr. Bartholomew's (John Bartholomew, who lived at Posham on the road to Minehead, rented Alfoxden and sub-let it to the Wordsworths). The wind blew so keen in our faces that we felt ourselves inclined to seek the covert of the wood. There we had warm shelter, and gathered a burthen of large rotten boughs blown down by the wind of the preceding night. The sun shone clear, but all at once a heavy blackness hung over the sea. The trees almost *roared*, and the ground seemed in motion with the multitudes of dancing leaves, which made a rustling sound, distinct from that of the trees. Still the asses pastured in the quietness under the hollies, undisturbed by these for-runners of the storm. The wind beat furiously against us as we returned. Full moon. She rose in uncommon majesty over the sea, slowly ascending through the clouds. Sat with the window open an hour in the moonlight.'

2nd Feb, 'Walked through the wood, and on the Downs before Dinner; a warm pleasant air. The sun shone, but was often obscured by straggling clouds. The redbreasts made a ceaseless song in the woods. The wind rose very high in the evening. The room smoked so that we were obliged to quit it. Young lambs in the green pasture in the Coombe, thick legs, large heads, black staring eyes.'

27th February, 'I walked to Stowey in the evening. William and Basil went with me through the wood. The prospect bright, yet mildly beautiful. The sea big and white, swelled to the very shores, but round and high in the middle. Coleridge returned with me, as far as the wood. A very bright moonlight night. Venus almost like another moon. Lost to us at Alfoxden long before she goes down the long wide sea.'

They lived so much within each other's hearts and spirits and minds. There was so much loving contact between all three Dorothy, William and Coleridge, that often Wordsworth's and Coleridge's poetry echo each other - and sometimes almost word for word echoing Dorothy's journal, which was full of poetic comments.

2nd April, 'A very high wind. Coleridge came to avoid the smoke; stayed all night. We walked in the wood and sat under the trees. The half of the wood perfectly still, while the wind was making a loud noise behind us. The still trees only gently bowed their heads, as if listening to the wind. The hollies in the thick wood unshaken by the blast; only, when it came with greater force, shaken by the rain drops falling from the bare oaks above.'

What a marvellous description of the wood, half of which was untouched by the wind: 'The still trees only gently bowed their heads, as if listening to the wind. The hollies in the thick wood unshaken by the blast.'

6th April, 'Went part of the way home with Coleridge. A pleasant, warm morning but a showery day. Walked a little distance up the lesser Coombe, with the intention of going to the source of the brook, but the evening closing in cold prevented us. The spring still advancing very slowly. The horse chestnuts budding, and the hedgerows beginning to look green, but nothing fully expanded.

' 7th April, 'Walked before dinner up the Coombe, to the source of the brook, and came home by the tops of the hills; a showery morning, at the hilltops; the view opened upon us very grand.'

Always the great delight in reading, the arrival of sent-for books. 14th April, 'Walked in the wood in the morning. The evening very stormy, so we stayed within doors. Mary Wollstonecraft's life, etc. came.'

15th April, 'Set forward after breakfast to Crockham, and returned to dinner at 3 o'clock. A fine cloudy morning. Walked about the Squire's grounds. Quaint waterfalls about, about which

Nature was very successfully striving to make beautiful what art had deformed - ruins, hermitages, etc., etc. In spite of all these things the dell romantic and beautiful, though everywhere planted with unnaturalised trees. Happily we cannot shape the huge hills, or carve out the valley according to our fancy.'

The huge hills and valleys were where her mind was free; so much colour; and friendship with Mrs. Coleridge too: 13th April, 'Walked in the wood in the morning. In the evening went to Stowey. I stayed with Mrs. Coleridge. William went to Poole's. Supped with Mrs. Coleridge.'

11th April, 'In the wood in the morning, walked to the top of the hill, then I went down into the wood. A pleasant evening, a fine air, the grass in the park becoming green, many green trees in the dell.'

12th April, 'Walked in the morning in the wood. In the evening up the Coombe, fine walk. The spring advances rapidly, multitudes of primroses, dog-violets, periwinkles, stitchwort.'

'Walked in the evening up the hill dividing the Coombes. Came home the Crookham way, by the thorn, and the 'little muddy pond'. Nine o'clock at our return. William all the morning engaged in wearisome composition. The moon crescent. Peter Bell begun.'

Dorothy, walking with William, and living with him, and caring for and looking after him, was very much aware of the work he put into his poetry composition. The little crescent moon was almost a symbol of good luck: 'Peter Bell begun ... ' 'On this day Coleridge too wrote a poem 'Fears in Solitude'.'

27th April: 'Coleridge breakfasted and drank tea, strolled in the wood in the morning, went with him in the evening through the wood, afterwards walked on the hills: the moon, a many-coloured sea and sky.'

Sunday 6th May: 'Expected the painter, and Coleridge. A rainy morning - very pleasant in the evening. Met Coleridge as we were walking out. Went with him to Stowey; heard the nightingale; saw a glow-worm.'

Always the beloved company of Coleridge coming to see them, they going to see him. Rare and beautiful events, 'heard the nightingale; saw a glow-worm.'

Also a walking expedition to Cheddar: 'Wednesday 16th of May Coleridge and William and myself set forward to the Cheddar rocks; slept at Bridgewater.'

'May 22 Thursday (or 24th, which was in fact the Thursday), 'Walked to Cheddar. Slept at Cross.' William went on alone from this expedition to see his publisher Cottle in Bristol.

Harrowed by their having to leave Alfoxden, Martha Ferguson however wrote, 'Dorothy is deeper in plays and poetry than ever.' This is shown by a letter of 5th of March in which Dorothy copied for Mary Hutchinson about 375 lines of 'The Ruined Cottage', which was growing, helped and inspired by Coleridge. Mary was warned 'not to let this poem go out of your own hands.' All copies were hand-made and represented a good deal of work, and so were treasured. By way of thanks Mary was sending ham and cheese from her brother's farm by wagon to William and Dorothy, Basil and Peggy. Dorothy's letter is ended very affectionately, 'God bless you dear Mary, William's very best love'. It is clear from the intimacy and affection of her letter that Mary was seen as part of the family. Dorothy and William were to leave Alfoxden in mid-summer; their chief concern was the loss of Coleridge's beloved society and companionship. To be as near him as possible, they hoped to find another home in Stowey.

Then suddenly Coleridge, typically, changed all their plans and with one of his brilliant shifts of fortune and focus, said he needed for his 'intellectual utility' to read German theologians and philosophers, especially Kant. Between 6th and 11th of March they formed their plan: the Coleridges, Wordsworths and friends would form a 'little colony' in Germany, to learn German and study 'natural science' - they would live in a village near a university in the mountains, near Hamburg, and so travel cheaply. 'Our present plan is to go into Germany for a couple of years' wrote Dorothy to Richard, who was probably horrified at this - to him - foolhardiness.

Their minds at ease about the future, Dorothy, William and Coleridge felt free to enjoy the beautiful summer countryside reading and writing poetry.

Dorothy wrote to Mrs. William Rawson to explain all this:

'My dear Aunt, you know that we are obliged to quit
Alfoxton at Midsummer. It is not, however, on account of the
taxes, for we could not get rid of them by appealing, but because
the house has been taken by another person. At first we regretted
the circumstances very much as everything has contributed to
attach us to this place, the society of Coleridge and the friendly
attentions of Mr. Poole who is a man of uncommon virtue and
good sense, the exceptional beauty of the countryside, and the
excellent opportunities we have of getting books; but as we
are now determined upon going into Germany along with Mr.
and Mrs. Coleridge and their family we are glad that we are
not shackled with the house.

We have long wished to go into that country for the
purpose of learning the language, and for the common
advantages to be acquired by seeing different people and
different manners. Coleridge has had the same wish; and we
have so arranged our plans that I hope we shall sail in two or
three months. Our first intention was to have gone immediately
to the neighbourhood of one of the universities; but as we
found the price of lodgings etc. is much greater in the towns
where there are universities we have resolved to go into some
small town or village, till we have acquired the language, which
we imagine we shall have a good knowledge of in about twelve
months, and afterward, to draw near a university when William
and Coleridge will then be better able to profit by the instruction
they may have an opportunity of receiving.

We are advised to go into Saxony. Some parts of that
country are extremely beautiful, and boarding is very cheap. It
is our intention (William's and mine) to board in some
respectable family for the benefit or rather the obligation of
talking German constantly. The Coleridges, if they can, will
take a ready-furnished house as they have two children and
must, of course, keep a servant.

Such are our plans for one year, at least; what we shall

do afterwards it is at present impossible to say. If the state of Europe will permit we shall endeavour to get into Switzerland; at any rate we shall travel as far as the tether of our slender income will permit. We hope to make some addition to our resources by translating from the German, the most profitable species of literary labour, of which I can do almost as much as my brother.'

She tells of Basil with her careful, loving awareness and attention, her understanding and pride in his development while living with William, herself and Peggy. Sadly they could neither take him with them, nor Peggy.

'Poor Basil! We are obliged to leave him behind, as his father, on account of having altered the course of his pursuit of the law, will not be able to pay the additional expenses which we should incur on his account. This, however, might be got over as he has friends who would do it for him, but as the experiment of taking a child of his age into a foreign country is at any rate hazardous and might be prejudicial if we were not so placed that he might see much of other children, we think upon the whole that it is better that he should not go, taking into calculation the certain expense.'
Dorothy then speaks wisely and understandingly of the care and education of children, always a great concern of hers. 'I am convinced that it is not good for a child to be educated alone after a certain age - Basil has in some respects, I think, suffered from it, though no doubt in others he has gained; he has a most excellent temper, is quite free from selfishness, is extremely active, and never fretful or discontented. Much of his good temper must be owing to our regularity of temper, and the constant equable treatment he receives from us. If he had been more with children whose minds were upon the same level as his own, *I think he could scarcely have been without selfishness. As to his activity, I believe that the solitude of Racedown tended considerably to increase it. Till a child is four*

*years old he needs no other companions than the flowers, g ...
the cattle, the sheep that scamper away from him when he makes
a vain, unexpected chase after them, the pebbles upon the road,
etc., etc. After the age of about four years, he begins to want
some other stimulus than the mere life that is in him - his efforts
would be greater but he must have an object, he would run but
he must run races, he would climb a wall but has no motive to
do it when he is alone; he must have some standard by which
to compare his powers or he will have no pleasure in exercising
them, and he becomes lifeless and inactive.*

*Basil, as to bodily exertion, has had this great advantage
ever since we came to Alfoxton; he has played a great deal
with a little boy who lives near us. He is a very naughty, spoiled
child but I think Basil has not suffered so much from him morally,
as we expected, and has certainly gone on improving in physical
strength. The situations of the two children at home are so totally
different as to prevent all comparison, one source of selfishness
and Basil is so convinced that to be (good ...?)'*

Here Dorothy's letter breaks off and is resumed three weeks
later when they had left Alfoxton and were in Bristol.

The only possible way to pay for this journey was for William
to sell his poems, and so they looked for a publisher. It was on 23rd
March that Coleridge read the now completed 'Ancient Mariner'
to William and Dorothy. This historic occasion took place in the
panelled parlour at Alfoxden House. His reading of this poem was
haunting and impressive as always; Mary Shelley - the writer, author
of *Frankenstein* daughter of Mary Wollstonecraft and Godwin and
Shelley's second wife - remembered having hidden behind a sofa
with Clare her stepsister and her stepbrother, as a child in her father
William Godwin's house, while Coleridge read this poem. She and
the other children were forbidden by their oppressive stepmother to
hear this beautiful poem, but the children were determined to listen
and so hid in the dark behind the sofa and heard it all. Mary Shelley
said she was haunted by the poem all her life. Coleridge said that
such was the second Mrs. Godwin's oppression of the children in

that house that it was 'quite catacombish'.

At this time William only spoke little of his poetry, and that merely to Coleridge and Dorothy, but she noted that his powers seemed to grow every day and 'his ideas flow faster than he can express them'.

They all hoped that Joseph Cottle, who had heard some of William's work on a visit to Stowey and had liked it, would publish William's poems. They invited Cottle, whom Dorothy liked, to visit them at Alfoxden and to hear readings of William's new poems under the great trees in the park. They all seemed to accept the fact that Cottle would publish, and Dorothy walked to Stowey with William to have his picture taken by the visiting artist W. Shuter - William's first known portrait. Coleridge gave this to Cottle. Dorothy and Coleridge, as she says in her diary, then walked with William to Cheddar, as he went on his way to see Cottle in Bristol.

From 24th May Dorothy stayed with Sara Coleridge, whose second child Berkley had been born about ten days earlier. William, having visited Bristol, returned bringing Joseph Cottle.

Cottle recounts that he drove with William and Coleridge in a gig bringing a noble loaf and a stout cheese and a bottle of brandy to Alfoxden. On the road from Stowey a beggar smelt the cheese and stole it; while Coleridge and Wordsworth were very incompetently unharnessing the horse in the courtyard, the bottle of brandy fell and was broken. Peggy had to rescue them and unharness the horse properly. So for supper that evening Dorothy could only set out the noble loaf, a plate of her own home-grown beautiful coss lettuce and an empty plate where the cheese should have been. They drank clear water instead of the brandy. That was the last entertaining of publishers that Dorothy tried; henceforth the village a mile away provided Cottle's meals, with Coleridge and William for company. But at the end of May Dorothy could report to Richard that 'William has sold his poems very advantageously'.

Cottle, Coleridge and William had discussed their plan for their book while taking Cottle on a tour to Lynton. This time Dorothy stayed at home. 'The Ancient Mariner' was first in the book, and then three others by Coleridge, one a dramatic poem; these joined

William's book of lyrics, in which Cottle said he found 'a peculiar but decided merit'. Eventually there were four earlier poems of William's - or parts of poems - included, but the great contributions to the character of the book were the lyric poems which William wrote at Alfoxden, the harvest of all Dorothy's loving care of him, her devoted housekeeping and copying and encouragement.

William wrote later, 'I published these poems for money and for money alone'. Coleridge and he in the preface were called 'The Author' and were anonymous.

After his stay at Alfoxden, Cottle went back to Bristol, taking 'The Ancient Mariner' and some of William's poems with him. William then followed him for further discussions.

By that time the Wordsworths had to leave Alfoxden, 'that dear and beautiful place' as Dorothy said.

Portrait of William Wordsworth 1798 by Robert Hancock
Reproduced with the kind permission of
The National Portrait Gallery

Dorothy (aged 62), ill but still writing her journal

CHAPTER 4

On 25th June they went to stay for a week at the Coleridges and then went on to Bristol, where they probably stayed with Joseph Cottle in wine Street. Dorothy grieved for the country in that noisy city, 'You cannot conceive,' she wrote to her Aunt Rawson, 'how the jarring contrast between the sounds which are now for ever ringing in my ears and the sweet sounds of Alfoxton make me long for the country again.'

Dorothy set out the finances for their journey to Germany to reassure her Aunt Rawson (and herself): 'When I am just upon the point of concluding my letter, I recollect that you may perhaps think that we are going upon an expensive scheme into Germany and that our income will not suffice to maintain us. I must put you to the expense of a double letter to explain this to you. Notwithstanding Mr. Montagu (from having changed the course of his application to the law) has not been able to fulfil his engagement respecting Basil, we have lived upon our income and are not a farthing poorer than when we began housekeeping. We can live for less money in Germany while we are stationary than we can in England, so that you see our regular income (independent of what we may gain by translation) will be sufficient to support us when we are there, and we shall receive, before our departure much more than sufficient to defray the expenses of our journey, from a bookseller to whom William has sold some poems that are now printing, for which he is to have a certain present price and is to be paid afterwards in proportion to their sale. Our expense last year £23 for rent, our journey to London, clothes, servants wages included, only amounted to £110. We have parted from our servant. Poor Girl! It was a hard trial for her. She would have gone to the world's end with us. I believe she was much more attached to us than to any other beings in the world. She was married a year ago and is now with child so she would have left us, if we had even been in England.'

She speaks of Coleridge and Southey, and of Mr. Rawson: 'I wonder whether we are likely to see Mr. Rawson during our two months residence in this neighbourhood. I fear there is not much chance of it as he generally makes his journey later. I need not say what pleasure it would give me to see him. I wish he had ever contrived to visit us at Alfoxden, if he had had no other motive than that of seeing an interesting country he would not have been disappointed. I have not often felt more regret than when we quitted Alfoxden: I should however have felt much more if we were not likely in so short a time to have again the pleasure of Coleridge's society, an advantage which I prize the more I know him.

'You ask me if I am acquainted with Southey. I know a little of him personally, that is I dined three times at his house when I was in town and called there once or twice; and I know a good deal of his character from our common friends. He is a young man of the most rigidly virtuous habits and is, I believe, exemplary in the discharge of all domestic duties, but though his talents are certainly very remarkable for his years (as far as I can judge) I think them much inferior to the talents of Coleridge.'

The Ferguson relations seemed a bit doubtful about it all, 'The Plan which you may think a curious one ... ' Dorothy lays it all down in a very agreeable manner ' ... and I wish it may answer to their views.' They were, however, delighted and completely reassured by the fact that William was going to publish his poems. 'I believe he has got a good price from a bookseller,' cousin Edward informed cousin Samuel admiringly. 'Cottle,' Dorothy told them the next month, 'has given 30 guineas for William's share of the volume'.

Though busy in Bristol with the printing of 'Lyrical Ballads', the Wordsworths took two trips, one into Wales with Coleridge and Thelwell on his farm in Brecknockshire, and another to Tintern Abbey, about which Wordsworth wrote his beautiful poem 'Lines Composed a Few Miles Above Tintern Abbey', with its tribute to Dorothy, his 'dear, dear sister':

' ... Therefore let the moon
Shine on thee on thy solitary walk;
And let the misty mountain winds be free
To blow against thee: and in after years,

When these wild ecstasies shall be matured
Into a sober pleasure; when thy mind
Shall be a mansion for all lovely forms,
Thy memory be as a dwelling place
For all sweet sounds and harmonies; oh! then,
If solitude, or fear, or pain, or grief,
Should be thy portion, with what healing thoughts
Of tender joy wilt thou remember me,
And these my exhortations! Nor, perchance -
If I should be where I can no more hear
Thy voice, nor catch from thy wild eyes these gleams
Of past experience - wilt thou then forget
That on the banks of this delightful stream
We stood together; and that I, so long
A worshipper of Nature, hither came
Unwearied in that service: rather say
With warmer love - oh! with far deeper zeal
Of holier love. Nor wilt thou then forget,
That after many wanderings, many years
Of absence, these steep woods and lofty cliffs,
And this green pastoral landscape, were to me
More dear, both for themselves and for thy sake!'

This marvellous poem was the last in the new book. Though
it makes one sad when reading it to think of the actual mental and
physical illness that darkened and marred Dorothy's last years - her
loss of memory and self-awareness. The only comfort, however,
was that she was very well and lovingly cared for by William and
Mary, practising their love and concern in a very good way with
instinctive psycho-geriatric nursing and attentive treatment.
    Returning from Tintern Abbey, Bristol seemed more noisy
and dirty than ever. Luckily James Losh, an acquaintance from
William's Paris days who was now in Bath for health reasons, sub-
let them a cottage at Shiehampton just outside the city. They stayed
there waiting while the poems were in the press. Then, in the last
week in August, they set out for London, stopping to see Blenheim

63

and Oxford. Dorothy wrote from London, 13th September that the poems were 'printed but not published in one small volume'. By the day of publication, Wordsworth and Coleridge and Dorothy were at sea heading for Germany.

Coleridge had eventually decided to leave his family at home, and wrote that 'Mrs. Coleridge's wishes tend the same way'. The only other person who came with them was a young neighbour from Stowey, John Chester, who adored Coleridge, 'attracted to Coleridge's discourse as flies are to honey,' said Hazlitt.

'Wordsworth shockingly ill,' reported Coleridge of their sea-voyage, 'his sister worst of all - vomiting and groaning unspeakably, and I neither sick nor giddy but gay as a lark'. In spite of it all Dorothy stuck courageously to her determination to keep a travel diary. She wrote of the Tuesday morning when they were in the still waters of the Elbe delayed by fog, 'The air cold and wet, the decks streaming, the shores invisible, no hope of clear weather.' The fog cleared, the ship slowly sailed upstream, and from Altona a rowing boat landed them at the quay of Hamburg on the Thursday afternoon.

Dorothy's observer's eye immediately began to enjoy the variety of human beings passing by: 'While we stood in the street which was open on one side of the Elbe, I was much amused by the various employments and dresses of the people who passed before us. There were Dutch women with immense straw bonnets, with flat crowns and rims in the shape of oyster shells, without trimming, or with only a plaid riband round the crown, and literally as large as a small-sized umbrella. Hamburger girls with white caps, with broad overhanging borders, showing all the face, and standing upright, a profusion of riband. Fruit-women, with large straw hats in the shape of an inverted bowl, or white handkerchiefs tyed round their head like a bishop's mitre. Jackets the most common; often the petticoat and jacket of different colours. The ladies without hats, in dresses of all fashions. Soldiers with dull-looking red coats, and immense cocked hats. The men little different from the English, except they generally have a pipe in their mouths.

'After waiting about an hour we saw William re-appear.' William had gone to seek lodgings and Dorothy, Coleridge and John

Chester guarded the luggage. 'Two porters carried our luggage in a sort of wheel-barrow, and we were conducted through the narrow, dirty, ill-paved stinking street to an inn, which with great difficulty, and after long seeking lodgings, had been procured for us.'

Life was difficult travelling, especially for someone as insular as Dorothy: 'the first impression an Englishman receives on entering a Hamburg inn is that of filth and filthy smells.'

'On our inquiring we found we could have no dinner, for dinner was over.

'I went upstairs to dress, a man servant brought up napkin water, etc. - My room at the top of the house contained a small bed, a chest of drawers, a table, four chairs and a stove in the corner. The floor just washed but I could see that the process had spread or plastered the coating of dirt - no carpet - floor painted brown - a large looking glass - four marks (a marks was 6 pence) the price of this room and Chester's and Coleridge's. When I returned I found the party below eating cold beef - no cloth spread, no vegetables, but some bad cucumbers pickled without vinegar. Very good wine at one mark four sous the bottle.'

In the ensuing days they got to know Hamburg. Dorothy wrote, 'Roused by the sound of the market. I could not but observe, notwithstanding the dirt of the houses, that the lower orders of women seemed in general much cleaner in their persons than the same rank in England.

'Breakfasted with Mons. de Loutre. Chester and I went to the promenade. People of all ranks, and in various dresses, walking backwards and forwards. Ladies with small baskets hanging on their arms, some without handkerchiefs and their necks entirely exposed, long shawls of various colours thrown over their shoulders. The women of the lower orders dressed with great modesty. Fruit and cakes of all kinds to be sold. English hardware - we asked the price of a plain leather inkstand. It was three marks. After spending three hours very pleasantly we returned home.'

Dorothy was horrified, 'the disposition is to cheat,' she said of the Hamburg shopkeepers; 'the honest shopkeeper a Jewess,' she notes.

65

On Wednesday September 26th they 'dined with Mr Klopstock. Had the pleasure of meeting his brother the poet, a venerable old man, retaining the liveliness and alertness of youth, though his legs are swelled immensely and he evidently cannot be very far from the grave. His second wife much younger than he, a fine, fresh-looking woman, but with an unpleasant expression of countenance, vain and not pleasing in her manners. Mr. Klopstock the merchant, very polite and kind; his wife who cannot speak a word of either English or French appears a very interesting woman; They have a little girl of 7 years old. She was dressed in a coloured frock, and her neck covered up with a thick handkerchief. (N.B. Mrs. Klopstock, the poet's lady, much exposed.) The child seemed indulged. The teeth of all the family very bad, their complexions fair. The rest of the party consisted of a young German who spoke a little English, a niece of Mr. Klopstocks, William and myself. We were conducted through the warehouse and counting house into a large low room with two windows at the end, and a glass door opening upon a balcony, which overlooks a part of the Elbe. The room hung with gilt, leather, a picture of Lessing, some other portraits, a bust of his brother in one corner. Floor painted brown, no carpet, mahogany tables, desks, chairs, etc. We had scarcely sat three minutes before we were called to dinner in the next room to which we were led in by folding doors. We sat round the table without order; Mrs. Klopstock distributed the dishes in succession. Soup first and second stewed veal without vegetables, third sausages with cabbage, fourth oysters with spinach, fifth fowls with salad and currant jelly, dessert grapes, biscuits, pears, plums, walnuts; afterwards coffee. A woman servant in the Hanoverian cap waited at table. She seemed more at her ease and more familiar than an English servant. She laughed and talked with the little girl. We withdrew into the next room and had tea. Mr. Klopstock's niece brought in the candles and washed up the tea things in a sort of passage or lobby. The party talked with much interest of the French comedy and seemed fond of music. The poet and his lady were obliged to depart soon after six. He sustained an animated conversation with William the whole afternoon. Poor old man! I could not look upon him, the benefactor of his country, the father of German poetry, without the most sensible emotion. We returned a little after seven. I had a bad headache and went to bed at nine.'

September 27th, Thursday, 'a bad headache. William and I set forward at 12 o'clock to Altona.' Dorothy describes what pleased her: 'The entrance to the town of Altona is very pleasant, the street is only built on one side and overlooks the Elbe - afterwards it becomes narrow and crowded. The walk between Hamburg and Altona is very pleasant, sandy and dry. The view towards Hamburg pleasing, a large branch of the Elbe winding through the flat country, the spire of Hamburg and gently rising grounds behind. The Elbe in the vicinity of Hamburg is so divided and spread out, that the country looks more like a plain overflowed by heavy rains than the bed of a great river. We went about a mile and a half beyond Altona; the roads dry and sandy and a causeway for foot passengers. The country in general immediately around us not rich or highly cultivated. The peasants were taking up their potatoes which appeared to have been ill-managed, they were very small. The houses on the banks of the Elbe, chiefly of brick, seemed very warm and well-built. Some gentlemen's houses are of white stone, the English fashion. The small cottage houses seemed to have little gardens, and all the gentlemen's houses were surrounded by gardens quaintly disposed in beds and curious knots, with ever-twisting gravel paths and bending poplars. The view of the Elbe and the spreading country must be very interesting in a fine sunset. There is a want of some atmospheric irradiation to give a richness to the scene. We met a drunken man on returning home, and were accosted by the first beggar whom we have seen since our arrival in Hamburg. He was an old man, a woman who seemed connected with him sate near him under a hedge, but did not make any petition.' Dorothy noticed beggars, the wild wanderers of the earth. 'We got some cakes at a French pastry cook's and after going nearly as far as the French Theatre bought some bread. I lay down till Coleridge returned from Ratzburg, a beautiful place but very dear.'

She also wrote about what displeased her in this strange place: Sept. 28th, Friday: 'Settled the account with Monsr. de Loutre. Still had a headache. Sought Coleridge at the booksellers and went to the promenade. Dined at the ordinary. All the Hamburgers full of Lord Nelson's victory. Our landland no very pleasing object to us while he sat with his greasy face at the head of the table, laughing with landlord-like vulgarity and complaisance, at the jokes of his guests, or while he exercised the force of his mind in deliberating the best way of cutting the beef. He had cheated us in our bill of not less than four guineas. Yesterday saw a man of about fifty years of age beating a woman decently dressed and about 37 years of age. He struck her on the breast several times and beat her with his stick. The expression in her face and attitude were half of anger and half of a spirit of resistance. What her offence had been we could not learn. It was in the public street. He was better dressed than she was, and evidently a stranger and this brutal treatment did not excite the smallest indignation in the breast of the spectators. They seemed rather to take the man's part. Called at a baker's shop. Put two shillings into the baker's hands, for which I was to have four small rolls. He gave me two and I let him understand that I was to have four, and with this view I took one shilling from him, pointing to it and to two loaves, and at the same time offering it to him, again I took up two others. In a savage manner he half-knocked the rolls out of my hand, and when I asked him for the other shilling he refused to return it, neither would he suffer me to take bread, nor give me back my money, and on these terms I quitted the shop. I am informed that it is the boast and glory of these people to cheat strangers; that when a feat of this kind is successfully performed the man goes from his shop into his house, and triumphantly relates it to his wife and family. The Hamburg shopkeepers have three sorts of weights, and a great part of their skill as shopkeepers, consists in calculating upon the knowledge of the buyer, and suiting him with scales accordingly.'

Sept. 29th: 'We took our places in the morning in the Brunswick coach for Wednesday. The fare 12 marks. We had two small trunks which we wished to have conveyed to the post, the distance about 3 hundred yards. A porter had the audacity to demand 20d for carrying them, and was very insolent when William refused to give it to him. He offered him 8d, which was more than a London porter would have expected. William carried them himself through a very heavy shower of rain.'

September 30th: 'Coleridge and Chester went to Ratzberg at 7 o'clock in the morning. Coleridge had a violent contest with the postilion who insisted on his paying 20p a mile for each horse, instead of a mark, the established fare. He was obliged to yield - but whether he can get redress or not I know not.'

Ratzberg was just outside Hamburg, a lovely island resort on a lake. There Dorothy said they were 'all in high life among Barons and Countesses,' ... 'we should be ruined.' Coleridge had his annuity from Wedgwood to give him more freedom of movement than William and Dorothy, who 'must find obscurer and cheaper lodgings without boarding.' Also it made sense to separate from Coleridge and concentrate on their learning German. 'I hear the two noble Englishmen have parted no sooner than they set foot on German earth,' wrote Lamb to Southey.

Without Coleridge Hamburg seemed even sadder and more oppressive than ever, Dorothy writing, 'William and I set forward at half past 11 with an intention of going to Blankenese. It was a fine morning but very windy. When we had got nearly through the town we saw a surly-looking German driving a poor Jew forward with foul language, and making frequent use of a stick which he had in his hand - The countenance of the Jew expressed neither anger nor surprise nor agitation; he spoke, but with meekness, and unresisting, pursued his way, followed by his inhuman driver, whose insolence we found was supported by law: the Jew had no right to reign in the city of Hamburg, as a German told us in broken English. The soldiers who are stationed at the drawbridge looked very surly at him, and the countenances of the bystanders expressed cold unfeeling cruelty.' With such a history of anti-semitism in Germany one thinks of the Holocaust, and the accepting attitude towards it of some Germans.

William wrote to Poole that Hamburg was a 'sad' place - and asked his friend if they might return to Alfoxden. This, however, did not happen.

As they were preparing for their next journey, William called at his friend the poet, Klopstock's, to ask about the way into Saxony - and at Remnant's English bookshop bought Burger's poems and Percy's Reliques of English Poetry. At 5 in the evening of the third of October they took the diligence to Brunswick.

They had a very miserable journey; Dorothy writes, 'our carriage was more than half-covered and lined with leather within, luxuries which I have since found are not often to be met with in a German diligence, though when we entered it I was much more inclined to observe the wretched crazy appearance of the whole, the crevices in the upper part (which was made of wood), the basketwork below, and the great space all round for the winds to blow through on every side, than to congratulate myself upon our good luck. Before we had got four miles from Hamburg the shaking of the carriage gave me a violent pain in my bowels, which was followed by sickness.'

Dorothy and William journeyed to Brunswick staying at wretched inns and seeing the countryside all by moonlight. They admired the Brunswick gardens produced by much industry from the sandy soil; and potato and turnip fields. The inn at Brunswick was welcome to them providing a good meal, a neat parlour in the English style and excellent beds and blankets. Here Dorothy must have recovered.

They took their places in the Goslar diligence in order to set off at 8 in the morning.

So after they had dined on the day of their arrival, they walked about and looked at Brunswick. It seemed quiet and dull. Dorothy says, 'We saw none of the gaiety and bustle of Hamburg ...' 'The Duke's palace is a large white building. There is nothing of elegance in its external appearance, but the gardens seemed as if they would be very pleasant. We peeped through a gateway, but were told it was too late to enter. When we left our inn William carried the portmanteau, and I the small parcel. He left them under my charge and went in search of a baker's shop. He brought me his pockets full of apples, for which he had paid two bon gros, and some excellent bread. Upon these I breakfasted and carried Kubla to a fountain in the neighbouring market place, where I drank some excellent water.'

(Kubla was the nickname Dorothy gave all water carrying vessels she used, after Coleridge's poem 'Kubla Kahn'). 'It was on Saturday the 6th of October when we arrived at Goslar between five and six in the evening.'

They arrived at Goslar after a journey which lasted from eight in the morning to eight at night. It was four months before they could bear to travel again.

Goslar was a decaying small town 'once the residence of emperors' William wrote, 'now the residence of grocers and linen drapers'. Dorothy described it as 'a lifeless town'. They settled in cheap lodgings with a drapers widow Frau Depperman in Brietstrasse. 'Provisions very cheap and lodgings cheap,' they told Coleridge - 'but no society'. They ate with only the two of them there, sat together by the iron stove, which kept the room very warm, and their society was their landlady, a French emigré priest, a young apprentice in the house, and a deaf and toothless neighbour. They had no invitations to go out. Coleridge said that as only married women went into society, 'His taking his sister with him was a wrong step - here a sister is considered only a name for mistress'.

Dorothy wrote to her brother Christopher Wordsworth: 'For more than two months past we have intended quitting Goslar in the course of each week, but we have been so frightened by the cold season, the dreadful roads, and the uncovered carts, that we needed no other motives (adding these considerations to our natural aversion to moving from a place where we live in comfort and quietness) to induce us to linger here. We have had a succession of excessively severe weather, once or twice interrupted with a cold thaw; and the cold of Christmas day has not been equalled in this climate during the last century. It was so excessive that when we left the room where we sit we were obliged to wrap ourselves up in greatcoats, etc., in order not to suffer much pain from the transition, though we only went into the next room or downstairs for a few minutes. No wonder then that we were afraid of travelling all night in an open cart! I do not believe that we should yet venture to move if we had not hit upon another plan, namely that of walking the first 30 or 35 miles of our journey, by which means we shall save the distance of

20 miles, a circuit of which the diligence makes, and shall also travel through much pleasanter country. Nordhausen, a city in Upper Saxony, is the place to which our footsteps tend. We shall there meet with covered diligences to all the considerable towns of Saxony. We are not yet exactly decided whither we shall go. We have letters to Weimar, but there are other places which seem to promise equal advantages, and where living is much cheaper as Erfurt, Eisnach, etc. ...'

'We have gone on advancing in the language, the main object of our journey, in tolerably regular progress, but if we had had the advantages of good society we should have done much more, this, however, is a benefit which we have now given up all expectation of attaining, as we find that when a man and woman are received into society, they are expected, being considered as a sort of family, to give entertainments in return for what they receive. Now this, in conjunction with the expense of travelling, is absolutely out of our power, though I believe we could do it, being stationary, for as little expense as we could live for, entirely without company in England. We have then bounded our desires to seeing a little more of this country and getting into a family pretty much resembling this, in which we are now with whom, as now, we may talk upon common subjects.'

"The climate of this part of Germany appears to me to be much colder than that of England, but I daresay the difference *seems* to be greater than it is, on account of the stoved rooms, whose summer warmth makes a contrast with the external air, that sets the flesh acreeping, even when you go through the passages and staircases. Our room has never been heated by so many degrees as the rooms of Goslar in general are, but I got a severe cough in the seasoning. I am now however quite well and can bear any transitions. We walk at least an hour every day, often much more. William has a green gown lined throughout with fox's skin, and I wrap myself up in furs that defy the cold.'

'The woman of this house who is a civil and good kind of respectable woman in her way could not refrain from cheating us of half-pence and farthings when we first came. She is a widow with 5 children, and keeps a linen draper's shop, which I daresay barely serves to support them decently. Yet she dresses herself out very fine in artificial flowers on a Sunday, and spent half a Louis on a jaunt in a traineau (sledge), a luxury which I suppose it would be a disgrace not to enjoy once in a winter. When the snow first fell, the whole town was in commotion, traineaus everywhere! But the people are not rich enough to keep it long, all is now quiet. Coleridge is in a very different world from what we stir in, he is all in high life, among barons, counts and countesses. He could not be better placed than he is at Ratzberg for attaining the object of his journey; but his expenses are much more than our conjointly. I think however he has done perfectly right in consenting to pay so much, as he will not stay longer in Germany than till March or April. It would have been impossible for us to have lived as he does; we should have been ruined.'

'William has been mixing with his German employment a good deal of English poetical composition. We have lived very happily and comfortably, but not sufficiently different from our English way of life. A young man, an apprentice in the house, comes up to sit with us every evening, but we have no other society but that of a French emigré priest, and what we find in our daily intercourse with this family.'

For inspiration William used to walk about in the moonlight, all in his fur gown and black fur hat, Dorothy said he looked like 'a grand Signior'.'

Coleridge sent them some poems to amuse them addressed to 'dear William and dear Dorothy', a line in them is, 'Dorothy eager of soul, my most affectionate sister'. In return William sent Coleridge 'two or three little Ryme poems which I hope will amuse you.' These were his mysterious 'Lucy' poems. One beginning, 'Strange fits of passion ... ' and one, 'She dwelt among the untrodden ways'. The third is the lovely poem:

'A slumber did my spirit seal;
I had no human fears:
She seemed a thing that could not feel

The touch of earthly years.
No motion has she now, nor force;
She neither hears nor sees;
Rolled round in earth's diurnal course
With rocks, and stones, and trees.'

No one knows who 'Lucy' was. Coleridge says in a letter to Tom Poole, writing about the death of his baby Berkley at home in Nether Stowey: 'Some months ago Wordsworth transmitted to me a most sublime epitaph, whether it had any reality I cannot say. Most probably, in some gloomier moment he had fancied the moment in which his sister might die.' There was perhaps all the grief felt at the death of Peggy Hutchinson, sister of Mary and Sara, who had recently died young of consumption. She had been a dear friend to both Dorothy and William since their childhood in Penrith. Otherwise the Lucy poems are a mystery of William's imagination.

Dorothy was quiet and deeply attentive to William's poetry, to the conditions of his creativity, as she had learned to be at Racedown and Alfoxden. So it was in this freezing, limited, but in some ways strange and happy time of their dwelling at Goslar.

When the snow thawed and the sun shone William and Dorothy set off, walking through the Harz Forest, seeing the moss bright green after the snow. Having sent their luggage on ahead, this was their little pilgrimage from town to town, that Dorothy had hoped for when writing to Christopher, before returning to Hamburg and sailing home. It was expensive in Germany, even for their simple way of living, and their German was not progressing as they had hoped. They kept at this time a joint journal, which Coleridge hoped to incorporate into a book about Germany for Longmans, but nothing came of it and William and Dorothy's journal was lost.

Dorothy, however, tells of their adventures in a letter to Coleridge written from Nordhausen. 'Goslar lies on the edge of some high hills; mountains they cannot be called, at the skirts of the Hartz Forest. After walking about a mile we began to ascend through a pine forest which with the accompaniments of a tiny waterfall alias "Kittenrachs" (Coleridge's name for a small cateract) might as

74

William says remind a traveller of the Alps in the same way as a little kitten may suggest a full-grown tiger.'

She tells of when they were 'saluted with the song of the lark, a pair of larks, a sweet, liquid and heavenly melody heard for the first time after so long and severe a winter. I ought to have said that before this we had a view of the Brocken, the Mont Blanc of the Hartz Forest, and the glory of all this part of Germany. I cannot speak of its height compared with any of our British mountains, but from the point from which we saw it, it had nothing impressive in its appearance. The day continued cheering and delightful, and we walked through a country presenting forest views of hill and valley, one of which a deep valley with a village built of wood scattered in the bottom, was very interesting. We lingered under the shades of the trees and did not arrive at Osterode till four o'clock in the afternoon. It is also a Hanoverian possession, a small *city* lying at the edge of the Hartz Forest, in a kind of low, wide valley. The appearance of the people as we passed through the streets was very little favourable, they looked dirty, impudent, and vulgar, and absolutely the whole town being at the windows or in the streets as we unluckily met them coming from church. We were stared completely out of countenance, at least I was; William stoutly denies that he was at all uncomfortable; however this was we had not the courage to stop at an inn till we had walked through the whole town, and just on the other side of the city gates, we called at one where they told us they could give us nothing to eat. While we stood pondering what we should do, inquiring for another Wirthaus, and half resolved to go a league further we were told we could be accommodated, one of the under-officers of the town, who was drinking with a sort of rabble, in the Wirthaus where we had been refused admittance, accosted us, and civilly assured us that we should be admitted into the house, but he brought one of his comrades a little step above him in place and about equal in self-importance and insolence, who questioned us respecting our business etc., etc., and would not let us pass without a passport. He conducted William to the Burgomaster who promised to grant him the said passport in the morning after he had seen our letters which were to come by the post wagon, with our trunk in the evening. In the mean time I was left in one of those towers which you always see at the entrance of cities, amongst a set of soldiers who were furbishing their dress, a woman who was engaged in some kind of Taylors business, and a man who had an iron ring and chain hanging to his hand, I suppose as a punishment for some felony. You may be sure I was not a little impatient for William's return. He brought back his friend the officer in great good humour both with himself and him, for he took care to flatter his vanity, and we were admitted into the Wirthaus where we had some cold veal for supper, decentish beds, and a large quantity of excellent coffee in the morning for the value of one shilling and eleven pence English money. Though we rose at seven o'clock, owing to the delays of office, we did not leave our inn till after ten. It was a mild morning, the sun shone occasionally through the patches of broken clouds, the larks regaled us with a never-ceasing song. Westill had the Hartz Forest on our left, and crossed a very delightful valley through which our road ought to have taken us but the floods had swept away the bridge. The country through which we passed was in general pleasant and tolerably peopled, but the ways dreadful, we were often obliged to walk as in the mines at Stowey, above the ankles in water, and sometimes as high in clay. We left the town of Hartzberg on our left; it had a huge decaying castle, built upon the edge of a steep hill richly wooded and commanding a fine prospect of hills clothed with Beech wood, and a wide meadow valley through which runs a respectable river, after we left this place the roads grew worse and worse, the darkness came on, and we were near being stopped by a water when a wagon overtook us which conducted us safely to an inn at Schazefeld, where we got a good supper, that is cold beef, indifferent soup, and cabbage, straw beds and coffee and bread and butter for one shilling and ten pence. In the night we had a hard frost and the first part of our yesterday's journey was very delightful, the country charming, something like the widest of the Welsh valleys, the widest and tamest, but afterwards the roads grew worse, still however we had a pleasant walk, and reached our inn at four in the afternoon. We had sausages and boiled milk for supper, coffee, etc. for one shilling and nine pence, we slept in company with our host and hostess and four children, a facetious shoe-maker, a Prussian tax-gatherer and a journeyman hat maker, who had travelled all over Germany working a month here, and a few days there, to see the world. Our landlord had been in the Prussian service, a fine-looking man, extremely fond of his children, and seeming to be very happy with a very good-tempered wife. We were struck with the extreme folly of people who draw conclusions respecting national character from the narrow limits of common observation. We have been much with German hosts and hostesses and notwithstanding the supposed identifying tendency first of national manners, and of particular occupations, these persons appeared in every respect as if made in contrast to each other, but this will be a more proper subject for conversation ... ' 'This morning was very rainy, so we got into the post wagon, in which conveyance we travelled ten miles and arrived at the posthaus in the afternoon. We are now at a tolerable inn but we don't know what we have to pay; I have thus brought down the little history of our lives since Saturday morning. I now come to something of more importance, the subject of your letters - but let me first speak of the joy we felt at seeing your handwriting again; I burst open the seals and could almost have kissed them in the presence of the post master, but we did not read a word till we got to the inn where we devoured them separately, for at least two hours. With the experience we have had of the possibility of travelling for a very trifling expense, we cannot but think you have done wisely in quitting Ratzberg, both on your own account and that of Chester. Gottingen seems to be the best possible place for your purpose.

'William now takes the pen. God bless you, Dear, Dear Coleridge.'

Dorothy's letter has her beautiful seeing and describing their way out adventures of random travel-met people: on twentieth of April they reached Gottingen and saw their beloved Coleridge after six months' separation; William was almost in tears, Dorothy grieved deeply over the death of Coleridge's baby Berkley (who she'd helped to bring into the world). Berkley had died of tuberculosis far in the damp cottage at Nether Stowey while she and William had been so

77

terribly cold in Goslar.

They spent a day together and Coleridge walked five miles with them to delay their parting. Coleridge found both William and Dorothy 'melancholy and hypped', and very impatient to return to England. He also sometimes felt 'a huge craving for Alfoxden' and Dorothy imagined them all together 'in the north of England amongst the mountains whither we wish to decoy you'. Always their plans for the future were for the three of them together, their endless enchanted walks and talks and poetry making, their first marvellous friendship when they'd made 'Lyrical Ballads'.

William and Dorothy went home to Mary Hutchinson, their old and dear friend who would share her home with them until they had one of their own.

CHAPTER 5

Dorothy and William went by diligence to Hamburg, by river-boat to Cuxhaven, and a good quiet passage to Yarmouth. They landed on 1st of May 1799 and set out straight away for the north; to the Hutchinson's farmhouse Sockburn.

Dorothy wrote to Thomas Poole, 'we are now staying with some of our early friends on the banks of the Tees'. Sockburn farm was isled by the river Tees. There lived Mary Hutchinson, Sara and Joanna her sisters, Mary's two younger brothers Tom the farmer and George, John Hutchinson lived at Stockton and Henry was at sea. Dorothy and William lived with the Hutchinsons at Sockburn farm from May till December. While they were 'still quite undetermined where we shall reside,' they though maybe they'd take a house nearby. Aunt Rawson wondered 'how they propose to add to their income I cannot tell.'

Their beloved quiet brother John returned safely from the sea from his trading voyage to Bengal in The Duke of Montrose.

Uncle Christopher Crackenthorpe died, and Dorothy mourned sincerely. As he had been truly fond of her, he had left her one hundred pounds in his will, and she was the only one of her family to whom he had left anything. She thought, 'I daresay he would have done much more had he been a free agent.'

During this time William lost his revolutionary beliefs and feelings. Coleridge also deeply distrusted Napoleon. Their lack of faith grew with Napoleon's ascendancy and tyranny which they saw as betrayal of the revolution. They began to feel that England, in defying Napoleon was defending liberty. Dorothy with William and Coleridge began to distrust the French, except of course for 'poor Annette'.

Towards the end of October Coleridge arrived at Sockburn with Cottle and met the Hutchinsons, Mary, of whom he had heard so much from Dorothy and William, and Sara her sister who a month later was to become the love of his life.

On 27th of October William, with Coleridge and Cottle, set

out on a walking tour of the Lakes, joined by his brother John, who had come north for Uncle Christopher Crackenthorpe's funeral. Dorothy stayed with Mary, and letters arrived from the walkers. Coleridge was enchanted by the beauty of the Lakes, 'Why were you not with us Dorothy, why were not you Mary with us?' he wrote. Coleridge was deeply interested in Dorothy and William's brother John, his shyness, his gentleness, his deep quiet feeling for beauty, his intellect. 'Your brother John is one of you' he wrote, 'he interests me much.' William wrote that they were staying at an inn at Grasmere.

John had offered to buy land for £40, and William thought of 'building a house by the lakeside', and with Dorothy's legacy buying furniture. Then he wrote, 'There is a small house at Grasmere empty which we might perhaps take and purchase furniture - But I shall write again when I know more on the subject.' By 26th of November when William returned to Sockburn Farm and to Dorothy he had begun to negotiate for the house at Grasmere.

Dorothy was delighted. In a month's time 'His father's children had once again a home together' she wrote. This was the desire of her heart. On the cold evening of 20th December 1799 the Wordsworths arrived at their home. 'A little white cottage gleaming from the midst of trees, with a vast and seemingly never-ending series of ascents rising above it to the height of more than three thousand feet.' This and a few other cottages formed the hamlet of Town End, the southern limit of Grasmere town; the road from Ambleside to Keswick ran past their door. The front windows looked directly over the lake; and behind the house their garden 'their little domestic slip of mountain' with a tiny orchard rose up the steep.

William had rented the cottage from the owner Benson of Tail End. This cottage Town End, Grasmere, had once been the inn of the hamlet - 'The Dove and Olive Branch' - hence its present name 'Dove Cottage'. It was a strong cottage built of local stone, white-washed with latticed windows and sturdy chimneys. When they arrived Dorothy wrote, 'We found no preparations except beds, without curtains, in the room upstairs, and a dying spark in the grate of the gloomy parlour.' This must have been daunting in the early dark of the cold winter evening in December. But Dorothy's inner delight and spirit were strong, 'we were young and healthy and had attained our object long desired, we had returned to our native mountains there to live.'

The front door opened into the kitchen, once the bar of the inn. This led into a stone flagged room which became Dorothy's bedroom, with a camp bed, then a scullery. Upstairs above the kitchen was their sitting room, and William's bedroom where the fire smoked dreadfully. There was also built on a sort of out-jutting lumber room and a small low un-ceilinged room, which Dorothy papered and put a bed into; it was a rough working cottage in the tradition of the district, a small country inn.

Molly Fisher, who lived with her married brother in the neighbouring cottage, had lit the fire for them that first evening. She became their servant and she loved Dorothy from the first dark cold evening she saw her; Molly was kind and warm-hearted, and did not ask very high wages. She worked for two shillings a week and her dinners, for two hours a day, and Dorothy taught her much. Molly learned to 'boil vegetables and watch the meat'. She could also, alone, 'shake carpets and clean everything upstairs' - She loved especially 'Maister John' and spoke of him being far away at sea, with tears in her eyes. She was very happy to help the Wordsworths. She was simple and unsophisticated and Coleridge and Hazlitt teased her, especially when she insisted they did not muddy the floor with their boots.

Coleridge called her, 'that drollery belonging to the Cottage' and Hazlitt mocked her that she had never heard of the French Revolution. Molly was sixty-two and though simple and ignorant, she was sure in her love for Dorothy.

Dorothy worked tremendously hard - with Molly's help - 'to get the cottage habitable for them'. Undaunted by a bad cold and toothache she battled on for three hard weeks, 'so much work that she is absolutely buried in it' and 'so much work that she has scarcely been out since our arrival' William wrote. She worked over Christmas Day, her 28th birthday, and the following weeks. But, thank heavens, before the end of January blessed help was at hand - her dear, quiet, practical brother John arrived. He was waiting for his chance of command of a ship The Earl of Abergavenny. So he came to Grasmere to stay with Dorothy and William for the eight months until his ship sailed. So gentle and sensitive was he and so respectful of his admired brother and sister's intimacy and solitude that when he first approached the cottage 'twice did he approach the door, and lay his hand on the latch, and stop, and turn away without the courage to enter. 'This', Dorothy said, 'will give you a notion of the depths of his affections, and the delicacy of his feelings'. In the next eight months he was a great help to them, with carpentry, with catching lake trout and pike, with an understanding of the practicalities of the cottage as if it were a ship he was fitting out - with laying out and helping to work in the garden.

Before the end of February Mary Hutchinson, their dear and faithful friend, came and stayed six weeks. When she left Coleridge came for a month, then a friend of Basil Montague's came for a short visit. Coleridge, as always, wished to live near Dorothy and William, and he returned to stay at their cottage in June, and in July he moved himself and his family to Greta Hall at Keswick, fifteen miles away. He now not only wished to be near William and Dorothy by living in the north, but also near Sara Hutchinson, Mary's sister, with whom he had fallen deeply in love while visiting Sockburn in November. Sara was small, red haired, very nice and intelligent and lively; a great walker on the fells Coleridge once said 'the entertainingness of her'; she was not conventionally pretty but had great character. This love, though vastly enriching Coleridge's life, caused him much pain and conflict; his married life did not go well - and it all affected his friendship with William and Dorothy - 'a heartrending letter from Coleridge', wrote Dorothy, 'William wrote to him'. William was not well himself at this time. When he wrote poetry, 'when he makes any effort of mind he feels a pain in his side ...'

Dorothy, however, was inspired by their new home and surroundings to begin her journal again while at Grasmere. This journal is contained in 4 notebooks. The first is a book of less than 4" x 6", its boards covered in mottled brown paper. It begins, 'William and John set off into Yorkshire ...' and then three 'Amens' to test the sharpness of her pen. Dorothy drew a full line across the page after each entry.

This notebook Dorothy had used before. She had first used it at Goslar - jottings and sums on the inside covers, lists of clothes, shirts, nightcaps, handkerchiefs, furs for the cold, also lists for groceries, bread, sugar, rum. Conversion sums from German currency, and odd phrases of English and German written and rewritten in a small elaborate script, Dorothy's practising of 18th century German script, 'with Peter' in tiny script (William had been employed in hewing down Peter Bell), so is 'industry' and 'Madam Deppermann', who was 'the good kind of respectable woman - a widow with five children and keeps a linen drapers shop' with whom Dorothy and William lodged at Breitstrasse Goslar. Lists of clothes to be packed, then 6 pages have been cut out at the front and five at the back, some probably were more lists and accounts.

Dorothy next used the notebook from the back - on their return from Germany, when they were staying with the Hutchinsons at Sockburn, Co. Durham. Dorothy copied out four epitaphs, two from a 'Life' of Benjamin Franklin (1st edition), one from Hutchinson's 'History of Durham', and one from the churchyard at Marske, Yorkshire, thirty miles from Sockburn. Alongside the first epitaph and also filling up small spaces amongst the items on the back cover are two tiny drawings of a church, one with a churchyard and tombstones. After the epitaphs Dorothy had copied out five verses of the 'Complaint of the Forsaken Indian Woman'. These verses meet the December entries of the Grasmere journal as it comes from the front of the book.

Grasmere Journal 1800-1803:

Dorothy began her journal because she missed William and John who had set off into Yorkshire to visit the Hutchinsons, and because 'poor old Molly did but ill supply to me the place of our good and dear Peggy', and she was worried about William and Coleridge, 'I resolved to write a journal of the time till William and John return, and I set about keeping my resolve, because I will not quarrel with myself, and because I shall give William pleasure by it when he comes home again.'

Her writing brought her into harmony with herself, away from all her conflict and stress. But she did not give it up when William and John returned. She kept it up for two and a half more years, and totally unconsciously, with no such intent, it is one of the masterpieces of such writing in English literature.

She 'sat a long time on a stone at the margin of the lake - and after a flood of tears my heart was easier. The lake looked to me I know not why dull and melancholy, the weltering on the shores seemed a heavy sound - I walked as long as I could amongst the stones of the shore.' Then she began to comfort herself with the wild flowers, 'the wood rich in flowers. A beautiful yellow, palish yellow flower, that looked thick and round and double, and smelt very sweet - I supposed it was ranunculus - Crowfoot, the grass-leaved rabbit-toothed white flower, strawberries, Geranium, scentless violets, anemonies, two kinds orchises, primroses. The heckberry very beautiful as a low shrub. The crab coming out'; this first entry is full of poor people and beggars, with whom Dorothy always had immediate sympathy. 'Met a blind man driving a very large beautiful bull and a cow - he walked with two sticks. Came home by Clappergate ... at Rydale a woman of the village, stout and well-dressed, begged a half penny - she had never, she said, done it before but these were hard times! Arrived at home with a headache and set some slips of privet. The evening cold, had a fire - my face now flame-coloured. It is nine o'clock, I shall soon go to bed. A young woman begged at the door - she had come from Manchester on Sunday morning with two shillings and a slip of paper which she supposed a bank note - it was a cheat. She had buried her husband and three children within a year and a half - all in one grave - burying very dear - paupers all put in one place - 20 shillings paid for as much ground as will bury a man - a gravestone to be put over it or the right will be lost. 11/6 each time the grave is opened. O that I had a letter from William.'

Thursday 16th: 'After tea went to Ambleside - a pleasant cool but not cold evening. Rydale was very beautiful with spear-headed streaks of polished steel. No letters! Only one newspaper. I returned by Clappersegate. Grasmere was very solemn in the last

"But when I came to Grasmere I felt it did me good"

glimpse of twilight, it calls home the heart to quietness. I had been very melancholy in my walk back. I had many of my saddest thoughts and I could not keep the tears within me. But when I came to Grasmere I felt it did me good. I finished my letter to M.H. (Mary Hutchinson), ate hasty pudding and went to bed. As I was going out in the morning I met a half-crazy old man - He showed me a pincushion, and begged a pin, afterwards a halfpenny. He began in a half indistinct voice in this manner, "Matthew Jobson's lost a cow. Tom has two good horses strained - Jim Jones's cow's broken her horn, etc., etc." He went into Aggy's and persuaded her to give him some whey and let him boil some porridge. She declares he ate two quarts.'

'Aggy' was Molly Fisher's sister, also a friend and helper of Dorothy and William.

Saturday 17th: 'Incessant rain from morning till night. T. Ashburner brought us coals. Worked hard and read Midsummer Night's Dream, Ballads - sauntered a little in the garden. The skobby sat quietly in its nest rocked by the winds, beaten by the rain.'

Sunday 19th (18th): 'Went to church, slight showers, a cold air. The mountains from this window look much greener, and I think the valley is more green than ever. The corn begins to shew itself. The ashes are still bare. Went part of the way home with Miss Simpson - A little girl from Coniston came to beg. She had lain out all night - her stepmother had turned her out of doors. Her father would not stay at home, "she flights so" ...'

These wonderful journals with all their telling of stray poor people, and marvellous descriptions of nature, and hard work in the house and garden, of moods, and beautifully clear observation were published in 1897 as The Journals of Dorothy Wordsworth in two volumes. Thanks to this we can love and enjoy them. The editor was Professor William Knight, who was the author of a Life of William Wordsworth, in which he used lengthy extracts from Dorothy's journals. 'Aggy' was Molly Fisher's sister also a friend and helper of Dorothy and William.

Dorothy continued reading and working, watching, adoring nature, becoming sad.

Monday 19th: 'Sauntered a good deal in the garden, bound carpets, mended old clothes, read Timon of Athens. Dried linen - Molly weeded the turnips, John stuck the peas. We had not much sunshine or wind but no rain until about 7 o'clock when we had a slight shower just after I had set out upon my walk. I did not return but walked up into the Black Quarter. I sauntered a long time among the rocks above the church. The most delightful situation possible for a cottage commanding two distinct views of the vale and the lake is amongst those rocks - I strolled on gathering mosses, etc. The quietness and still seclusion of the valley affected me even to producing the deepest melancholy - I forced myself from it. The wind rose before I went to bed. No rain - Dodwell and Wilkinson called in my absence.

'Tuesday morning (20th): A fine mild rain - after breakfast the sky cleared and before the clouds passed from the hill I went to Ambleside - It was a sweet morning - Everything green and overflowing with Life, and the streams making a perpetual song with the thrushes and all the little birds, not forgetting the stone-chats.'

The black quarter was the name the Wordsworths gave to Easedale, the north-western arm of the valley. They named the rocks and hills, thus making the valley their own.

John, who was helping Dorothy by sticking the peas, was John Fisher - Molly Fisher's brother. He was registered on his marriage to Aggy as 'Cordwainer' and said by Coleridge to be a shoemaker - 'a fine enthusiastic, noble-minded creature'. He was a small estatesman and had an apprentice. He was registered on his death as 'yeoman'.

After his wife Aggy's death he kept 'but one cow - just enough for Molly to manage'.

Dorothy's journal continues: 'Thursday 22nd: A very fine day with showers - dried the linen and starched and drank tea at Mr. Simpsons. Brought down Batchelors Buttons (Rock Ranunculous) and other plants - went part of the way back - A showering mild evening - all the peas up ...'

'Sunday 25th: A very fine warm day - had no fire. Read

87

Macbeth in the morning. Sate under the trees after dinner.'

'Monday May 26th: A very fine morning, worked in the garden until after 10 when old Mr. Simpson came and talked to me until after 12. Molly weeding. Wrote letters to JH, Coleridge, C Li and W. I walked towards Rydale and turned aside at my favourite field. The air and the lake were still - one cottage light in the vale, had so much of the day left that I could distinguish objects, the woods, trees and houses. Two or three different kinds of birds sang at intervals on the opposite shore. I sate till I could hardly drag myself away I grew so sad. "When pleasant thoughts, etc." '

'Friday (30th): In the morning went to Ambleside, forgetting the post does not come till evening - how was I grieved when I was so informed - I walked back resolving to go again in the evening. It rained very mildly, sweetly in the morning as I came home, but came on a wet afternoon and evening - luckily I caught Mr. Oliff's lad as he was going for letters, he brought me one from William and twelve papers. I planted London Pride upon the wall and many things in the borders. John sodded the wall. As I came past Rydale in the morning I saw a heron swimming with only its neck out of the water. It beat and struggled amongst the water when it flew away and was long in getting loose.'

John Fisher it was who sodded the wall. The recently built supporting wall for the new platform or small terrace in the garden orchard behind the house.

'Saturday (31st): A sweet mild rainy morning. Grundy the carpet man called. I paid him 1/10. Went to the blind man's for plants. I got such a load I was obliged to leave my basket in the road and send Molly for it. Planted, etc. After dinner when I was putting up the valances Miss Simpson and her visitors called - I went with them to the Brathay Bridge. We got Broom in returning, strawberries, etc. and came home by Ambleside - Grasmere looked divinely beautiful. Mr., Miss Simpson and Tommy drank tea at 8 o'clock - I walked to the Potters with them.'

Sunday June 1st, 'Rain in the night - a sweet mild morning - Read Ballads, went to church. Singers from Wytheburn. Went part of the way home with Miss Simpson. Walked upon the hill above

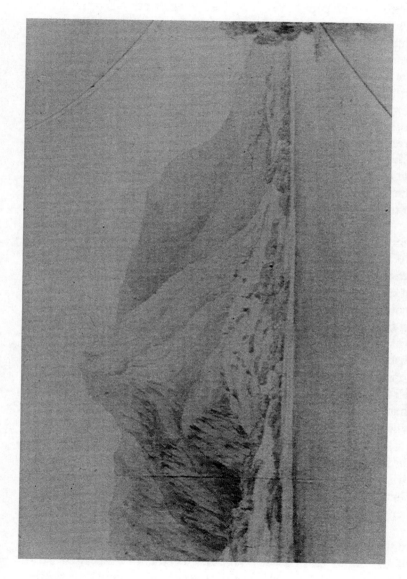

Hill Gray on Grasmere Lake: John White Abbot

the house till dinner-time - Went again to church - a christening and singing which kept us very late. The pewside came down with me. Walked with Miss Simpson nearly home. After tea went to Ambleside, round the lakes - a very fine warm evening. I lay upon the steep of Loughrigg my heart in what I saw when I was not startled but recalled from my reverie by a noise as of a child paddling without shoes. I looked up, saw a lamb close to me - it approached nearer and nearer, as if to examine me and stood a long time. I did not move - at last it ran past me and went bleating along the pathway, seeming to be seeking its mother - I saw a hare in the high road. The post not come in - I waited in the road till Johns the apprentice came with a letter from Coleridge and three papers. The moon shone upon the water - reached home at 10 o'clock - went to bed immediately. Molly brought daisies and we planted.'

Monday (2nd): 'A cold dry windy morning. I worked in the garden and planted flowers, etc. Sate under the trees after dinner till tea-time. John Fisher stuck peas, Molly weeded and washed. I went to Ambleside after tea, crossed the stepping stones at the foot of Grasmere and pursued my way on the other side of Rydale and by Clappergate. I sate a long time to watch the hurrying waves and to hear the regularly irregular sound of the dashing waters. The waves round about the little 'island' seemed like a dance of spirits that rose out of the water, round the small circumference of shore. I inquired about lodgings for Coleridge, and was accompanied by Mrs. Nicolson as far as Rydale. This was very kind, but God be thanked I want not company by a moonlight lake. It was near 11 when I reached home. I wrote to Coleridge and went late to bed.'

It is good to see and hear Dorothy on her own at home, with the animals, the friendly people who lived near and were part of her life - with her beloved nature, her best companion, and books - all her reading, and tasks at home, her moods and walks and wanderings, her contemplations, her expectancy of letters from her loved ones.

Miss Simpson was Elizabeth Jane Simpson, younger daughter of the Revd. Joseph Simpson of High Broadraine, Grasmere, vicar of the small church of Wythburn. Elizabeth then aged 36 in December 1803 did, said Dorothy, 'a very foolish thing' - she married the son of the Ambleside-based artist Julius Caesar Ibbetson, a young man 'little more than half her age', and by the next autumn she was dead of consumption, and her baby daughter died shortly afterwards.

Mr. Simpson, according to recollections by William Green, was a most cheerful and entertaining companion, and frequently walked after he was eighty to Ambleside and back the same day. He died suddenly on 27th June 1807, aged 92. Dorothy describes him in September 1800 as going 'afishing in the Tarns on the hill-tops with my Brothers and he is as active as many men of 50'.

Tommy was the Revd. Joseph Simpson's grandson, son of his eldest daughter Mary and her first husband, a builder, Thomas Jameson, shortly to die. By 1868, through the encouragement of John Harden of Brathay Hall, Tommy was an aspiring artist in London.

'The blind man is Matthew Newton, the honest itinerant bread-merchant, 'who lost his eyes, by an unfortunate blast' at the White Moss Slate Quarry between Grasmere and Rydale. Matthew Newton had been blind for some 20 years when Dorothy came to Grasmere, and was about 70 years old. He lived with his wife and sister and died in 1816. In fact the final entry in Dorothy's Grasmere journal is about him: 1803 (Sunday 16th) Intensely cold. Wm had a fancy for some gingerbread.'

Mrs. Nicolson, who had so unwantedly accompanied her, for Dorothy needed no society by the moonlight, Agnes Nicolson was post mistress of Ambleside. In 1850 she remembered how her husband Joseph, the first post master, would get up late at night and let Mr. and Miss Wordsworth into the parlour or kitchen, where they would have 'the letter out of the box - and sit up reading and changing, until they had made it quite to their minds.'

'Wednesday 4th, very fine day. I sate out of doors most of the day, wrote to Mr. Jackson. Ambleside Fair. I walked to the lakeside in the morning, took up some plants and sate upon a stone reading Ballads. In the evening I was watering plants when Mr. and Miss Simpson called - I accompanied them home - it was very interesting in the twilight. I brought home lemon thyme and several other plants, and planted them by moonlight. I lingered out of doors in the hope of hearing my brother's tread.

'Thursday (5th), I sate out of doors great part of the day and worked in the garden - had a letter from Mr. Jackson, and wrote another to Coleridge. The little birds busy making love and pecking the blossoms and bits of moss off the trees as I lie under them. Molly went out to tea - I would not go from the house expecting my brothers - I rambled on the hill above the house gathering wild thyme and took up roots of wild columbine. Just as I was returning with my 'load' Mr. and Miss Simpson called. We went again upon the hill, got more plants, set them, and went to the Blind Man's for London Pride for Miss Simpson. I went with them as far as the blacksmith's. A fine lovely moonlit night.

'Saturday 7th, A very warm cloudy morning, threatened to rain. I walked up to Mr. Simpsons to gather gooseberries. It was a very fine afternoon ... Little Tommy came down with me, ate gooseberry pudding and drank tea with me. We went up the hill to gather sods and plants and went down to the lakeside and took up orchises, etc. I watered the garden and weeded. I did not leave home in the expectation of William and John, and sitting at work till after 11 o'clock I heard a foot go to the front of the house, turn round and open the gate. It was William - after our first joy was over we got some tea. We did not go to bed till 4 o'clock on the morning so he had the opportunity of seeing our improvements - the birds were singing, all looked fresh though not gay. There was a greyness of earth and sky. We did not rise till near to ten in the morning. We were busy all day in writing letters to Coleridge, Montague, Douglass, Richard. Mr. and Miss Simpson called in the evening, the little boy carried our letters to Ambleside, we walked with Mr. and Miss Simpson home on their return. The evening was cold and I was afraid of the tooth-ache for William. We met John on our return home.'

'Monday 9th, in the evening Wm cut down the winter cherry tree, I sowed French beans and weeded. A coronetted Landau went by when we were sitting upon the sodded wall. The ladies (evidently Tourists) turned an eye of interest upon our little garden and cottage. We went to R Newtons for pikefloats and went round to Mr. Bell's boat and on to lake to fish. We caught nothing - it was extremely cold. The reeds and bullrushes or bullpipes of a tender soft green making a plain whose surface moved with the wind. The reeds not yet tall, the lake clear to the bottom, but saw no fish. In the evening I stuck peas, watered the garden and planted broccoli - did not walk for it was very cold. A poor girl called to beg who had no work at home and was going in search of it to Kendal. She slept in Mr. Benson's lathe and went off after breakfast in the morning with 7p and a letter to the Mayor of Kendal.

'On Tuesday May 27th a very tall woman, tall much beyond the measure of tall women, called at the door. She had a very long brown cloak; and a very white cap without bonnet - her face was excessively brown, but it had plainly once been fair. She led a little bare-footed child about two years old by the hand and said her husband who was a tinker was gone before with the other children. I gave her a piece of bread. Afterwards on my road to Ambleside, beside the bridge at Rydale, I saw her husband sitting by the roadside, his two asses feeding beside him and the two young children at play upon the grass. The man did not beg - and I passed and about a quarter of a mile further I saw two boys before me, one about 10 the other about eight years old at play chasing a butterfly. They were wild figures, not very ragged, but without shoes and stockings; the hat of the elder was wreathed round with yellow flowers, the younger whose hat was only a rimless crown, had stuck it round with laurel leaves. They continued to play till I drew very near and addressed me with the begging cant and the whining voice of sorrow - I said I served your Mother this morning (the boys were so like the woman who had called at the door that I could not be mistaken) - Oh! says the elder, you could not serve my mother for she's dead and my father's on at the next town - he's a potter. I persisted in my assertion that I would give them nothing. Says the elder, "Come, lets away," and away they flew like lightening. They had however sauntered so long in their road that they did not reach Ambleside before me, and I saw them go up to Matthew Harrison's house with their wallet upon the elder's shoulder, and creeping with a beggar's complaining foot. On my return through Ambleside I met in the street the mother driving her asses; in the two panniers of one of which were the two little children whom she was chiding and threatening with a wand which she used to drive on her asses, while the little things hung in wantoness over the pannier's edge. The woman had told me in the morning that she was of Scotland where her accent proved, but she lived (I think at Wigton) that they could not keep a house, and so they travelled.'

Dorothy's beggars are seen with interest and compassion, and are also in the safekeeping appreciation of her imaginative understanding (as they are in that of William too). But with Dorothy it is more than that. They are like her subconscious feelings about herself thrust out of her parent's house when her mother died when Dorothy was six, never again to be welcomed back along with her brothers - outcast, wandering; so vividly are these people described, somewhere in tune with her own wild desolate being, but held in her art as a writer, or like wonderful paintings or sculpted figures.

This description of the beggar woman and her husband was written two weeks after Dorothy met them, and was probably a result of her telling William about the beggars as they walked to Ambleside.

Almost two years later William wrote his poem 'Beggars' (1802) and he told Miss Fenwick in 1842 that the beggars were 'met and described to me by my sister, near the Quarry at the head of Rydale Lake, a place still a chosen resort of vagrants travelling with their families.'

'Monday 16th, Wm and I went to Brathay by little Langdale and Collath and Skelleth. It was a warm mild morning with threatenings of rain. The vale of little Langdale looked bare and unlovely - Collath was wild and interesting, from the peat carts and peat gatherers, - a valley all perfumed with gale and wild thyme. The woods about the waterfall veined with rich yellow broom. A succession of delicious views from Skelleth to Brathay. We met near Skelleth a pretty little boy with a wallet over his shoulder. He came from Hawkeshead and was going to 'late' a lock of meal. He spoke gently and without complaint. When I asked him if he got enough to eat he looked surprised and said "Nay". He was 7 years old but seemed not more than 5. We drank tea at Mr. Ibbestons and returned by Ambleside. Sent 3-9-0 to the Potters at Kendal. Met John on our return home at about 10 o'clock. Saw a primrose in blossom.'

'... not more than 5.' Dorothy would remember this child and his going to beg a measure of meal on 12th Feb. 1802. She associated him with Basil Montagu, and was very sad at his worsened plight.

The Mr. Ibbeston with whom they drank tea, was Julius Caesar Ibbeston, a Yorkshireman, assistant to a London picture dealer then a landscape painter. He ran away from his London debts and the deaths of 8 children and a wife, and came to live at Clappersgate, Ambleside. He painted scenes and inn signs, and married a local girl, 18 years old Bella Thompson. That year he painted a good and happy picture of Grasmere with long-horned cattle, milkmaids, spilt milk, and the white church below Helm Crag. Dorothy and William didn't continue to call. In 1802 the Ibbestons moved to Troutbeck and in 1804 Dorothy told Lady Beaumont that she believed Ibbeston proud and high-spirited, 'I know nothing ill of him except that he is addicted to drinking violently, by fits, and I have been told that his conversation in the company of women is unbecoming and indecent. We have seen nothing of him for at least three years.'

'Saturday 21st, in the morning William and I went to Ambleside to get his tooth drawn, and put in - a fine clear morning but cold - Wm's tooth drawn with very little pain, he slept till three o'clock. Young Mr. S. drank tea and supped with us. They fished in Rydale water and they caught two small fishes - W. no bite, John 2. Miss Simpson and three children called - I walked with them to Rydale. The evening cold and clear and frosty, but the wind was falling as I returned. I stayed at home about an hour and then walked up the hill to Rydale Lake. Grasmere looked so beautiful that my heart almost melted away. It was quite calm, only spotted with sparkles of light. The church visible. On our return all distant objects had faded away - all but the hills. The reflection of the light bright sky above black quarter was very solemn. Mr. S did not go until 12 o'clock.'

'Monday 23 - Mr. Simpson called in the morning, Tommy's father dead. Wm and I went to Langdale to fish. The morning was very cold - I sate at the foot of the lake till my head ached with cold. The view exquisitely beautiful, through a gate and under a sycamore tree beside the first house going into Loughrigg - Elter water looked barren, and the view from the church less beautiful than in winter. When W went down to the water to fish I lay under the wind, my head pillowed upon a mossy rock and slept about 10 minutes, which relieved my headache. We ate our dinner together then parted again, Wm was afraid he had lost his line and sought me. An old man saw me just after I had crossed the stepping stones and was going thro a copse - "Ho, where are you going?" "To Ellerwater Bridge." "Why," says he, "it's well I saw you, ye were gane to Little Langdale by Wrynose, and several other places," - which he ran over, with a mixture of triumph, good nature and wit. "It's well I saw you or you'd have been lost." The evening grew very pleasant, we sate on the side of the hill looking over to Eller water. I was much tired and returned home to tea - W went to fish for pike in Rydale. John came in when I had done tea, and he and I carried a jug of tea to William. We met him in the old road from Rydale - he drank his tea upon the turf - the setting sun threw a red purple light upon the rocks and stone walls of Rydale which gave them a most interesting beautiful appearance.'

'Wednesday 25th, a very rainy day - I made a shoe - Wm and John went to fish in Langdale. In the evening I went above the house and gathered flowers which I planted, foxgloves, etc. On Sunday (29th June 1800) Mr. and Mrs. Coleridge and Hartley came. The day was very warm and we sailed to the foot of Loughrigg. They staid with us three weeks and till the Thursday following, i.e. till the 23 (24) of July. On the Friday preceding their departure we drank tea at the island. The weather was delightful - and on the Sunday we made a great fire, and drank tea at Baibriggs with the Simpsons ...'

June 1800 till 23 (24th) July: after noting the flowers and foxgloves of that Wednesday, Dorothy wrote nothing for a time, and then left a deeper than usual space below her last line of writing, as she began her scant summary of Coleridge's 3 ½ week visit.

96

James Bourne-Grasmere

CHAPTER 6

From letters to the printers we know that during his visit with them, Coleridge, Dorothy and William spent a lot of time preparing the text for the second edition of Lyrical Ballads; and from Coleridge's notebooks we learn of excursions to Dungeon Gyll, Watenlath, of his noticing ladies reading Gilpin's Observations on the Picturesque 'while passing by the very places instead of looking at the places', and that, like William, he had been impressed by the man 'in peasant's garb idly fishing during hay-time: Come near - thin, pale, can scarce speak - or throw out his fishing rod', and by William's poem 'A narrow girdle of rough stones'. By 24th July the Coleridges had left for Greta Hall and on the following day Dorothy resumed her journal.

Coleridge also describes the great bonfire of 20th July: 'Mountains seen through the smoke of our wild fire, made of fir apples - Alder bush outmost twigs smouldering in sparks green ling - column of smoke - the twigs and boughs heaved up by the smoke'. And Coleridge's letter of 25th July to Davy describing the island picnic and 'glorious bonfire' of fir apples with the 'ruddy laughing faces in the twilight' of 'us that danced round it'.

Young Mr. S. was Bartholomew Sympson, son of the Revd. Joseph Sympson; 'an interesting man,' said Dorothy, 'about 40, manages his father's glebe land, reads a little and spends much time in fishing.'

Dorothy's Journal resumes: 'Sunday morning 26th (27th), very warm - Molly ill - John bathed in the lake. I wrote out Ruth in the afternoon, in the morning I read Mr. Knight's landscape. After tea we rowed down to Loughrigg Fell, visited the white foxglove, gathered wild strawberries, and walked up to view Rydale. We lay a long time looking at the lake, the shores all embrowned with the scorching sun; the ferns were turning yellow, that is here and there one was quite turned. We walked round by Benson's wood home. The lake was now most still and reflected the beautiful yellow and blue and purple and grey colours of the sky. We heard a strong sound in Bainrigg's wood as we were floating on the water. It seemed in the wood, but it must have been above it, for presently we saw a raven very high above us - it called out and the dome of the sky seemed to echo the sound - it called again and again as it flew onwards, and the mountains gave back the sound, seeming as if from their centre a musical bell-like answering to the bird's hoarse voice. We heard both the call of the bird and the echo after we could see him no longer. We walked up to the top of the hill again in view of Rydale - met Mr. and Miss Simpson on horseback. The crescent moon which had shone upon the water was gone now. Returned to supper at 10 o'clock.'

So they lived their quite paradisical life, threaded with pain of toothache and headache and tiredness and illness, deaths of friends like Tommy's father; and working hard fishing, cobbling, gardening, cooking, sewing, but always with Dorothy's marvellous appreciation of and delight in nature and her descriptions of it and people like the old man met in the copse, visits from the Coleridges and picnics with them and the Simpsons, bathing and caring for each other. William and Dorothy and John, Dorothy and John taking tea to William. Dorothy refreshed from her headache after ten minutes' sleep with her head on a mossy stone - trust in nature as a mother - having been so early deprived of their own. Reading, mending, writing and copying, publishing poetry with Coleridge.

'Monday morning (28th), received a letter from Coleridge enclosing one from Mr. Davy about Lyrical Ballads - intensely hot. I made pies in the morning. Wm went into the wood and altered his poems. In the evening it was so very warm that I was much too tired to walk.'

Tuesday (29th), still very hot. We gathered peas for dinner. We walked up in the evening to find out Hewetson's cottage but it was too dark. I was sick and weary.'

'Wednesday (30th), gathered peas for Mrs. Simpson - John and I walked up with them - very hot - Wm had intended to go to Keswick. I was obliged to lie down after dinner from excessive heat and headache. The evening was excessively beautiful - a rich reflection of the moon, the moonlight clouds and the hills, and from the Rays gap a huge rainbow pillar. We sailed upon the lake till it was 10 o'clock.'

'Thursday (31st), all the morning I was busy copying poems - gathered peas, and in the afternoon Coleridge came very hot, he brought the 2nd volume of the Anthology - The men went to bathe and we afterwards sailed down to Loughrigg, read poems on the water and let the boat take its own course - we walked a long time upon Loughrigg and returned in the grey twilight. The moon just setting as we reached home.'

The 'Anthology' Coleridge brought was the second and last of two anthologies of modern verse edited by Robert Southey. His friends contributed and Southey wrote many of the poems. This volume had in it many poems by Coleridge, and this was the first time William and Dorothy would see Coleridge's great poem 'This Lime Tree Bower' in print.

'Friday 1st August. In the morning I copied *The Brothers* - Coleridge and Wm went down to the lake. They returned and we all went to Mary Point where we sate in the breeze and the shade and read Wm's poems altered 'The Whirlblast' etc. Mr. Simpson came to tea and Mr. B. Simpson afterwards - we drank tea in the orchard.'

Mary Point was a 'heath-clad rock' in Bainriggs Wood at the foot of Grasmere, named after MH - an 'eminence' close by was named after Sara.

'The Whirlblast, etc.' - 'A whirlblast from behind the hill' was a poem composed 18 March 1798 when Dorothy had written in her Alfoxden journal: 'sheltered under the hollies, during a hail-shower. The withered leaves danced with the hailstones. William wrote a description of the storm.' Their writing so often echoed each other's.

'Saturday morning 2nd, Wm and Coleridge went to Keswick. John went with them to Wythburn and stayed all day fishing and brought home 2 small pikes at night. I accompanied them to Lewthwait's cottage and on my return papered Wm's room. I afterwards lay down till tea time and after tea worked at my shifts in the orchard. A grey evening - about 8 o'clock it gathered for rain and I had the scatterings of a shower, but afterwards the lake became of a glassy calmness and all was still. I sate till I could see no longer and then continued my work in the house.'

All the time William was working at his poems and reading them to Dorothy and John around the countryside; all the time Dorothy was weaving among her hard work in the garden and kitchen and her walking and her fine, original observations: 'Friday evening (29th), we walked to Rydale to inquire for a letter. We walked over the hill by the Firgrove. I sate upon a rock and observed a flight of swallows gathering together high above my head. They flew towards Rydale. We walked through the wood over the stepping stones - The lake of Rydale was very beautiful, partly still. John and I left Wm to compose an inscription - that about the path. We had a very fine walk by the gloomy lake. There was a curious yellow reflection in the water as of cornfields - there was no light in the clouds from which it appeared to come.'

'Sunday 29th (31st), Anthony Harrison and John left us at ½ past seven, a very fine morning. A great deal of corn cut in the vale, and the whole prospect though not tinged with a general autumnal yellow, yet softened down into a mellowness of colouring which seems to impart softness to the forms of hills and mountains. At 11 o'clock Coleridge came when I was walking in the still, clear moonshine in the garden - he came over Helvellyn - Wm was gone to bed and John also, worn out with his ride round Coniston. We sate and chatted till 1/2 past three, W in his dressing gown. Coleridge read us part of 'Christabel'. Talked much about the mountains, etc., etc., Miss Thrale's hatred - Losh's opinion of Southey - the first of poets.'

Anthony Harrison - son of Anthony Harrison a surgeon of Penrith, was a contemporary of William at Hawkeshead; he and his brother John each donated 10s 6d to The New School Library in 1792. He was a Penrith lawyer who published Poetical Recreations 2 vols (1806); and in 1808 he helped proof read 'The Friend' for Coleridge.

They all liked to sit up late and inhabit the night and talk, loving the night, the moon, the stars; they loved to walk in the

101

moonlight. Coleridge's poem 'Frost at Midnight' was written when
he was sitting up late beside his sleeping baby:

'Or if the secret ministry of frost
Shall hang them up in silent icicles
Quietly shining to the quiet Moon.'

'Monday morning 1st September, we walked in the wood by
the lake. W read 'Joanna' and 'The Firgrove' to Coleridge. They
bathed. The morning was delightful with somewhat of an autumnal
freshness. After dinner Coleridge discovered a rock seat in the
orchard, cleared away the brambles. Coleridge obliged to go to bed
after tea. John and I followed Wm up the hill and then returned to
go to Mr. Simpson's - we borrowed some bottles for bottling rum.
The evening somewhat frosty and grey but very pleasant, I broiled
Coleridge a mutton chop which he ate in bed. Wm was gone to bed
- I chatted with John and Coleridge till near 12.'

'Tuesday 2nd, In the morning they all went to Stickel Tarn. A
very fine, warm sunny beautiful morning. I baked a pie for dinner -
little Sally was with me. The fair day. There seemed very few people
and very few stalls yet I believe there were many cakes and much
beer sold. My brothers came home to dinner at 6 o'clock. We drank
tea immediately after by candlelight. It was a lovely moonlight night.
We talked much about a house on Helvellyn. The moonlight shone
upon the village. It did not eclipse the village lights and the sound of
dancing and merriment came along the still air - I walked with
Coleridge and Wm up the lane and by the church, I then lingered
with Coleridge in the garden. John and Wm were both gone to bed
and all the lights out.'

Dorothy tells of how on 27th September they heard of the
Abergavenny's arrival. This was John's ship:

'On Monday John left us. Wm and I parted with him in sight
of Ullswater. It was a fine day, showery but with sunshine and fine
clouds - poor fellow, my heart was right sad - I could not help thinking
we should see him again because he was only going to Penrith.'

Friday 10th October, In the morning when I arose the mists

were hanging over the opposite hills - and the tops of the high hills were covered with snow. There was a most lovely combination at the head of the vale - of the yellow autumnal hills wrapped in sunshine, and overhung with partial mists, the green and yellow trees and the distant snow-topped mountains. It was a lovely morning'. The beautiful autumn went on.

'Saturday 11th, The colours of the mountains soft and rich with orange fern - the cattle pasturing upon the hill-tops, kites sailing as in the sky above our heads - sheep bleating and in lines and chains and patterns scattered over the mountains. They come down and feed on the little green islands in the beds of the torrents and so may be swept away. The sheepfold is falling away, it is built nearly in the form of a heart unequally divided. Look down the brook and see the drops rise upwards and sparkle in the air, at the little falls, the higher sparkles the tallest. We walked along the turf of the mountains till we came to a cattle track - made by the cattle which come upon the hills. We drank tea at Mr. Simpson's, returned at about nine - a fine mild night.'

'Sunday 12th October, Beautiful day. Sate in the house writing in the morning while Wm went to the wood to compose. Wrote to John in the morning - copied poems for the LB. In the evening wrote to Mrs. Rawson. Mary Jameson and Sally Ashburner dined. We pulled apples after dinner, a large basketful. We walked before tea to Bainriggs to observe the many coloured foliage, the oaks dark green with yellow leaves - The birches generally still green, some near the water yellowish. The sycamore crimson and crimson-tufted - the mountain ash a deep orange - the common ash lemon colour, but many ashes still fresh in their summer green. Those that were discoloured chiefly near the water. William composing in the evening. Went to bed at 12 o'clock.'

'Monday 20th, William worked in the morning at the sheep-fold. After dinner we walked to Rydale, crossed the stepping stones and while we were walking under the tall oak trees the Lloyds called out to us. They went with us on the western side of Rydale. The lights were very grand upon the woody Rydale Hills. Those behind dark and topp'd with clouds. The two lakes were divinely beautiful

- Grasmere excessively solemn and the whole lake was calm and dappled: with soft grey dapple. The Lloyds stayed with us till 8 o'clock. We then walked to the top of the hill at Rydale - very mild and warm - about 6 glow-worms shining faintly. We went up as far as the grove. When we came home the fire was out. We ate our supper in the dark and went to bed immediately. William was disturbed in the night by the rain coming into his room, for it was a very rainy night. The ash leaves lay across the road.'

For two months after 11 October William thought about and composed 'Michael', the final poem in 'Lyrical Ballads 1800', and the replacement for 'Christabel'. He and Dorothy went to find the actual sheepfold 'on which so much of the poem turns', the ruins of it were, and maybe still are, by Greenhead Ghyll. William had known about the unfinished Grasmere sheepfold from his boyhood, because Ann Tyson, his Hawkeshead 'Dame' had worked as a girl for a family of Grasmere origin, the Knotts, then living at Rydale (at the house William himself was to live in, Rydale Mount). It was Ann Tyson who told William the story of the Grasmere shepherd.

Coleridge settled at nearby Greta Hall with his family. He was sad and ill, unhappy and quarrelling with his wife. He was still in love with Sara Hutchinson, but his basic Christian morality forbade him to commit adultery or divorce his wife. He became more and more dependent upon laudanum, and Dorothy - his dear friend - grieved for him:

'Tuesday 10th (1801), Poor C left us and we came home together. We left Keswick at 2 o'clock and did not arrive at G till 9 o'clock - drank tea at John Stanley's very comfortably. I burnt myself with Coleridge's Aquafortis. Mary's feet sore. C had a sweet day for his ride - every sight and sound reminded me of him, dear, dear fellow -of his many walks with us by day and by night - of all dear things. I was melancholy and could not talk, but at last I eased my heart by weeping - nervous blubbering says William. It is not so - O how many, many reasons have I to be anxious for him.'

'Sunday 15th (Nov), Walked in the morning to Churnmilk Force nearly, and went upon Hiefer Crags. The valley of its wintry yellow, but the bed of the brook still in some places almost shaded with leaves - the oaks brown in general, but one that might be almost called green - the whole prospect was very soft and the distant view down the vale very impressive, a long vale down to Ambleside - the hills at Ambleside in mist and sunshine - all else grey. We sate by the fire and read Chaucer, (Thompson Mary read) and Bishop Hall. Letters from Sara and Mrs. Clarkson last night.'

Monday 16th November, A very dankish, misty, wettish morning - Mary and Molly ironed all day. I made bread and called at Mr. Oliffs - Mr. O at home - the prospect soft from the windows. Mrs. O observed that it was beautiful even in winter! The Luffs passed us. W walked backwards and forwards in the orchard field. William somewhat weakish but, upon the whole, pretty well - he is now at 7 o'clock reading Spenser. Mary is writing beside me. The little syke murmurs. We are quiet and happy but poor Peggy Ashburner is very ill and in pain. She coughs as if she would cough her life away. I am going to write to Coleridge and Sara. Poor C! I hope he was in London yesterday. Molly has been very witty with Mary all day. She says 'Ye may say what ye will but there's nothing like a gay auld man for behaving weel to a young wife. Ye may laugh but this wind blows no favour' - and where 'there's no love there's no favour'. On Sunday I lectured little John Dawson for telling lies. I told him I had heard that he charged Jenny Baty falsely for having beaten him. Says Molly - she says 'it's not so that she never lifted her hand till him, and she should speak truth you would think in her condition' - She is with child. Two beggars today.'

Little John Dawson of How Top (bapt 3 Mar. 1799) seems too young for either Dorothy's lecture or his accusation of Jenny Baty. Jenny defends herself against the charge, but, significantly, ill-treatment of a parish apprentice by 'one of our near neighbours' is discussed at some length by Dorothy in 1808. The boy in this case came 'from a distant place' and so the Parish officers did not monitor his treatment. Dorothy describes the boy's nursing his mistress's numerous children, his slavish condition, the lack of religious instruction, the 'almost savage ignorance with bold vice', despite the traces of natural sense and good temper. The boy was 16 in 1808, and thus would be 7 or 8 when Dorothy lectured a boy for lying and for charging Jenny Baty with beating him. If this was that same boy (and the name John Dawson is common and could be entirely unconnected with the little boy at How Top), then perhaps he was not lying, and was ultimately vindicated by Dorothy herself in the Green story. Dorothy observes him again on 20th February and 1st June 1802.

'Wednesday 18th, We sate in the house in the morning reading Spenser. I was unwell and lay in bed all the afternoon. Wm and Mary walked to Rydale - very pleasant moonlight, the Lakes beautiful. The church an image of Peace. Wm wrote some lines upon it. I in bed when they came home. Mary and I walked as far as Sara's gate before supper - we stood there a long time, the whole scene impressive, the mountains indistinct, the Lake calm and partly ruffled - large island and sweet sound of water falling into the quiet Lake. A storm was gathering at Easedale, so we returned but the moon came out and opened to us the church and village. Helm crag in shade, the larger mountains dappled like the sky - we stood long upon the bridge, wished for Wm - he stayed at home being sickish - found him better. We went to bed.'

Sara Hutchinson had an eminence, a seat, a rock and here a gate. She had had the gate, generally known as the Wishing Gate, since her visit of March 1801. William wrote to Mary Hutchinson about it in April, 'You will recollect that here is a gate just across the road, directly opposite the firgrove, this gate is always a favourite station of ours; we love it far more now on Sara's account. You know that it commands a beautiful prospect; Sara carved her cypher upon one of its bars and we call it her gate. We will find out another place for your cypher.' On 31st October 1802 Dorothy is again at Sara's gate with Mary, now William's wife.

In November 1801 when Dorothy and Mary stood on the bridge and wished for William, Dorothy was sharing the freedom and vision of days and nights in the countryside with Mary, who was her lifelong friend and sister. They loved the moonlight; opening to them the village, the mountains 'dappled like the sky.'

"Tuesday 24th, A rainy morning. We were well except that my head ached a little and I took my breakfast in bed. I read a little of Chaucer, prepared the goose for dinner, and we all walked out - I was obliged to return for my tippet and spenser, it was so cold. We had intended to go to Easedale, but we shaped our course to Mr. Gell's cottage. It was very windy and we heard the wind everywhere, the walls sheltered us - John Green's house looked pretty under Silver How - as we were going along we were stopped at once, at the distance perhaps of 50 yards from our favourite Birch tree it was yielding to the gusty wind with all its tender twigs, the sun shone upon it and it glanced in the wind like a flying sunshiny shower - it was a tree in shape with stem and branches but it was like a spirit of water - The sun went in and it resumed its purplish appearance, the twigs still yielding to the wind but not so visibly to us. The other birch trees that were near it looked bright and cheerful - but it was a creature by its own self among them. We could not get into Mr. Gell's grounds - the old tree fallen from its undue exaltation above the gate. A shower came on when we were at Bensons. We went through the wood - it became fair, there was a rainbow which spanned the lake from the island house to the foot of Bainriggs. The village looked populous and beautiful. Catkins were coming out and palm trees budding - the alder with its plum coloured buds. We came home near the stepping stones - reached home at dinner time. Sent Peggy Ashburner some goose. She sent me some honey - with a thousand thanks - 'alas the gratitude of men has etc.' I went in to set her right about this and sate a while with her. She talked about Thomas having sold his land - 'Ay', says she, 'I said many a time He's not come from London to buy our land however,' - then she told me with what pains and industry they had made up their taxes, interest, etc., etc. - how they all got up at 5 o'clock in the morning to spin and Thomas carded and that they had paid off a hundred pounds of the interest. She said she used to take such pleasure in the cattle and sheep - 'O how pleased I used to be when they fetched them down, and when I had been a bit poorly I would gang out upon the hill and look ower t' fields and see them and it used to do me so much good you cannot think' - Molly said to me when I came in, 'poor Body! She's very ill but one doesn't know how long she may last: many a fair face may gang before her.' We sate by the fire without work for some time, when Mary read a poem of Daniell upon Learning. After tea William read Spenser now and then a little aloud to us. We were making his waistcoat. We had a note from Mrs. C with bad news from poor C very ill. William walked to John's grove - I went to meet him - moonlight but it rained. I met him before I had got as far as John Baty's, he had been surprised and terrified by a rushing of winds which seemed to bring earth, sky and lake together, as if the whole were going to enclose him in - he was glad that he was in a high road.'

'Alas the gratitude of men' quoted by Peggy Ashburner is from the last two lines of William's poem, 'Simon Lee':

'Alas! the gratitude of men
Has oftener left me mourning.'

In speaking of our walk on Sunday evening, the 22nd November, I forgot to notice one most impressive sight - it was the moon and the moonlight seen through hurrying, driving clouds immediately behind the stone man upon the top of the hill on the Forest side. Every tooth and every edge of the rock was visible, and the Man stood like a giant watching from the roof of a lofty castle. The hill seemed perpendicular from the darkness below it. It was a sight I could call to mind at any time, it was so distinct.'

The stone man was Stone Arthur, 'the loneliest place we have among the clouds,' as William calls it in his 1800 poem on the Naming of Places. 'There is an Eminence', Mary Hutchinson and Sara had been 'given' rocky hillocks near the lake; this was William's. Dorothy had made it his, had said, 'This lonesome peak shall bear my Name'.

'Sunday 6th December 1801, A very fine beautiful sunshiny morning - William worked a while at Chaucer then we set forward to walk into Easedale. We met Mr. and Mrs. Oliff who were going to call upon us. They turned back with us and we parted at White Bridge. We went up into Easedale in that flat field which makes the second circle of Easedale with that beautiful rock in the field beside us, and all the rock and the woods and the mountains enclosing us round. The sun was shining among them, the snow thinly scattered upon the tops of the mountains. In the afternoon we sate by the fire - I read Chaucer aloud, Mary read the first Canto of the Fairy Queen. After tea Mary and I walked to Ambleside for letters - reaching home by 11 o'clock - we had a sweet walk, it was a sober starlight evening, the stars not shining as it were with all their brightness when they were visible and sometimes hiding themselves behind small greyish clouds that passed soberly along. We opened C's letter at Wilcock's door, we thought we saw that he wrote in good spirits, so we came happily homewards where we arrived two hours after we left home. It was a sad, melancholy letter and prevented us all from sleeping.'

'Monday morning, 7th, We rose by candlelight, a showery unpleasant morning after a downright rainy night. We determined however to go to Keswick if possible, and we set off a little after 9 o'clock. When we had been upon the Rays it snowed very much and the whole prospect closed in upon us like a moorland valley upon a moor - very wild - but we were at the top of the Rays, we saw the mountains before us, the sun shone upon them here and there and the Wythburn vale, though wild, looked soft. The rain went on cheerfully and pleasantly, now and then a hail shower attacked us but we kept up a good heart for Mary is a famous jockey. We met Mrs. Barcroft - she had been unwell in 'The Liverpool complaint' and was riding out for the benefit of her health. She had not seen Mrs. C. 'The weather had been such as to preclude all intercourse between neighbours.' - We reached Greta Hall at about one o'clock. Met Mrs. C in the field, Derwent in his cradle asleep, Hartley at his dinner - Derwent pale image of his father, Hartley well. We wrote to C. Mrs. C left us at 1/2 past 2 - we drank tea by ourselves, the children played about us. Mary said to Hartley, 'Shall I take Derwent with me?' 'No,' says H, 'I cannot spare my little brother' in sweetest tone possible, and he cannot do without his Mama. 'Well,' says Mary, 'why cannot I be his Mama'. Can't he have more Mamas than one? 'No', says H. What for? Because they do not love as Mothers do. What is the difference between Mothers and Mamas, looking at his sleeves. Mothers wear sleeves like this, pulling his own tight down, and Mamas (pulling them up making a bustle about his shoulders) so - We parted from them at 4 o'clock. It was a little of the dusk when we set off. Cotton Mills lighted up - the first star at Nadal fell, but it was never dark - we rode very briskly, snow upon the Rays, reached home far sooner than we expected at 7 o'clock. William at work with Chaucer, the God of Love, sate latish. I wrote a little to C.'

'Thursday 10th December, A very fine sunny morning - not frosty. We walked into Easedale to gather mosses, and then we went past to Aggy Fleming's and up the gill, beyond that little waterfall - it was a wild scene of crag and mountain. One craggy point rose above the rest irregular and ragged and very impressive it was. We called at Aggy Fleming's, she told us about her miserable house, she looked shockingly with her head tyed up. Her mother was there - the children looked healthy. We were very unsuccessful in our search after mosses. Just when the evening was closing in Mr. Clarkson came to the door - it was a fine frosty evening. We played at cards.'

Dec 10th 1801, 'Aggy Fleming's', Gillside, below Helm Crag. Aggy had married John Fleming, slater from Ulverston in 1788. He died in 1798 when the youngest child was a year old. A son William died in 1805, and Aggy Fleming still a widow, died in Jan 1808.

Saturday 12th December, 1801: 'A fine frosty morning - snow upon the ground - I made bread and pies. We walked with Mrs. Luff to Rydale and came home the other side of the lake. Met Townley with his dogs - all looked cheerful and bright - Helm Crag rose very bold and craggy, a being by itself, and behind it was the large ridge of mountain smooth as marble and snow-white - all the mountains looked like solid stone on our left going down from Grasmere i.e. White Moss and Nab Scar. The snow hid all the grass and all signs of vegetation and the rocks shewed themselves boldly everywhere and seemed more strong than rock and stone. The birches on the Crags beautiful, red brown and glittering - the ashes glittering spears with their upright stems - the hips very beautiful and so good! and dear Coleridge - I ate twenty for thee.' Dorothy the quiet, the brilliant natural observer, with an instinctive tenderness for natural creation and children.

February 8th 1802, Monday morning, 'It was very windy and rained very hard all the morning. William worked at his poem and I read a little in Lessing and the grammar - a chaise came past to fetch Ellis the carrier who had hurt his head ...'

' ... We walked on very wet through the clashy cold roads in bad spirits at the idea of having to go as far as Rydale, but before we had come again to the shore of the lake we met our patient bow-bent Friend, with his little wooden box at his back, "Where are you going?" said he. "To Rydale for letters." "I have two for you in my box." We lifted up the lid, and there they lay. Poor fellow, he straddled - pushed on with all his might, but we soon outstripped him, for when we had turned back with our letters, we were very thankful that we had not to go on for we should have been sadly tired - In thinking this I could not help comparing lots with him! He goes on that slow pace every morning, and after wrought a hard day's work returns at night, however weary he takes it all quietly, and though perhaps he feels neither thankfulness nor pleasure, when he eats his supper, and has no luxury to look forward to but falling asleep in bed - He seems mechanized to labour. We broke the seal of Coleridge's letter, and I had light just to see that he was not ill. I put it in my pocket, but at the top of White Moss I took it to my bosom, a safe place for it. The night was wild. There was a strange, mountain lightness when we were at the top of White Moss. I have often observed it there in the evenings, being between the two valleys. There is more of the sky there than in any other place. It has a strange effect sometimes along with the obscurity of evening or night. There was not much wind till we came to John's Grove and then it roared out of the grove; all the trees were tossing about. C's letter somewhat damped us, it spoke with less confidence about France. Wm wrote to him (NB the moon came out suddenly when we were at John's Grove, and a star or two beside.'*

February 9th, Tuesday, 'A funeral came by of a poor woman who had drowned herself, some say because she was badly treated by her husband; others that he was very decent, and she had been an indifferent wife. However this was, she had only been married to him last Witsuntide and had had very indifferent health ever since.

* From The Ancient Mariner 1.265: "Softly she was going up, And a star or two beside ..."

111

She had got up in the night and drowned herself in the pond. She had requested to be buried beside her mother, and so she was buried beside her mother, and so she was brought in a hearse. She was followed by several decent-looking men on horseback, her sister, Thomas Fleming's wife in a chaise, and some others with her, and a cart full of women. Molly says 'folk thinks of their mothers. Poor body. She has been little thought of by any body else.' We did a little Lessing, I attempted a fable but my head ached, my bones were sore with the day before and I was downright stupid: we went to bed, but not till William had tired himself.'

February 11th 1802, Thursday, 'A very fine clear sunny frost, the ground white with snow. William rose before Molly was ready for him, I rose a little after nine. William sadly tired and working still at the 'Pedlar'. Miss Simpson called when he was worn out - he escaped and sate in his own room till she went. She was very faint and had had a tooth drawn and had suffered greatly. I walked up with her past Gawain's. The sun was very warm till we got past Lewthwait's then it had little power, and had not melted the roads. As I came back I felt the vale like a different climate. The vale was bright and beautiful. Molly had linen hung out. We had pork to dinner sent us by Miss Simpson. William still poorly. We made up a good fire after dinner, and Wm brought his mattress out; and lay down on the floor. I read to him the life of Ben Johnson, and some short poems of his, which were too interesting for him, and would not let him go to sleep. I had begun with Fletcher, but he was too dull for me. Fuller says in his Life of Johnson (speaking of his plays) 'if his latter were not so spiritual and vigorous as his first pieces; all that are old, and all who desire to be old, should excuse him therein'. He says he 'beheld' wit combats between Shakespear and Johnson, and compares Shakespear to an English Man of War, Johnson to a great galleon.'

Dorothy had often 'beheld' (witnessed) combats of wit between William and Coleridge. Coleridge, who was like a great river, William like a great rock.

This is Dorothy whom Coleridge had described to Southey after his first Racedown meeting with her, her first visit and William's to Coleridge's cottage at Nether Stowey: 'Miss Wordsworth is a most exquisite young woman in her mind and heart'.

February 12th, Friday, 'A very fine, bright, clear hard frost. Wm working again. I recopied 'The Pedlar' but poor Wm all the time at work.

'Molly tells me "What, Little Sally's gone to visit at Mr. Simpson's. They say she's very smart, she's got on a new bedgown that her cousin gave her; it's a very bonny one they tell me, but I've not seen it. Sally and me's in luck." In the afternoon a poor woman came, she said, to beg rags for her husband's leg, which had been wounded by a slate from the roof in the great wind - but she has been used to go abegging for she has often come here. Her father lived to the age of 105. She is a woman of strong bones - with a complexion that has been beautiful, and remained very fresh last year, but now she looks broken, and her little boy - a pretty little fellow, and whom I have loved for the sake of Basil - looks thin and pale, I observed this to her. 'Aye,' says she, 'we have all been ill. Our house was unroofed in the storm nearly, and so we lived in it for more than a week." The child wears a ragged drab coat and a fur cap, poor little fellow, I think he seems scarcely at all grown since the first time I saw him. William was with me; we met him in a lane going to Skellwith Bridge. He looked very pretty. He was walking lazily in the deep narrow lane, over-shadowed by the hedgerows, his meal poke hung over his shoulder. He said he "was going a laiting". Poor creature. He now wears the same coat he had at that time. When the woman was gone, I could not help thinking that we are not half thankful enough that we are placed in that condition of life in which we are. We do not so often bless God for this, as we wish for this £50 - that £60, etc., etc. We have not however to reproach ourselves with ever breathing a murmur. This woman's was just a common cause! The snow still lies upon the ground. Just at the closing of the day, I heard a cart pass the door, and at the same time the dismal sound of a crying infant. I went to the window, and had light enough to see that a man was driving a cart, which seemed not to be very full, and that a woman with an infant in her arms was following close behind and a dog close to her. It was a wild and melancholy sight. Wm rubbed his table after candles were lighted, and we sate a long time with the windows unclosed. I almost finished writing 'The Pedlar', but poor Wm wore himself and me out with labour. We had an affecting conversation. Went to bed at 12 o'clock.'

Dorothy is heartbreaking and marvellous in her descriptions of her tender-heartedness towards the poor; her humility, she who had hardly any money of her own, who worked herself to the bone for a good and decent household for herself, her brother and her friends - the procession of misery passes her door and she reacts to it with unending helpfulness and gentleness and grieving.

On February 14th William went to Penrith to despatch some letters for Mary and for Mrs. Clarkson. Fortified by apples. Molly sent for the horse. Dorothy was left to herself walking and met these beautiful travellers: 'I stood at Sara's gate and when I came in view of Rydale I cast a long look upon the mountains beyond. They were very white, but I concluded that Wm would have a very safe passage over Kirkstone, and I was quite easy about him. After dinner, a little before sunset, I walked out about 20 yards above Glow-worm Rock. I met a carman, a Highlander I suppose, with 4 carts, the first two belonging to himself, the last evidently to a man and his family who had joined company with him, and who I guessed to be potters. The carman was cheering his horses and talking to a little lass about 10 years of age who seemed to make him her companion. She ran to the wall, and took up a large stone to support the wheel of his carts, and ran before with it in her arms to be ready for him. She was a beautiful creature, and there was something uncommonly impressive in the lightness and joyousness of her manner. Her business seemed to be all pleasure - pleasure in her own motions, and the man looked at her as if he too were pleased, and spoke to her in the same tone in which he spoke to his horses. There was a wildness in her whole figure, not the wildness of a mountain lass, but a road lass, a traveller from her birth, who had wanted neither food nor clothes.'

The beauty and love of and sheer painting the portrait of this girl: 'Her mother followed the last cart, with a lovely child, perhaps about a year old, at her back, and a good-looking girl, about 15 years old walking beside her. All the children were like the mother. She had a very fresh complexion, but she was blown with fagging up the hill: with the steepness of the hill and thro the bairn that she carried. Her husband was helping the horse to drag the cart up by pushing it with his shoulder. I got tea when I reached home; and read German till about 9 o'clock. Then Molly went away and I wrote to Coleridge. Went to bed at about 12 o'clock. Slept in Wm's bed, I slept badly.'

So much did she love children. Like the little boy she loved for Basil's sake. Dorothy so delighted in these people. She felt such kinship with them, just for their own sake, in her wonderful descriptions of them: she returned home, so dependent was she on the security and safety that William's presence gave her that in his absence she slept in his bed; and grieved in her separation from him that she slept badly, her thoughts full of longing for his return.

Tuesday 16th. 'A fine morning but I had persuaded myself not to expect him. I believe because I was afraid of being disappointed. I ironed all day. He came in just at tea time, had only seen Mary H for a couple of hours between Eamont Bridge and Hartshorn tree. Mrs. C better. He had had a difficult journey above Kirkstone and came home to Threlkeld and his mouth and breath were very cold when he kissed me. We spent a sweet evening. He was better, had altered 'the Pedlar'.

Coleridge knew, almost prophetically, before his time, about conservation, 'green ecology', and psychology, the 'study of creativity'. Dorothy lovingly respected during these years Coleridge's rare creativity and William's marvellous deep gift, but she also had her own unique, loving, wholly original vision, her astonishing observations in nature and of the travelling people, beggars, children, itinerant potters, discharged servicemen, and this was her own and no one else's.

William was very deeply discouraging to Coleridge, refusing to have 'Christabel' in the second edition of 'Lyrical Ballads', and relegating 'The Ancient Mariner' to the back of the book. Coleridge came to the Lakes to help Wordsworth edit the second edition of LB; and received in return this rejection. It shook his confidence in his own imaginative gifts, which perhaps did not go so easily with Wordsworth's poetry, his mysticism of nature, his care for ordinary rural people; but maybe Coleridge would not have become so lost, so addicted to laudanum if he had been encouraged by Wordsworth to see his great and unique range as a poet during this time. Shelley described Coleridge as a marvellous bird 'with his own internal lightenings blind'. Sadly Wordsworth, though of course an incomparable poet, was egotistical. This was testified to by De Quincy who knew him well and lived for a time in Dove Cottage when the Wordsworths moved to Rydal Mount; and also by Keats, who met Wordsworth in London, and was disappointed in him.

But it is through the inspiration of Dorothy's faithfulness, tenderness, of her magical way of putting things, that both her beloved brother William and her dear friend Coleridge wrote much of their poetry.

William wrote a poem 'Louisa' about February 1802, in which he was almost certainly thinking of Dorothy - this was a favourite play of theirs to 'hunt the waterfalls':

'I met Louisa in the shade,
And having seen that lovely maid,
Why should I fear to say
That, nymph-like, she is fleet and strong,
And down the rocks can leap along
Like rivulets in May?

She loves her fire, her cottage home;
Yet o'er the moorland she will roam
In weather rough and bleak;
And, when against the wind she strains,
Oh! might I kiss the mountain rains
That sparkle on her cheek.

Take all that's mine 'beneath the moon',
If I with her but half a noon
May sit beneath the walls
Of some old cave, or mossy nook,
When up she winds along the brook
To hunt the waterfalls.'

Never, never do we forget Dorothy's travellers, her beggars, her discharged soldiers and sailors, her poor people, and particularly their children.

Feb 16th, 'We went to bed pretty soon and Mr. Graham said he wished Wm had been with him the other day. He was riding in a post chaise and he heard a strange cry that he could not understand, the sound continued and he called to the chaise-driver to stop. It was a little girl that was crying as if her heart would burst. She had got up behind the chaise, and her cloak had been caught by the wheel, and was jammed in and it hung there. She was crying after it, poor thing. Mr. Graham took her to the chaise, and the cloak was returned from the wheel, but the child's misery did not cease, for her cloak was torn to rags; it had been a miserable cloak before, but she had no other, it was the greatest sorrow that could befall her. Her name was Alice Fell. She had no parents. At the next town Mr. G left money with some respectable people in the town to buy her a new cloak.'

Feb 21st, Saturday, 'A very wet morning. I wrote the 2nd prologue to 'Peter Bell', then went to Mrs. Olliff's. After dinner I wrote the 1 and 2 prologue. William walked to the tailor's, while I was at Mrs. O's - it rained all the time. Snowdrops quite out, but cold and wintry; yet, for all this, a thrush that lives in our orchard has shouted and sung its merriest all day long. In the evening I wrote to Mrs. Clarkson, and to Br. Richard. Wm went to bed exhausted.'

Feb 23rd, Tuesday, 'A misty rainy morning - the lake calm. I baked bread and pies. Before dinner worked a little at Wm's waistcoat - after dinner read German grammar. Before tea we walked into Easedale. We turned aside in the Parson's field, a pretty field with pretty prospects. Then we went to the first large field, but such a cold wind met us as that we turned again. The wind seemed warm when we came out of our door. That dear thrush was singing upon the topmost of the smooth branches of the ash tree at the top of the orchard. How long it has been perched on that same tree I cannot tell, but we have heard its dear voice in the orchard these days through, along with the cheerful undersong made by our dear friends the robins. We came home by Goans - I picked up a few mosses by the roadside, which I left at home. We came to John's grove, there we sate a little while looking at the fading landscape, the lake, though the objects on the shore were fading, seemed brighter than when it is perfect day, and the island pushed itself upwards, distinct and large. All the shores marked. There was a sweet, sea-like sound in the trees above our heads. We walked backwards and forwards for some time for dear John's sake, then we walked to look at Rydale. Darkish when we reached home, and we got tea immediately with candles. William now reading in Bishop Hall - I going to read German. We have a nice singing fire, with one piece of wood. Fletcher's carts are arrived but no papers from Mrs. Coleridge.'

'That dear thrush' is like Coleridge's romantic portrait of Dorothy:

'A most gentle maid
Who dwelleth in her hospitable home
Hard by the castle, and at latest eve
(Even like a lady vowed and dedicate
To something more than nature in the grove
Glides thro the pathways, she knows all the notes'

March 4th, Thursday: Dorothy is always made desolate by William's going away. Her old childhood fear of abandonment is still strong in her. Dorothy writes: 'Before we had quite finished breakfast Calvert's man brought the horses for William. He had a deal to do , to shave, pens to make, poems to put in order for writing, to settle the dress, pack up, etc. and the man came before the pens were made, and he was obliged to leave me with only two. Since he has left me at half past eleven (it is now 2) I have been putting the drawers in order, laid by his clothes which we had thrown here there and everywhere, filed two months newspapers and got my dinner, two boiled eggs and two apple tarts and I have set Molly to clear the garden a little and I myself have helped. I transplanted some snowdrops - the bees are busy. Wm has a nice bright day. It was hard frost in the night. The robins were sweetly singing. Now for my walk - I will be busy, I will look well, and be well when he comes back to me. O the Darling! Here is one of his bitten apples. I can hardly find it in my heart to throw it into the fire. I must wash myself. Then off. I walked round two lakes, crossed the stepping stones at Rydale foot. Sate down where we always sit. I was full of thoughts about my darling. Blessings on him. I came home at the foot of our own hill under Loughrigg. They are making sad ravages in the woods. Bensons Wood is going, and the wood above the river. The wind has blown down a small fir tree on the rock that terminates John's path, I suppose it was the wind on Wednesday night. I read German after my return till tea-time. I worked and read LB, enchanted with the 'Idiot Boy' - Wrote to Wm; then went to bed. it snowed when I went to bed.'

March 5th, Friday, 'First walked in the garden and orchard, a frosty sunny morning. After dinner I gathered mosses in Easedale. I saw before me sitting in the open field upon his sack of rags the old ragman that I know. His coat is of scarlet in a thousand patches. His breeches knees untied. The breeches have been given to him by someone else - he has a round hat, pretty good, small round hat but large-rimmed. When I came to him he said, 'is there a brigg yonder that'll carry me ow'r t'water?"

So picturesque, so Gypsy, so wild. So almost like a hallucination, this meeting with the ragman is Dorothy's beautiful and imaginative description of it. So like a folk song. Dorothy continues: 'He seemed half-stupid. When I came home Molly had shook out the carpets and cleaned everything upstairs. When I see her so happy in her work, and exulting in her own importance, I often think of that affecting expression which she made use of to me one evening lately. Talking of her good luck in being in this house: 'Aye, Mistress, them 'ats low laid would have been a proud creature could they have (seen) where I is now, fro what they thought mud be my doom' ...

Dorothy's love and tenderness and delight in Molly's pride in her life with herself and William is all Dorothy's own. As is Molly's love and pride in Dorothy.

'I was tired when I reached home. I sent Molly Ashburner to Rydale. No letters! I was sadly mortified. I expected one fully from Coleridge. Wrote to William. Read the LB, got into sad thoughts, tried at German, but could not go on - Read LB. Blessings on that brother of mine! Beautiful new moon over Silver How.'

March 7th, Sunday morning, 'A very fine clear frost. I stitched up 'The Pedlar'; wrote out 'Ruth'; read it with alterations, then wrote to Mary H. Read a little German, got my dinner. Mrs. Lloyd called at the door, and in came William. I did not expect him till tomorrow. How glad I was. After we had talked about an hour and I gave him his dinner, a beef steak we sate talking and happy. Mr. and Miss Simpson came in at tea time. William came home very well - he had been a little fatigued with reading his poems. He brought two new stanzas for Ruth. We went to bed pretty soon and slept well.

March 8th, Monday morning, a soft rain and mist. We walked to Rydale for letters. The vale looked very beautiful in excessive simplicity, yet, at the same time, in uncommon obscurity. The church stood alone, no mountains behind. The meadows looked calm and rich, bordering on the still lake and island. Found a very affecting letter from Montague, also one from Mary. We read Montague's in walking on - sate down to read Mary's - I came home with a bad headache. I lay down - I slept, but rose little better. I have got tea and am now much relieved. On Friday evening the moon hung over the northern side of the highest point of Silver How, like a gold ring snapped in two, shaved off at the end, it was so narrow. Within this ring lay the circle of the round moon, as distinctly to be seen as ever the enlightened moon is. William had observed the same appearance at Keswick, perhaps at the very same moment, hanging over Newland Fells. Sent off a letter to Mary H, also to Coleridge and Sara, and re-wrote in the evening the alteration to 'Ruth', which we sent off at the same time.'

March 11th, Thursday, 'A fine morning. William worked at the poem on the 'Singing Bird'. Just as we were sitting down to dinner we heard Mr. Clarkson's voice. I ran down. William followed. He was so finely mounted that William was more intent on the horse than the rider, an offence easily forgiven, for Mr. Clarkson was very proud of it himself as he well could be. We ate our dinner, then Mr. Clarkson came, we walked with him round by the White Bridge after dinner - the Vale in mist, rather the mountains big with rain, soft and beautiful. Mr. C was sleepy and went soon to bed.'

March 12th, Friday: 'A very fine morning, we went to see Mr. Clarkson off. Then we went up towards Easedale but a shower drove us back. The sun shone while it rained, and the stones of the walls and the pebbles of the road glittered like silver. When William was at Keswick I saw Jane Ashburner driving the cow along the high road from the well where she had been watering it - she had a stick in her hand and came tripping along in the jig-step as if she were dancing. Her presence was bold and graceful, her cheeks flushed with health, her countenance was free and gay. William finished the poem of the 'Singing Bird'. In the meantime I read the remainder of Lessing. In the evening after tea William wrote 'Alice Fell', he went to bed tired with a wakeful mind and weary body. A very sharp clear night.'

Dorothy with whom each person's art was safely and well held and loved - Jane Ashburner's dancing, William's poetry.

March 13th, Saturday morning, 'It was as cold as ever it has been all winter, very hard frost. I baked pies and bread and seed-cake for Mr. Simpson. William finished 'Alice Fell', and then he wrote a poem of 'The Beggar Woman', taken from a woman I had seen in May (now nearly two years ago) when John and he were at Gallow Hill. I sate with him at intervals in the morning, took down his stanzas, etc. After dinner we walked to Rydale for letters. It was terribly cold - we had two or three brisk hard showers - the hail stones looked clean and pretty upon the dry clean road. Little Peggy Simpson was standing at the door catching the hail stones in her hand. She grows very like her mother, when she is sixteen years old I dare say that to her grandmother's eye she will seem as like to what her mother was, as any rose in her garden is like the rose that grew there years before.'

Dorothy's enchanting picture of Jane Ashburner dancing and of little Peggy Simpson standing in the door catching hail stones in

121

her hand, depicted by the rose simile, shows her clear and enchanting vision of people around her.

'No letters at Rydale. We drank tea as soon as we reached home. After tea I read to William that account of the little boy belonging to the tall woman, and an unlucky thing it was, for he could not escape from those very words, and so he could not write the poem. He left it unfinished, and went tired to bed. In our walk from Rydale he had got warmed with the subject, and had half cast the poem.'

March 14th, 'William had slept badly - he got up at nine o'clock, but before he rose he had finished 'The Beggar Boys', and while we were at breakfast that is (for I had breakfasted) he, with his basin of broth before him untouched, and a little plate of bread and butter, he wrote the poem 'To a Butterfly'! He ate not a morsel, nor put on his stockings, but sat with his shirt neck unbuttoned, his waistcoat open till he did it. The thought first came upon him as we were talking about the pleasure we both always feel at the sight of a butterfly. I told him that I used to chase them a little, but that I was afraid of brushing the dust off their wings, and did not catch them. He told me he used to kill all the white ones when he went to school, because they were Frenchmen. Mr. Simpson came in just as he was finishing the poem. After he was gone I wrote it down and the other poems, and I read them all over to him.'

March 16th, Tuesday, 'A very fine morning. Mrs. Luff called. William went up into the orchard while she was here and wrote part of 'The Emigrant Mother'. After dinner I read him to sleep. I read Spenser while he leaned upon my shoulder. We walked to look at Rydale. Then we walked towards Goans. The moon was a good height above the mountains and she seemed far and distant in the sky; these were two stars beside her, that twinkled in and out, and seemed almost like butterflys in motion and lightness. They looked to be far nearer to us than the moon.'

March 17th, Wednesday, 'William went up into the orchard and finished the poem. Mrs. Luff and Mrs. Oliff called. I was with Mrs.O at the top of White Moss. Mr. O met us and I went to their house, he offered me manure from the garden. I went and sat with

William and walked backwards and forwards in the orchard till dinner time. He read me his poems, I broiled beefsteaks. After dinner I made a pillow of my shoulder. I read to him and my beloved slept. I afterwards got him pillows, he was lying with his head on the table when Miss Simpson came in. She stayed to tea. I went with her to Rydale - no letters! A sweet evening, as it had been a sweet day, a grey evening and I walked quietly along the side of Rydale Lake with quiet thoughts - the hills and the lake were still - the owls had not begun to hoot, and the little birds had given over singing. I looked before me and I saw a red light upon Silver How as if coming out of the vale below:

There was a light of most strange birth
A light that came out of the earth,
And spread along the dark hill-side.

This was going on when I saw the shape of Beloved in the road at a little distance. We turned back to see the light but it was fading almost gone. The owls hooted when we sate on the wall at the foot of white Moss; the sky broke more and more, and we saw the moon now and then. John Green passed by with his cart. We sate on when we came in sight of our own dear Grasmere, the vale looked fair and quiet in the moonshine, the church was there and all the cottages. There were huge slow-travelling clouds in the sky, that threw large masses of shade upon some of the mountains. We walked backwards and forwards and between home and Oliff's, till I was tired. William kindled and began to write the poem. We carried cloaks into the orchard and sate a while there. I left him and he nearly finished the poem. I was tired to death - he came down to me, I read the poem. A sailor begged here today, going to Glasgow. He spoke cheerfully in a sweet tone.'

March 18th, 'A very fine morning. A sun shone. I felt myself weak and William charged me not to go to Mrs. Lloyds.'

Dorothy did not stay in the safety of William's instructions. She rested and walked over to see the Lloyds regardless, 'I seemed indeed to myself unfit for it, but when he was gone, I thought I would get the visit over if I could, so I ate a beefsteak thinking it would strengthen me, so it did, and I went off. I had a very pleasant walk - Rydale Vale was full of life and motion. The wind blew briskly, and the lake was covered over with bright silver waves that were each the twinkling of an eye, then others rose up and took their place as fast as they went away. The rocks glittered in the sunshine, the cows and ravens were busy, the thrushes and little birds sang. I went thro the fields and sate half an hour afraid to pass a cow. The cow looked at me and I looked at the cow, and whenever I stirred the cow gave over eating. I was very much tired when I reached the Lloyds - I walked in the garden. Charles is all for agriculture - Mrs. L in her kindest way. A parcel came in from Birmingham, with Lamb's play for us, and for C. They came with me as far as Rydale. As we came along Ambleside Vale in the twilight was grave evening. There was something in the air that compelled me to serious thought - the hills were large, closed in by the sky - it was nearly dark when I parted from the Lloyds, that is night was come on, the moon was crescent. But, as I climbed Moss (White Moss Common) the moon came out from behind a mountain mass of black clouds - O, the unutterable darkness of the sky, and earth below the moon! And the glorious brightness of the moon itself! There was a vivid sparkling streak of light at the end of Rydale Water, but the rest was very dark, and Loughrigg Fell and Silver How were white and bright, as if they were covered in hoar frost. The moon retired again and appeared and disappeared several times before I reached home. Once there was no moonlight to be seen but upon the island house and the promontory of the island where it stands, 'That needs must be a holy place', etc., etc. I had many very exquisite feelings and when I saw the lowly building, the waters, among the dark and lofty hills, with that bright, soft light upon it, made me more than half a poet. I was tired when I reached home, and could not sit down to reading and tried to write verses, but alas I gave up expecting William, and went soon to bed. Fletcher's carts came home later.'

March 19th, 'A very rainy morning. I went up into the lane to collect a few green mosses to make the chimney gay against my darling's return. Poor C, I did not wish for, or expect him, it rained so. Mr. Luff came in. Before my dinner we had a long talk - He left

124

me before 4 o'clock, and about half an hour after Coleridge came in
- his eyes were a little swollen with the wind - I was much affected
with the sight of him, he seemed half-stupefied. William came in
soon after. Coleridge went to bed late and William and I sate up late
till four o'clock. A letter from Sara sent by Mary. They disputed
about Ben Johnson. My spirits were agitated very much.'

Coleridge was sad because he had just left Sara Hutchinson.
He had been staying with her in her own home, but had then
renounced her except as an ideal and platonic love and a dear friend.

* * * * * * *

Dorothy used to sing this to her niece Dora, William and
Mary's child

"The Cottager to her infant"
"The days are cold, the nights are long,
The north wind sings a doleful song:
Then hush again upon my breast;
All merry things are now at rest;
Save thee, my Pretty love.

The kettle sleeps upon the hearth,
The crickets long have ceased their mirth;
There's nothing stirring in the house
Save one wee, hungry, nibbling mouse;
Then why so busy, thou?
Nay! Start not at that startling light;
Tis but the moon that shines so bright
On the window-pane bedropped with rain.
Then Darling! Sleep again,
And wake when it is day."

So close were Dorothy and William that Dorothy was almost
William's muse and her voice and his inspiration; and her writing all
the time was inspired by his living; writing poetry, all the time so

125

intimately with her.

Coleridge was wholly good about the Jews. On his journey in Germany, he said, he observed the touching sight of a family of 12 itinerant Jews sharing a miserable bed of straw at an inn, with their dogs sleeping at their feet: 'there was a very beautiful Boy among them, fast asleep, with the softest conceivable opening of the mouth, with the right beard of his Grandfather on his right cheek. The Jews are horribly unnaturally oppressed and persecuted all through Germany.'

Dorothy, 20th March: 'A tolerably fine morning after 11 o'clock, but when I awoke the whole vale was covered in snow. William and Coleridge walked to Burwick's. I followed but did not find them - I came home and they were here. We had a little talk about going abroad. We sate pleasantly enough. After tea William read 'The Pedlar'. After supper we talked about various things - christening the children, etc., etc. Went to bed at 12 o'clock.'

March 21st, Sunday: 'A showery day. Coleridge and William lay long in bed. We sent up to Mackareth's for the horse to go to Keswick, but we could not have it. Went with C to Burwick, where he left us. William was very unwell this evening. We had a sweet, tender conversation. I wrote to Mary and Sara.'

March 22nd, Monday, 'A rainy day. William very poorly. Mr. Luff came in after dinner and brought us letters from Sara H and one from poor Annette. I read Sara's letter while he was here, I finished my letter to M and Sara and wrote to my brother Richard. We talked a good deal about C and other interesting things. We resolved to see Annette, and that Wm should go to Mary. Wm wrote to Coleridge not to expect us till Thursday or Friday.'

March 23rd, Teusday, 'A mild morning. William worked at the Cuckoo poem, I sewed beside him. After dinner he slept. I read German, at the closing of the day I went to sit in the orchard, he came to see me and walked backwards and forwards. We talked about C. Wm repeated the poem to me. I left him there, and in 20 minutes he came in, and rather tired after attempting to write. He is now reading Ben Johnson. I am going to read German. It is about 10 o'clock, a quiet night. The fire flutters, the clock ticks, hear nothing else save the breathing of my Beloved, he now and again pushes his book forwards and turns over a new leaf. Fletcher is now come home. No letter from C.'

This is the perfect harmony and peace of people who love each other. At one with their own selves, with their light and life; in their own close work, writing and reading and studying, in their worshipping lakes and mountains. Firelight and time peaceably passing.

Friday 26th March, 'A beautiful morning. William wrote to Annette, then worked at Cuckoo. I was ill and in bad spirits. I sate two hours in the orchard. William and I walked together after tea, first to the top of White Moss then to Mr. Oliffs. I left Wm, and while he was absent wrote out poems. I grew alarmed and went to seek him - I met him at Mr. Oliffs. He had been trying without success to alter a passage in Silver How poem. He had written a conclusion just before he went out. While I was getting into bed he wrote 'The Rainbow'.'

March 27th, 'A divine morning. At breakfast William wrote part of an ode. Mr. Oliff sent the dung and we went to work in the garden. We sate all day in the orchard.'

March 31st, Wednesday, 'Very unwell. We walked to Portinscale, lay upon the turf, and saw into the vale of Newlands up to Borrowdale, and down to Keswick - a soft Venetian view. I returned better. Calvert and Wilkinson dined with us. I walked Mrs. W to the Quaker meeting; met William and we walked in the field together.'

April 2nd, Friday, 'Wm and I sate all the morning in the field. I nursed Derwent. Drank tea with Miss Cockins.'

April 3rd, Friday, 'Went to Skiddaw with C. We dined at Calverts. Fine day.'

April 9th, Friday, 'Mrs. C planting. Sent off letters. A windy morning - rough lake - sun shines, very cold - a windy night. Walked in Dunmallet. Marked out name on a tree.'

April 12th, Monday, 'Had the mantua-maker. The ground covered with snow. Walked to T. Wilkinsons and sent for letters. The woman brought me one from William and Mary. It was a sharp windy night. Thomas Wilkinson came with me to Barton, and questioned like a catechizer all the way. Every question was like the snapping of a little thread about my heart - I was so full of thought of my half-read letter and other things. I was glad when he left me. Then I had time to look at the moon while I was thinking my own thoughts. The moon travelled through the clouds, tinging them with yellow as she passed along, with two stars near her, one larger than the other. These stars grew and diminished as they passed from, or went into the clouds. At this time William, as I found next day, between Middleham and Barnard Castle, having parted from Mary. I read over my letter. When I got to the house Mr. and Mrs. C were playing at cards.'

April 15th, Thursday: The day they saw the daffodils, and Dorothy wrote about them with equal beauty: 'It was a threatening misty morning but mild. We set off after dinner for Eusemere. Mrs. Clarkson went a short way with us but turned back. The wind was furious, and we thought we must have returned. We first rested in a large boat house, then under a furze bush - opposite Mr. Clarkson's - Saw the plough going in a field. The wind seized our breath. The lake was rough. There was a boat by itself, floating in the middle of the bay below Water-Millock. We rested again in Water Millock Lane. The hawthorns are black and green, the birches here and there greenish but there is yet more of purple to be seen in the twigs. We got into a field to avoid some cows - people working. A few primroses by the roadside, wood-sorrel flowers, the anemone, scentless violets and strawberries, and that starry yellow flower which Mrs. C calls pilewort. When we were in the woods, beyond Gowberry Park, we saw a few daffodils close to the waterside. We fancied that the lake had floated the seeds ashore, and that the little colony had so sprung up: But as we went along, there were more and yet more; and at last, under the boughs of the trees, we saw that there was a long belt of them along the shore, about the breadth of a country turnpike road. I never saw daffodils so beautiful. They grew among mossy stones; some rested their heads upon these stones as on a pillow for weariness; and the rest turned and reeled and danced, and seemed as if they verily laughed with the wind that blew upon them over the lake; they looked so gay, ever glancing, ever changing. The wind blew directly over the lake to them. There was here and there a little knot, and a few stragglers a few yards higher up; but were so few, as not to disturb the simplicity, unity, and life of that one busy highway. We rested again and again. The bays were stormy and we heard the waves at different distances. In the middle of the water like the sea.'

It is not surprising that in her last, long illness, it was thought locally that Dorothy was worn out with writing all William's poetry for him - which began so often with Dorothy's vision and prose.

April 16th, 'After William had shaved we set forward; the valley is at first broken by little rocky woods, knolls that make retiring places, fairy valleys in the vale; the river winds along under the hills, travelling, not in a bustle but slowly, to the lake. We saw a fisherman in the flat meadow on the other side of the water. He came towards us and threw his line over the two-arched bridge. It is a bridge of heavy construction, almost bending inwards in the middle, but it is grey and there is a look of ancientry in the architecture of it that pleases me. As we go on the vale opens out more onto one vale, with somewhat of a cradle bed. Cottages with groups of trees, on the side of the hills. We passed a pair of twin children - 2 years old. Sate on the next bridge which we crossed - a single arch. We rested again upon the turf, looked at the same bridge. We observed arches in the water, occasioned by the larger stones sending it down in two streams. A sheep came plunging through the river, stumbling up the bank, and passed close to us. It has been frightened by an insignificant little dog on the other side. Its fleece dropped in a glittering shower under its belly. Primroses by the road-side, pilewort that shone like stars of gold in the sun, violets, strawberries, retired and half-buried among the grass. When we came to the foot Brothers Water, I left William sitting on the bridge, and went along the path to the right side of the lake through the wood. I was delighted at what I saw. The water under the boughs of the bare old tree, the simplicity of the mountains, and the exquisite beauty of the path. There was one grey cottage. I repeated 'The Glow Worm' as I went along' (this was William's poem 'Among all lovely things my love had been'). 'I hung over the gate, and thought I could have stayed for ever. When I returned, I found William writing a poem descriptive of the sights and sounds we saw and heard' ('The cock is crowing'). 'There was the gentle flowing of the stream, the glittering, lively lake, green fields without a living creature to be seen on them, behind us a flat pasture with 42 cattle feeding - to our left, the road tending to the hamlet. No smoke there. The sun shone on the bare roofs. The people were at work, ploughing, harrowing, sowing; the lasses spreading dung, a dog barking now and then, cocks crowing, and birds twittering the snow in patches at the top of the highest hills; purple and green twigs on the birches, ashes with their glittering spikes quite bare. The hawthorn is bright green with black stems under the oak. The moss of the oak glossy.'

April 17th, Saturday, 'A mild warm rain. We sate in the garden all the morning. William dug a little - I transplanted a honeysuckle. The lake was still. The sheep on the island reflected in the water like the grey deer we had seen at Gowbarrow Park. We walked after tea by moonlight. I had been in my bed in the afternoon, and William had slept in his chair. We walked towards Rydale first, then backwards and forwards below Mr. Oliff's. The village was beautiful in the moonlight, Helm Crag was observed very distinct. The dead hedge round Benson's field bound together at the top by an interlacing of ash sticks which made a chain of silver when we faced the moon. A letter from C and also from SH. I saw a robin chasing a scarlet butterfly this morning.'

April 18th, Saturday, 'I lay in bed late, again a mild grey morning, with rising vapours. We sate in the orchard. William wrote a poem on the Robin and the Butterfly. I went to drink tea at Luff's, but as we did not dine till 6 o'clock it was late. It was mist and small rain all the way, but very pleasant. William met me at Rydale. Aggie accompanied me thither. We sate up late. He met me with the conclusion of the poem of the Robin. I read it to him in bed. We left out some lines! ...'

So Dorothy would join in with William in writing his poetry, together they 'left out some lines'!

April 21st, Wednesday, 'William and I sauntered a little in the garden. Coleridge came to us and repeated the verses he wrote to Sara.' This was Coleridge's magnificent poem 'Dejection' about his sadness and written to Sara Hutchinson; this sadness caused Dorothy to grieve for her dear friend. Several personal stanzas were published with this poem in 1937.

Dorothy says she was affected by these poems at this time; she was on the whole not feeling well and in miserable spirits: 'The sunshine, the green fields and the fair sky made me sadder; even the little happy sporting lambs seemed but sorrowful for me. The pilewort spread out on the grass a thousand shining stars.' Dorothy grieved for her great friend Coleridge, and William also was troubled. But his rejection of 'Christabel' for 'Lyrical Ballads' had deeply damaged Coleridge's self-confidence as a poet and made him doubt his glowing and real talent, his idea of himself as a poet. His way was perhaps not Wordsworth's way, but both were equally marvellous poets - and Wordsworth's rejection of Coleridge's contribution, was partly responsible for Coleridge's depression and his opium addiction, his misery and illness.

'The primroses were there, and the remains of a few daffodils. The well, which we cleaned out last night, is still but a little muddy pond, though full of water - I went to bed after dinner, and could not sleep; went to bed again. Read Fergian's life and a poem or two - fell asleep for five minutes and awoke better. We got tea. Sate comfortably in the evening. I went to bed early.'

April 22nd, Tuesday, 'A fine mild morning. We walked to Eusedale. The sun shone. Coleridge talked of his plan of sowing the laburnum in the woods. The waters were high, for there had been a great quantity of rain in the night. I was tired and sate under the shade of a holly tree that grows upon a rock, sate there and looked down the stream. Then I went to the single holly tree that grows upon a rock, sate there and looked down the stream. I then went to the single holly behind that single rock in the field, and sate upon the grass till they came from the waterfall. I saw them there and heard Wm, flinging stones into the river, whose roaring was loud even where I was. When they returned William was repeating the poem 'I have thoughts that are fed by the sun'. It had been called to his

131

mind by the dying away of the stunning of the waterfall when he came behind a stone. When we had got into the vale the heavy rain came on. We saw a family of little children sheltering themselves under a wall before the rain came on. They sate in a row making a canopy for each other of their clothes. The servant lass was planting potatoes near them. Coleridge changed his clothes - we were all wet. Wilkinson came in while we were all at dinner. Coleridge and I after dinner drank black currants and water.'

April 23rd, 1802, Friday, 'It being a beautiful morning we set off at 11 o'clock, intending to stay out of doors all the morning. We went towards Rydale, and before we got to Tom Dawson's we determined to go under Nab Scar. It was very grand when we looked up, very strong, here and there a budding tree. William observed that the Umbrella Yew Tree, that breasts the wind, had lost its character as a tree, and had become something like solid wood. Coleridge and I pushed on before. We left William sitting on the stones, feasting with silence; and C and I sat down upon a rocky seat - a couch it might be under the bower of William's eglantine, Andrew's Broom. He, Wm, was below us and we could see him. He came to us and repeated his poems while we sate beside him on the ground. The poems were 'The Waterfall', 'The Eglantine', and 'The Oak and the Broom'. He had made himself a seat in the crumbling ground. After we had lingered long, looking into vales, Ambleside Vale with the copses, the village under the hill, and the green fields - Rydale with a lake all alive and glittering, but little stirred by breezes - our own dear Grasmere, making first a little round lake of nature's own, with never a house, never a green field, but the copses and bare hills enclosing it, and the river flowing out of it - above rose the Coniston Fells, in their own shape and colour - not man's hills, but all for themselves the sky and the clouds, and the few wild creatures. C went to search for something new. We saw him climbing up towards a rock. He called us, and we found him in a bower - the sweetest that ever was seen. The rock on one side is very high, and all covered in ivy, which hung loosely about, and bare branches and brown berries. On the other, it was higher than my head. We looked down upon Ambleside Vale that seemed to wind away from us, the village lying under the hill. The far island was reflected beautifully. We now first saw that the trees are planted in rows. About this bower there is mountain ash, common ash, yew tree, ivy, hills, hawthorns, mosses, and flowers and a carpet of moss. Above, at the top of the rocks there is another spot - it is scarce a bower, a little parlour only, not enclosed by walls, but shaped out for a resting place by the rocks, and the ground rising above it. It had a sweet moss carpet - we resolved to go and plant flowers in both these places tomorrow. We wished for Mary and Sara. Dined late. After dinner Wm and I worked in the garden. C read letter from Sara.'

April 29th, Thursday, 'A beautiful morning. The sun shone and all was pleasant. We sent off our parcel to Coleridge by the waggon. Mr. Simpson heard the Cuckoo today. Before we went out, I had written down 'The Tinker' which William finished this morning. Luff called - he was very lame, limped into the kitchen. He came on a little pony. We went to John's Grove, sate a while at first. Afterwards William lay, and I lay, in the trench under the fence - he with his eyes shut, and listening to the waterfalls and the birds. There was no one waterfall above another - it was a sound of waters in the air. William heard me breathing and rustling now and then, but we both lay still, and unseen by one another; he thought it would be sweet just to lie so in the grave, so near the peaceful sounds of the earth, and just to know that our dear friends are near. The lake was so still; there was our boat out. Silver How reflected with delicate purple and yellowish hues as I have seen Spar; lambs on the island, and running races together by the half-dozen (in the round field near us). The copses greenish, hawthorns green. Came home to dinner then went to Mr. Simpson's - we rested a long time under a wall, sheep and lambs were in the fields - cottages smoking. As I lay down on the grass I observed the glittering silver line on the ridge on the backs of the sheep, owing to their situation respecting the sun, which made them look beautiful, but with something of strangeness, like animals of another kind, as if of animals belonging to a more splendid world. Met old Mrs. S at the door - Mrs. S poorly. I got mullins and pansies. I was sick and obliged to come home soon. We went to bed immediately - I slept upstairs - the air coldish, where it was felt, somewhat frosty.'

April 30th, Friday, 'We came into the orchard directly after breakfast, and sate there. The lake was calm, the day cloudy. We saw two fishermen by the lakeside. William began to write the poem of 'The Celandine'. I wrote to Mary H sitting on the fur gown. Walked backwards and forwards with William - he repeated his poem to me, then he got to walk again and could not give over. He had not finished his dinner till five o'clock. After dinner we took up the gown into the Hollins above. We found there a sweet seat, and thither we will often go. We spread the gown, put on each a cloak, and there we lay. William fell asleep - he had a bad headache owing to his having been disturbed the night before, with reading C's letter which Fletcher had brought to the door. I did not sleep, but I lay with half-shut eyes, looking at the prospect as in a vision almost, I was so resigned to it. Loughrigg Fell was the most distant hill; then came the lake, slipping in between the copses, and above the copse the round swelling fields; nearer to me a wild intermixture of rocks, trees and slacks of grassy ground. When we turned the corner of our little shelter, we saw the church and the whole vale. It is a blessed place. The birds were above us on all sides - skobbies, robins, bull-finches. Crows now and then flew over our heads, as we were warned by the sound of the beating of the air above us. We stayed till the light of day was going, and the little birds had begun to settle their singing. But there was a thrush not far off; that seemed to sing louder and clearer than the thrush had sung when it was quite day. We came in at 8 o'clock, got tea, wrote to Coleridge, and wrote to Mrs. Clarkson part of a letter. We went to bed at 20 minutes past 11, with prayers that William might sleep well.'

May 1st, Saturday, 'Rose not till half past 8, a heavenly morning. I sowed the flowers, William helped me. Then we went and sate in the orchard till dinner time. After dinner we went again to our old resting place in the Hollins under the rock. We first lay under a holly, where we saw nothing but the holly tree, and a budding elm and the sky above our heads. But that holly had a beauty about it more than its own, knowing as we did where we were. When the sun had got low enough, we went to the rock shade. Oh, the overwhelming beauty of the vale below; greener than green! The ravens flew high, high in the sky and the sun shone upon them, their bellies and their wings, long after there was none of his light to be seen but a little space at the top of Loughrigg Fell - We went down to tea at 8 o'clock, had lost the poem and returned after tea. The landscape was fading: sheep and lambs quiet among the rocks. We walked towards the kings and backwards and forwards. The sky was perfectly cloudless. NB. Is it often so? Three solitary stars in the middle of the blue vault, one or two on the point of the high hills. Wm wrote 'The Celandine' 2nd part tonight. Heard the Cuckoo today - this first of May.'

May 4th, Tuesday, 'William had slept pretty well and though he went to bed nervous and jaded in the extreme - he rose refreshed. I wrote 'The Leech Gatherer' for him, which he had begun the night before, and of which he wrote several stanzas in the morning. It was very hot; we called at Mr. Simpson's door as we passed, but did not go in. We rested several times by the way, read and repeated 'The Leech Gatherer'. We were almost melted before we were at the top of the hill. We saw Coleridge at the Wythborn side of the water. He crossed the beck to us. Mr. Simpson was fishing there. William and I ate a luncheon, then went on towards the waterfall. It is a glorious wild solitude under that lofty purple crag. It stood upright by itself. Its own self, and its shadow below, one man - all else was sunshine. We went on further. A bird, at the top of the crags, was flying round and round, and looking in thinness, transparency, shape and motion, like a moth.

Dorothy is seen in her journal writing with all the fresh clarity of a true child of nature. She is perhaps in some ways the model for Coleridge's 'Christabel', an original, nature-loving, nature reverent person, known to Coleridge since Alfoxden days.

Dorothy and William, worried by Coleridge's melancholy and illness, encouraged his friendship and growing love for Sara Hutchinson when she was staying with them at Grasmere. Sara, to whom Coleridge gave the romantic code name of 'Asra', became his loved friend, secretary, helper, recording and even copying plant names in his private notebooks, a favour he allowed no one else. She read books with him, listened to his philosophy, and was his companion in his delight in nature. Once when he was ill and Sara visited, he sat up at once to read with her. When he knew of William's engagement to Mary Hutchinson, he craved reassurance from Asra that he was not to be left out of the circle of his beloved friends.

Coleridge did not, however, live with Sara as her lover. This was due to a great extent because of his love for his two children Hartley and Derwent. He would talk to and play with and teach Hartley for hours; some of his poems were inspired by conversations he had with his little child.

Coleridge arrived at Grasmere on 19th of March and Dorothy, worried, wrote: 'his eyes were a little swollen with the wind. I was much affected with the sight of him, he seemed half-stupefied.' He had just left Gallow Hill, where he had been helping nurse Sara, made ill by the disturbance his love letters caused her. He had renounced her after a fond and loving stay and he had 'wept aloud' when he left on the mail on 13th March. At Grasmere they stayed up late talking and Dorothy's spirits were 'much agitated'. A letter arrived from Asra at Gallow Hill.

Over the weekend they talked of Wordsworth's marriage, and of their plan to visit Annette Vallon and little Caroline, her and William's child before the marriage. Then Coleridge went back to Greta Hall, where the Wordsworths promised to come to him the week following.

When Dorothy and William arrived at Greta Hall, William brought with him the first four stanzas of his ode 'Intimations of Immortality', and Coleridge then wrote his 'Dejection, an Ode', written in the form of a letter to Sara Hutchinson. This ode of Coleridge's echoes and replies to William's. 'Dejection' is a sad and truly magnificent poem telling of Coleridge's melancholy with a wonderful description of the storm raging loudly outside, and plaintively as a lost child, that his faith and love are now in Sara Hutchinson.

CHAPTER 7

After staying with the Coleridges, Dorothy and William went on to stay with the Clarksons at Eusemere, and they caught the coach into Yorkshire for a visit to Mary and the Hutchinsons, farming at Gallow Hill near Malton. On the coach a storm came on but Dorothy and William buttoned themselves together into the guard's cloak, 'I never rode more snugly'. They walked the last stage of the journey over Hambledon Hills, Dorothy, though weary, delighted by looking down on the ruins of Rievaux Abbey, 'among a brotherhood of valleys'. From 16th to 20th July they stayed at the Hutchinsons, exploring the wolds in rain and sunshine. Sara was with Mary, and this was lucky as she helped Dorothy with clothes for France. Sara had ordered for herself from London 'a chip hat or bonnet of the very newest fashion - peagreen else lilac'. Sara was small, like Dorothy, so she lent Dorothy one or more white gowns to wear in France, the centre of fashion, and Dorothy trusted Sara's taste.

By 29th July Dorothy and William were in London, and two days later by six they caught the Dover coach at Charing Cross. 'It was a beautiful morning', Dorothy wrote. 'The city, St. Pauls, with river and a multitude of little boats, made a most beautiful sight as we crossed Westminster Bridge. The houses were not overhung by their cloud of smoke, and they were spread out endlessly, yet the sun shone so brightly with such fierce light, that there was even something like the purity of one of nature's own grand spectacles.' She was going at last to see her 'sister' Annette, to whom she had written so faithfully, to see her dear niece Caroline, William's child. William began 'on the roof of the coach' his beautiful sonnet 'Composed on Westminster Bridge', Sept 3rd 1802:

'Earth has not anything to show more fair:
Dull would he be of soul who could pass by
A sight so touching in its majesty:
This City now doth, like a garment, wear
The beauty of the morning; silent, bare,

137

Ships, towers, domes, theatres, and temples lie
Open unto the fields, and to the sky;
All bright and glittering in the sokeless air.
Never did sun more beautifully steep
In his first splendour, valley, rock, or hill;
Ne'er saw I, never felt, a calm so deep!
The river glideth at his own sweet will:
Dear God! the very houses seem asleep,
And all that mighty heart is lying still!'

On August 1st, 1802, they were on board ship in Calais
Harbour at 7.30 in the morning, but by almost 8.30 they had 'found
out Annette and C chez Madame Avril dans la Rue de la Tête
d'Or.' They were to be together one month. It was strange for
them to recognise each other: William grown more serious, shabby;
and Dorothy his sister, so enthusiastic in her letters, was very
workworn and thin. Annette had been bravely fighting in the cause
of the Royalists and Catholics in a resistance movement called The
Chouans. She called herself Madame William and brought up
Caroline bravely and well by herself. She, with her two sisters, had
hidden in the family house in Blois many many priests and royalist
refugees - someone later said she had saved his life by risking her
own. She went to Catholic services secretly, and rescued a prisoner
by a rope ladder. In police records she was 'Widow Williams of
Blois; gives shelter to Chuans'. She and William agreed on hating
Buonapart.
	Dorothy was moved by this history of courage and suffering,
though she followed William in being suspicious of Catholics. She
never lost her love and sympathy for 'poor, dear Annette' and her
loving concern for Caroline. She always loved children and especially
William's children. They walked on Calais sands in the evenings,
'delightful walks' Dorothy wrote, 'after the heat of the day was
passed away', and with them 'the dear child', little French Caroline,
'untouched by solemn thought' who looked so like William. Dorothy
was deeply involved and touched, writing 'The reflections in the
water were more beautiful than the sky itself, purple waves brighter

than precious stones, forever melting away upon the sands' on hot quiet nights she saw 'the little boats row out of the harbour with wings of fire, and the sail boats with the fiery track which they cut as they went along'. She saw with a child's vision, even as Caroline, the 'sparkles, balls, shootings and streams of glow-worm light. Caroline was delighted.'

During their stay with Annette in Calais they discussed a dowry for Caroline, and all in friendship and calm meeting and respect; with concern for Caroline's future. Dorothy continued faithfully to write to Annette thereafter, but William and Annette only met twice more in their lives. Dorothy saw Annette and Caroline as her own family.

On 29th August Dorothy and William left Calais and reached Dover 24 hours later, Dorothy being sick all the way. As August was very hot, they both had a bath and then sat on the cliffs thinking sadly of Annette and Caroline. Dorothy especially grieved at being parted from her niece, a child of her own family.

In London they stayed probably in Basil Montague's chambers, it being the law vacation, and nearby at Mitre Court Buildings lived Charles and Mary Lamb; Dorothy and William dined with them on 7th September. Lamb took them to 'Bartlemy Fair' for a special outing. Dorothy got a headache from the noise and crowds, but during their three weeks stay in London she developed a deep and lasting friendship and admiration for kindly, generous Mary Lamb. Dorothy was quick to understand the tragedy and faithful love of Charles and Mary Lamb, and Charles' care and devotion to his sister, who was afflicted with occasional bouts of insanity, during one of which she had killed their mother. The sympathy between these two women, Mary Lamb and Dorothy, led to a long-living friendship between their two families. Wordsworth later grieved at Lamb's death, saying, 'the Lamb, the frolic and the gentle.'

May 12th, Wednesday (1802), 'A sunshiny but coldish morning. We walked to Eusedale and returned by George Rawson's and the lane. We brought home heckberry blossom, crab blossom, the anemone nemorosa, marsh marigold, speedwell, that beautiful blue one, the colour of blue stone on glass used in jewellery - with its beautiful pearl-like chives. Anemonies are in abundance, and still the dear, dear primroses, violets in beds, pansies in abundance, and the little Celandine. Butterflys of all colours. I often see some small ones of a pale purple lilac, or Emperor's eye colour, something of the colour of that large geranium which grows by the lake-side. Wm observed the beauty of Geordy Green's house. We see it from our orchard. Wm pulled ivy - I put it over the chimney piece. Sate in the orchard the hour before dinner, coldish. We have now dined. My head aches. William is sleeping in the window. In the evening we were sitting at the table, writing, when we were roused by Coleridge's voice below. He had walked; looked paleish but not much tired. We sate up till one o'clock, all together; when William went, I sate with C in the sitting room (where he slept till past 1/4 past two o'clock. Wrote to MH.'

May 14th, Friday 1802, 'A very cold morning - hail and snow showers all day. We went to Brother's wood, intending to get plants, and to go along the shore of the lake to the foot. We did go a part of the way, but there was no pleasure in stepping along that difficult sauntering road in the ungenial weather. We turned again and walked backwards and forwards in Brother's wood. William teased himself with seeking an epithet for the cuckoo. I sate a while upon my last summer seat, the mossy stone. William's unemployed beside me, and the space between where Coleridge had so often lain ... ' Dorothy, with the ghosts of last summer, her own seat on her stone. There is almost a note of grieving here, of Coleridge going away from them. 'The oak trees are just putting forth yellow knots of leaves. The ashes with their flowers passing away, and leaves coming out. The blue hyacinth is not quite full-blown; gowans are coming out, march marigolds in full glory; the little star plant, a star without a flower. We took home a great load of gowans, and planted them in the cold about the orchard. After dinner, I worked bread, then came in and mended stockings beside William; he fell asleep. After tea I walked to Rydale for letters. It was a strange night. The hills were covered over with a slight covering of hail or snow, just so as to give them a hoary winter look with the black rocks. The woods looked miserable, the coppices green as grass, which looked quite unnatural, and they seemed half-shrivelled up, as if they shrank from the air. 'O', thought I, 'what a beautiful thing God has made winter to be, by stripping the trees, and letting us see their shapes and forms. What a freedom does it seem to give the storms! There are several new flowers out, but I had no pleasure in looking at them. I walked as fast as I could back again with my letter from SH which I skimmed over at Tommy Flemings. Met Wm at the top of White Moss. We walked a little beyond Oliff's. Near 10 when we came in. Wm and Molly had dug the ground and planted potatoes in my absence. We wrote to Coleridge. Sent off a letter to Annette, bread and frocks to the Cs. Went to bed at 1/2 past 11. William very nervous. After he was in bed, haunted with altering 'The Rainbow'.'

May 15th 1802, Saturday morning, 'It is now 1/2 past 10, and he is not up. Miss Simpson called when I was in bed. I have been in the garden. It looks fresh and neat in spite of the frost. Molly tells me they had thick ice on a jug at their door last night. A very cold and cheerless morning. I sate mending stockings all the morning. I read in Shakespear. William lay very late because he slept ill last night. It snowed this morning just like Christmas. We had a melancholy letter from Coleridge just at bed-time. It distressed me very much, and I resolved upon going to Keswick the next day!'

The following is written on the blotting paper opposite this date:

'S T Coleridge Dorothy Wordsworth. William Wordsworth Mary Hutchinson. Sara Hutchinson William. Coleridge Mary Dorothy Sara 16th May 1802 John Wordsworth'

Dorothy rehearsing the names of the members of their beloved commune, like telling her beads.

May 16th, 'William was at work all the morning. I did not go to Keswick. A sunny cold frosty day. A snow-shower at night. We were a good while in the orchard in the morning.'

May 17th, Monday: 'William was not well. He went with me to Wythborn Water. He left me in a post-chaise. Hail showers, snow and cold attacked me. The people were graving peats under Nadd Fell. A lark and thrush singing near Coleridge's home. Bancrofts there. A letter from MH.'

May 18th, Tuesday, 'Terribly cold. Coleridge not well. Froude called, Wilkinson called, I not well. C and I walked in the evening in the garden. Warmer in the evening. Wrote to M and S.'

They were all very often ill and wove their lives around their illness.

May 19th, Wednesday, 'A grey morning - not quite so cold. C and I set off at 1/2 past 9 o'clock. Met William near the 6-mile stone. We sate down by the roadside, and then went to Wythburn Water. Longed to be at the island. Sate in the sun. Colerige's bowels bad, mine also. We drank tea at John Stanley's. The evenings cold and clear. The glorious light on Skiddaw. I was tired. Brought a cloak down from Mr. Simpson's. Packed up books for Coleridge, then got supper - and went to bed.'

May 21st, Friday, 'A very warm gentle morning, a little rain. William wrote 2 sonnets on Buonapart, after I had read Milton's sonnets to him. In the evening he went with Mr. Simpson with Borwick's boat to gather ling in Bainriggs. I plashed about the well. Was much heated. I think I caught a cold.'

May 22nd, Saturday, 'A very hot morning. A hot wind, as if coming from a sand desert. We met Coleridge. He was sitting under Sara's rock when we reached him. He turned with us. We sate a long time under the wall of the sheep fold. Had some interesting melancholy talk about his private affairs. We drank tea at a farmhouse. The woman was very kind. There was a woman with three children travelling from Workingham to Manchester. The woman served them liberally. Afterwards she said that she never suffered any to go away without a trifle 'sec as we have'. The woman at whose house we drank tea the last time was rich and senseless - she said 'she never served anyone but their own poor'. C came home with us. We sate some time in the orchard. Then they came in to supper - mutton chops and potatoes. Letters from S and MH.'

May 23rd, Sunday, 'I sate with Coleridge in the orchard all morning. I was ill in the afternoon, took laudanum. We walked in Bainriggs after tea. Saw the juniper - umbrella-shaped. C went to S and M points, joined us in White Moss.'

May 28th, Friday, 'I was much better than yesterday, though poorly. William tired himself with hammering at a passage. After dinner he was better - and I greatly better. We sate in the orchard. The sky cloudy, the air sweet and cool. The young bull-finches in their party-coloured raiment bustle about among the blossoms, and poise themselves like wire-dancers, or tumblers, shaking the twigs and dashing off the blossoms. There is yet one primrose in the orchard. The stitchwort is fading. The wild columbines are coming into beauty, the vetches are in abundance, blossoming and seeding; that pretty little wavy-looking dial-like yellow flower, the speedwell, and some others, whose names I do not yet know. The wild columbines are coming into beauty, some of the gowans fading. In the garden we have lilies, and many other flowers. The scarlet beans are up in crowds. It is now between 8 and 9 o'clock. It has rained sweetly for two hours and a half; the air is very mild. The heckberry blossoms are dropping off fast, almost gone - barberries are in beauty - snowballs coming forward - May roses blossoming.'

May 29th, Saturday, 'I was much better - I made bread and a wee rhubarb tart and a batter pudding for William. We sate in the orchard after dinner. William finished his poem on going for Mary ('A Farewell'). I wrote it out. I wrote to Mary H, having received a letter from her in the evening. A sweet day. We nailed up the honey-suckles, and hoed the scarlet beans.'

May 31st, Monday, 'I was much better. We sate out all day. Mary Jameson dined. I wrote out a poem on 'Our Departure', which he seemed to have finished. In the evening Miss Simpson brought us a letter from MH; and a complimentary and critical letter to W from John Wilson of Glasgow post-paid. I went a little way with Miss S. My tooth broke today. They will soon be gone. Let that pass, I shall be beloved - I want no more.'

And indeed Dorothy was truly beloved by those whom she loved, by William and his family; and when she was ill and old she was cared for by William and Mary with the sweetest and most sensitive care which William and Mary knew.

June 1st, Tuesday, 'A very sweet day, but sad want of rain.

We went into the orchard after dinner; after I had written to MH. Then on to Mr. Oliff's intakes. We found some torn bird's nests. The Columbine was growing upon the rocks; here and there a solitary plant sheltered and shaded by the tufts and bowers of trees. It is a graceful slender creature, a female seeking retirement, and growing freest and most graceful where it is most alone. I observed the more shaded plants were always the tallest. A short note and gooseberries from Coleridge.' Dorothy too grew freest and most gracefully when most alone.

June 2nd, Wednesday, 'In the morning we observed that the scarlet beans were dropping in the leaves in great numbers. Owing, we guess to an insect. We sate a while in the orchard - then we went to the old carpenter's about the hurdles. Yesterday an old man called, a grey-haired man, above 70 years of age. He said he had been a soldier, that his wife and children had died in Jamaica. He had a beggar's wallet over his shoulders; a coat of shreds and patches, although of a drab colour; he was tall and tho his body was bent, he had the look of one used to having been upright. I talked a while and gave him a piece of cold bacon and a penny. Said he, 'You're a fine woman'. I could not help smiling; I suppose he meant 'you're a kind woman'. Afterwards a woman called, travelling to Glasgow. After dinner we went to Frank's field, crawled up the little glen and planned a seat, then went to Mr. Oliff's Hollins and sate there - found a beautiful shell-like purple fungus in Frank's field. After tea we walked to Butterlip How and backwards and forwards there. All the young oak trees leaves are dry as powder. A cold south wind, portending rain. I ought to have said that on Tuesday evening, namely June 1st, we walked upon the turf near John's Grove. It was a lovely night. The clouds of the Western sky reflected a saffron light upon the upper end of the lake. All was still. We went to look at Rydale. There was an Alpine fire-like red upon the tops of the mountains. This was gone when we came into view of the lake. But when we saw the lake in a new and most beautiful point of view, between two little rocks, and behind a small ridge that had concealed it from us. This White Moss, a place made for all kinds of beautiful works of art and nature, woods and valleys, fairy valleys and fairy tarns, and miniature mountains, alps above alps. Little John Dawson came in from the woods with a stick over his shoulder.'

June 3rd, 1802: Ellen was Mrs. Clarkson's housekeeper and companion. She lived at Eusemere and looked after the house while the Clarksons were away. When the Wordsworths 'ate our dinner' at the foot of Kirkstone, they were feasting upon pies which Ellen had made. It was also Ellen who gave Dorothy and Sara 'tea by the kitchen fire - nice bread and everything comfortable!' when they walked over from Park House.

Tuesday June 8th, 1802, 'Ellen and I rode to Windemere. We had a fine sunny day, neither hot nor cold. I mounted the horse at the quarry - we had no difficulties or delay but the gates. I was enchanted with some of the views. From the high Ray the view was very delightful, rich and festive, water and wood houses, groves, hedge-rows, green fields and mountains - white houses large and small - we passed 2 or 3 nice looking statesmen's houses. Mr. Curwen's shrubberies looked pitiful enough under the native trees. We put up our horses, ate our dinner by the water-side and walked up to the station. Then we went to the island, walked round it and crossed the lake with our horse in the ferry. The shrubs have been cut away in some parts of the island. I observed to the boatman that I did not think it improved. He replied, 'We think it is, for one could hardly see the house before.' It seems to me to be, however, no better than it was. They have made no natural glades; it is merely a lawn with a few miserable young trees, standing as if they were half-starved. There are no sheep, no cattle, upon these lawns. It is neither one thing or another - neither natural, nor wholly cultivated and artificial, which it was before. And that great house! Mercy upon us! If it could be concealed, it would be well for all who are not pained to see the pleasantest of earthly spots deformed by man. But it cannot be covered. Even the tallest of our old oak trees would not reach the top of it. When we went into the boat, there were two men standing at the landing place. One seemed to be about 60, a man with a jolly red face; he looked as if he might have lived many years in Mr. Curwen's house.'

June 9th, Wednesday, 'Wm slept ill. A soaking all day rain. We should have gone to Mr. Simpson's for tea but we walked up after tea. Lloyds called. The hawthorn of the mountainside like orchards in blossom. Brought rhubarb down. It rained hard. Ambleside fair. I wrote to Christopher and MH.'

June 10th, Thursday, 'I wrote to Mrs. Clarkson and Luff - went with Ellen to Rydale. Coleridge came in with a sack of books, etc. and a bunch of mountain ash. He had been attacked by a cow. He came over by Grisdale. A furious wind. Mr. Simpson drank tea. William very poorly - we went to bed lateish - I slept in the sitting room.' Coleridge into one of his bursts of energy and strength, carrying a sack of books all the way over to the Wordsworth despite cows and a furious wind undaunted.

June 13th, Sunday, 'A fine morning. Sunshiny and bright but with rainy clouds. William had slept better but not well, he had been altering the poem to Mary this morning, he is now washing his feet. I wrote out poems for our journey and I wrote a letter to my Uncle Cookson. Mr. Simpson came when we were in the orchard in the morning, and brought us a beautiful drawing which he had done. In the evening we walked first on our own path - there we walked a good while. It was a silent night. The stars were out by ones and twos, but no cuckoo, no little birds, the air was not so warm, and we have observed that since Tuesday 8th, when William wrote 'The sun has long been set', that we have had no birds singing after the evening is fairly set in. We walked to our new view of Rydale, but it put on a sullen face. There was an owl hooting at Bainriggs. Its first Haloo was so like a human shout that I was surprised when it made a second call tremulous - lengthened out, to find that the shout had come from an owl. The full moon (not quite full) was among a company of steady island clouds, and the sky bluer about it than the natural sky blue. William observed that the full moon, above a dark fir grove, is a fine image of the descent of a superior being. There was a shower which drove us into John's Grove before we had quitted our favourite path. We walked upon John's path before we went to view Rydale. We went to bed immediately on our return home. Dorothy writes to her brother Richard Wordsworth, Grasmere,

10th June 1802:

My dear Brother
William received your letter on Monday morning. I am
considerably better than I was when I wrote to you last, though
far from well. I have had the most severe cold I have ever had
in all my life, and it has taken both my strength and my looks.
I will make no comments upon the intelligence which William
communicated to you in his last, except that I do not doubt that
if his health is so good that he can go on with those employments
in which he has lately been engaged, his marriage will add to
his comfort and happiness. Mary Hutchinson is a most excellent
woman - I have known her long, and I know her thoroughly;
she has been a dear friend of mine, is deeply attached to William,
and is disposed to feel kindly to all his family.
As you express a desire to know what are my wishes or
expectations respecting a settlement upon me, I will explain to
you frankly how I feel, though, relying as I do and have ever
had reason to rely, upon the affection of my Brothers and their
regard for my happiness, I do not doubt that, according to their
power, they would meet the full extent of my wishes, without my
making them known myself. I shall continue to live with my
Brother William - but he, having nothing to spare nor being
likely to have, at least for many years, I am obliged (I need not
say how much he regrets this necessity) to set him aside, and I
will consider myself as boarding, through my whole life with an
indifferent person.'

Thus William's marriage was made possible by Dorothy's
asking nothing from him, but on the contrary to pay her share of his
household expenses. At 30 her character was set and formed in
habits of frugality, self-sacrifice and hard work. She says, 'Sixty
pounds a year is the sum which would entirely gratify all my desires.'
(This was actually the highest income free of income tax imposed
by Pitt to pay for the French wars.) Of this Dorothy had already '20
pounds' a year 'absent money' from John's East India Company

salary, and twenty pounds a year from Christopher out of his stipend as Fellow of Trinity, Cambridge. Dorothy was in fact begging from Richard. She says, 'I would be very loth to be oppressive to you or any of my Brothers, or draw on you for more than you can spare without straitening yourselves,' but she replied 'as I have every reason to rely upon her brother's affection'. She was destitute from the Lowther law suit, as William said, and this letter shows her utter destitution.

In fact, when next year Lord Lowther's heirs paid what was owed to the Wordsworth brothers and sister, after legal formalities, Dorothy's life changed but little, as her character was now set.

She continues the letter to Richard,

'Sixty pounds a year is the sum which would entirely gratify all my desires. With sixty pounds a year I should not fear any accidents or changes which might befall me. I cannot look forward to times when, with my habits of frugality, I could not live comfortably on that sum (observe I am speaking now of a provision or settlement for life, and it would be absurd at my age (30 years) to talk of anything else).' - so Dorothy sets aside all thoughts of marriage - *'At present with sixty pounds per ann, I should have something to spare to exercise my better feelings in relieving the necessities of others, I might buy a few books, take a journey now and then - all which things though they do not come under the article of absolute necessaries, you will perceive that it is highly desirable that a person of my age and my education should occasionally have in her power.*
You never talk of coming to see us - I wish you would. Grasmere is a sweet place, and you would have plenty of sport in fishing if you have not lost the art. We have been advised to send a statement of our case to Lord Lonsdale's Executors and Heirs. Mr. Clarkson talked to my Uncle Myers about it, who approves of its being done, but William will write to you about it. In a fortnight's time we are going into Yorkshire to Mr. Hutchinson's to spend a couple of months before William is married - he will be married just before our return home. Pray write before we go. I shall stand in need of the money which John intended for

me, having calculated upon it - the sum he gave me reason to expect to receive by this time was twenty pounds - God Bless you!

I am my dear Brother
   your affecte Sister D Wordsworth'

William's part of this letter followed hereafter.
Dorothy also wrote to Mrs. John Marshall:
Gallow Hill, September 29th, 1802

My dear Friend,

I cannot express how grieviously I am mortified at not having had the happiness of seeing you when you were at Scarborough. We reached Gallow Hill on Friday evening, and truly distressed I was indeed to learn that you had been here the Sunday before and were gone. What a pleasure would it have been to me to see my old Friend and her dear little children! My Brother desires me to send his kind remembrance to you and Mr. Marshall and to assure you that he was exceedingly sorry that he had not the pleasure of seeing you both.

I should have written to you from London, but that I always indulged the hope of meeting you here at Scarborough, and was always also unable to speak with any certainty of the time of our return. We were detained in London by a succession of unexpected events, first the arrival of my Brother Christopher, then of my Brother John, and last of all (which was indeed the only unfortunate one) by my being exceedingly unwell, in a violent cold caught by riding from Windsor in a long-bodied coach with 12 passengers. This cold detained us in town till last Wednesday. I am now perfectly well, except that I do not feel myself strong, and am very thin, but my kind Friends help me to take such good care of myself that I hope soon to become as strong as anybody.

We leave Gallow Hill on Monday morning, immediately after my Brother William's marriage, we expect to reach Grasmere on Wednesday evening. William, Mary and I go together in a post chaise, and after Mr. Hutchinson's harvest is over (when we shall have got completely settled in our own home) he and his sister Sara will follow us and spend some time at Grasmere and Keswick. My dear Jane, if this letter reaches you before next Monday you will think of me, travelling towards our own dear Grasmere with my most beloved Brother and his wife. I have long loved Mary Hutchinson as a sister, and she is equally attached to me, this being so, you will guess that I look forward with perfect happiness to this connection between us, but happy as I am, I half dread that concentration of all tender feelings, past, present and future, which will come upon me on the wedding morning. There never lived on earth a better woman than Mary H. and I have no doubt that that she is in every respect formed to make an excellent wife to my Brother, and I seem to myself to have scarcely anything left to wish for, but that the wedding was over, and we had reached our home again. We have indeed been a long time absent. It was, however, a delightful thing to see all our brothers, particularly John, after his return from India. He was in perfect health and excellent spirits. We spent two days with my Uncle and Aunt Cookson at Windsor, and saw Mary, and their youngest children, as good and sweet a set of children as ever I was with. Mary is a delightful, lovely, affectionate, and sensible girl. My Aunt and Uncle were both well, Uncle looks scarcely worse than when I left Forncett.'

Here Dorothy is travelling round her family greeting in peace her beloved brothers, and her old loved guardians, her uncle and aunt Cookson (now at Winsor) all friction past, and their lovely children - some of whom she had helped to bring up - grown strong and beautiful. Dorothy, who among her beloved wild Lake countryside home is all shadow and light and gleaming, wild eyes, is also very benevolent and harmonious, generous and affectionate.

Dorothy continues her letter to Jane:

'No doubt you will have heard we have every prospect of

settling our affairs with Lord Lowther entirely to our satisfaction. Our claim in law is as good as ever, and, what is of more consequence, Lord L is a just man and disposed to repair as much as lies within his power, the damage done by his predecessors. I am going to write to Mrs. Rawson this afternoon. Remember me kindly to your sister Catherine and all your sisters - again my love to your husband and kisses to all your children. God bless you my dear Jane! Your affectionate and faithful friend
D. Wordsworth'

Dorothy's Journal: December 24th, Christmas Eve, 'William is now sitting beside me at 1/2 past 10 o'clock. I have been beside him ever sine ten, running the heel of a stocking, repeating some of his sonnets to him, listening to his own repeating, reading some of Milton's and the Allegro and Penseroso. It is a quiet keen frost. Mary is in the parlour below attending to the baking of cakes, and Jenny Fletcher's pies. Sara is in bed with a toothache and so we are (?). My beloved William is turning over the leaves of Charlotte Smith's sonnets, but he keeps his hand to his poor chest, pushing aside his breastplate. Mary is well and I am well, and Molly is as blithe as this time last year. Coleridge came this morning with Wedgewood. We all turned out of Wms bedroom one by one to meet him. He looked well. We had to tell him of the birth of his little girl born yesterday morning at 6 o'clock.' Coleridge's daughter Sara. 'Wm went with them to Wythburn in the chaise, and M and I met Wm at the Rays. It was not an unpleasant morning to the feeling far from it.' Dorothy was born on 25th December, Christmas Day, and this new little Sara on 23rd December, the day before Christmas Eve. 'The sun shone now and then, and there was no wind, but all things looked cheerless and distinct. No meltings of sky into mountains, the mountains like stone-work wrought up by huge hammers. Last Sunday was as mild a day as I remember. We all set off together to walk. I went to Rydale and Wm returned with me. M and S went round the lakes. There were flowers of various kinds - the top most bell of a foxglove, geraniums, daisies, a buttercup in the water (but this I saw 2 or 3 days before), small yellow flowers (I do not know their name) in the turf, a large bunch of strawberry blossoms. Wm sate a while with me, then went to meet M and S. Last Saturday I dined at Mr. Simpsons, also a beautiful mild day. Monday was a frosty day and it has been frost ever since. It is today Christmas Day, Saturday 25th December 1802. I am thirty one years of age. It is a dull frosty day.'

'Again I have neglected to write my Journal - New Year's

Day is passed, old Christmas Day and I have recorded nothing. It is today Tuesday January 11th. On Christmas Day I dressed myself ready to go to Keswick in a returned Chaise but did not go. On Thursday 30th December, I went to K, William rode before me to the foot of the hill nearest K. There we parted close to an old water course, which was then noisy with water, but on my return a dry channel. We ate some potted beef on horseback and sweet cake. We stopped our horse close to the hedge, opposite a tuft of primroses, three flowers in full blossom and bud. They reared themselves up among the green moss. We debated long whether we should pluck them, and at last left them to live out their day, which I was right glad of at my return the Sunday following, for there they remained, uninjured by cold or wet. I stayed at K over New Year's Day, and returned on Saturday the 2nd of January. Wm Mackareth fetched me (M and S walked as far as John Stanley's) - Wm was alarmed at my long delay, and came to within 3 miles of Keswick. He mounted before me. It had been a sweet mild day and was a pleasant evening. C stayed with us till Tuesday, January 4th. Wm and I walked up to George Ms to endeavour to get the horse, then walked with him to Ambleside. We parted with him at Kirkstone. On Thursday 6 C returned, and on Friday 7th, he and Sara went to Keswick. W accompanied them to the foot of Wythburn. I to Miss Simpson's and dined, and called on Aggy Fleming sick in bed. It was a gentle day, and when Wm and I returned home just before sunset, it was a heavenly evening. A soft sky among the hills, and a summer sunshine above, blending with the sky, for it was more like the sky than clouds. The turf looked warm and soft.'

January 8th, 1803, Saturday, 'Wm and I walked to Rydale - no letters. Still as mild as spring - a beautiful moonlight evening and a quiet night; but before morning the wind rose, and it became dreadfully cold. We were not well, Mary and I.'

Jan 9th, Sunday, 'Mary lay long in bed and did not walk. Wm and I walked in Brother's wood. I was astonished with the beauty of the place for I had never been here since my return home - never since my return in June! Wrote to Mrs. Lamb.'

January 10th, 'I lay in bed to have a drench of sleep till one o'clock. Worked all day - petticoats - Mrs. C's wrists. Ran Wm's woollen stockings, for he put them on today for the first time. We walked to Rydale and brought letters from Sara, Annette and (?), furiously cold.'

January 11th, Tuesday, 'A very cold day. Wm promised me he would rise as soon as I carried him his breakfast, but he lay in bed till between 12 and 1. We talked of walking but the blackness of the cold made us slow to put forward, and we did not walk at all. Mary read The Prologue to Chaucer's Tales to me in the morning. William was working at his poem to C. (William's poem to Coleridge was 'The Prelude'). Letter from Keswick and from Taylor on Wm's marriage. C poorly, in bad spirits. Canaries. Before tea I sate 2 hours in the parlour. Read part of 'The Knight's Tale' with exquisite delight. Since tea Mary and I have been downstairs copying out Italian poems for Stuart. William has been working beside me, and here ends this imperfect summary. I will take a nice Calais Book, and will for the future write regularly and, if I can, write legibly; so much for this my resolution on Tuesday night, January 11th, 1803. Now I am going to take tapioca for my supper, and Mary an egg, and William some cold mutton - his poor chest is tired.'

In spite of Dorothy's New Year resolution, her Diary ends after the entry for January 12th, Wednesday: very cold and cold all the week.

January 16th, Sunday, 'Intensely cold. William had a fancy for some gingerbread. I put on Molly's cloak and my spenser, and we walked towards Matthew Newton's. I went into the house. The blind man and his wife and sister were sitting by the fire, and all dressed very clean in their Sunday clothes, the sister reading. They took their little stock of gingerbread out of the cupboard, and I bought 6 pennyworth. They were so grateful when I paid them for it that I could not find it in my heart to tell them we were going to make gingerbread ourselves. I had asked them if they had no thick - "No," answered Matthew, "there was none of Friday but we will 'endeavour' to get some." The next day the woman came just when we were baking, and we bought 2 pennyworth.'

Dorothy's lovely journey ends as we know when she and William went to get gingerbread from the blind man that cold day Sunday 16th 1803.

Thereafter she was to be busy and devoted to helping to nurse and care for William and Mary's children, whom she loved as her own. Always her love for William was the centre of her life, she wrote: 'fraternal affection has been the building up of my being, the light of my path.'

Their love for their working class neighbours, in whose houses they would sit and talk and listen to gossip by the hour, made them beloved by the local community. However, these same people were also made wary by the Wordsworth's eccentricities - their tramping about at all times and in all weathers and seasons; William murmering away to himself composing poetry in the woods and gazing by the hour at rainy fields whilst standing underneath an umbrella; Dorothy keeping open house to all her beloved friends who gave her such great delight. In their first ecstatic summer at Grasmere, a large rock on the banks of Thirlmere, on the way north over to Keswick, was carved with the initials W.W., M.H., D.W., S.T.C., J.W., S.H., as a monument to William, Mary Hutchinson, Dorothy, Coleridge, John Wordsworth and Sara Hutchinson. Dorothy called it The Rock of Names or Sara's Crag, and two years later, then the letters had been even more deeply carved by them, Dorothy wrote in her journal, 'I kissed them all'.

Dorothy sitting up talking to Coleridge and the others late at night, broiling a chop for Coleridge to eat in bed, Dorothy out in the garden in the moonlight with John and Coleridge, having the house full of their friends - they were all like an early, unself-conscious hippy commune. The fact that they did not work at anything visible or comprehensible made them seem well off. That William used to kiss Dorothy, Mary, Sara and Joanna when he bid them farewell for a bit to go on a walk on his own; their shabby second-hand clothes and boots covered in mud from long field-walks, their Gypsy rags and tatters, and Dorothy's childlike trust and hospitality, the fact that they went to bed and got up at all hours as it suited them, all struck the local people as strange and gave rise to the gossip of incest between William and Dorothy - a cruel and uncomprehending untruth, a myth and suspicion. It was like the suspicion they had caused around themselves at Alfoxden Park all over again, only in some ways more vicious.

Dorothy and William were indeed very close and essential to each other, and their love had some erotic elements, but it was truly platonic, they inspired each other. Dorothy was indeed very disturbed by William's marriage to their friend Mary Hutchinson, as we can see from her diary entry of that time - after a visit to see Annette and Caroline in France, William and Dorothy returned, and William married Mary Hutchinson. But Dorothy was sure that she was included in his marriage from the first. William assured her of this by slipping the ring on her finger before the wedding, allowing her to keep it on all the night before the wedding. Dorothy's long friendship with Mary Hutchinson stood her in good stead, and Mary was a sweet and generous, even a self-sacrificing person, so they both felt totally included, one with another.

When William and Dorothy returned from France and arrived at Mary's home, Dorothy wrote, 'Mary first met us in the avenue. She looked so fat and well we were made very happy by the sight of her - then came Sara and last of all Joanna. Tom was forking corn, standing upon the corn cart. We dressed ourselves immediately and got tea - the garden looked gay with asters and sweet peas - I looked at everything with tranquillity and happiness but I was ill both on Saturday and Sunday and continued to be poorly most of the time of our stay. Jack and George came on Friday evening first of October. On Saturday we rode to Hackness, William, Jack, George and Sara single, I behind Tom. On Sunday 3rd Mary and Sara were busy packing. On Monday 4th October 1802, my Brother William was married to Mary Hutchinson. I slept a good deal of the night and rose fresh and well in the morning - at a little after 8 o'clock I saw them go down the avenue towards the church. William had parted from me upstairs. I gave him the wedding ring - with how deep a blessing! I took it from my forefinger where I had worn it for the while of the night before - he slipped it again onto my finger and blessed me fervently. When they were absent my dear little Sara prepared the breakfast. I kept myself as quiet as I could, but when I saw the two men running up the walk, coming to tell us it was over, I could stand it no longer and threw myself on the bed neither hearing nor seeing anything, till Sara came upstairs to me and said, 'They are coming'. This forced me from the bed where I lay and I moved I knew not how straight forward, faster than my strength could carry me till I met my beloved William and fell upon his bosom. He and John Hutchinson led me to the house and there I stayed to welcome my dear Mary. As soon as we had breakfasted we departed. It rained when we set off. Poor Mary was much agitated when she parted from her Brothers and Sisters and her home. Nothing particular occurred till we reached Kirby. We had sunshine, showers, pleasant talk, love and cheerfulness. We were obliged to stay two hours at K, while the horses were feeding. We wrote a few lines to Sara and then walked out, the sun shone and we went to the churchyard, after we had put a letter into the Post Office for the York Herald. We sauntered about and read the gravestones. There was one to the memory of 5 children, who had all died within five years. There was another stone erected to the memory of an unfortunate woman (as we supposed, by a stranger). The verses engraved upon it expressed that she had been neglected by her Relations and counselled the Readers of those words to look within and recollect their own frailties. We left Kirby at about 1/2 past two. There was not much variety of prospect from K to Helmsely but the country is very pleasant, being rich and woody, and Helmsely itself stands very sweetly at the foot of the rising grounds of Duncomb Park which is scattered all over with tall woods and lifting itself above the common buildings of the town stands Helmsely Castle, now a ruin, but formerly inhabited by the gay Duke of Buckingham. Every foot of the road was, of itself, interesting to us, for we had travelled along it on foot Wm and I - when we went to fetch our dear Mary, and had sate upon the turf by the roadside more than once. Before we reached Helmsely our driver told us that he could not take us any further, so we stopped at the same inn where we had slept before. My heart danced at the sight of its cleanly outside, bright yellow walls, casements overshadowed with jasmine and its low, double gavel-ended front. We were not shewn into the same parlour where Wm and I were, it was a small room with a drawing over the chimney piece which the woman told us had been bought at a sale. Mary and I warmed ourselves at the kitchen fire, then we walked into the garden, and looked over the gate up to the old ruin which stands at the top of the mount, and round about it the moats are grown into soft green cradles, hollows surrounded with green grassy hillocks and these are overshadowed by old trees, chiefly ashes. I prevailed upon William to go up with me to the ruins. We left Mary sitting by the kitchen fire. The sun shone, it was warm and very pleasant. One part of the castle seems to be inhabited. There was a man mowing nettles in the open space which had most likely once been the Castle court. There was one gateway exceedingly beautiful - children were playing upon the sloping ground. We came home by the street. After about an hour's delay we set forward again, had an excellent driver who opened the gates so dexterously that the horses never stopped. Mary was very much delighted with the view of the castle from the point where we had seen it before. I was pleased to see again the little path which we had walked upon, the gate I had climbed over, and the road down which we had seen the two little boys drag a log of wood, and a team of horses struggle under the weight of a great load of timber. We had felt compassion for the poor horses that were under the governance of oppressive and ill-judging drivers, and for the poor boys who had seemed of an age to have been able to have dragged the log of wood merely out of love of their own activity, but from poverty and bad food they panted for weakness and were obliged to fetch their father from the town to help them.'

Here Dorothy remembers herself and William on their way together to fetch Mary. 'Duncomb House looks well from the road, a large building, though I believe only 2 thirds of the original designs are completed; we rode down a very steep hill to Ryvaux Valley, with woods all round us. We stopped upon the bridge to look at the

Abbey and again when we had crossed it. Dear Mary had never seen a ruined Abbey before except Whitby. We recognised the cottages, houses and little valleys as we went along, we walked upon a long hill, the road carried us up the cleft or valley with woody hills on each side of us. When we went to GH. I had walked down this valley alone. Wm followed me. It was not dark evening when we passed the little publick house, but before we had crossed the Hambledon Hills and reached the point overlooking Yorkshire it was quite dark. We had not wanted, however, fair prospects before us. As we drove along the flat plain of the high hill, far far off us in the Western sky we saw shapes of castles, ruins among groves, a great spreading wood, rocks and single trees, a minster with its tower unusually distinct, minarets in another quarter, and a round Grecian temple also - the colours of the sky of a bright grey and the forms of a sober grey, with a dome. As we descended the hill there was no distinct view but of a great space, only near us, we saw the wild and (as people say) bottomless tarn in the hollow at the side of the hill. It seemed to be made visible to us only by its own light, for all the hill about us was dark. Before we reached Thirsk we saw a light before us which we at first thought was the moon, then lime kilns, but when we drove into the market place it proved a large bonfire with lads dancing round it, which is a sight I dearly love. The inn was like an illuminated house - every room full. We asked the cause and were told by the girl that it was 'Mr. John Bell's birthday, that he had hired his Estate'. The landlady was very civil. She did not recognise the despised foot-travellers. We rode nicely in the dark, and reaching Leming Lane at 11 o'clock. I am always sorry to get out of a chaise when it is night. The people of the house were going to bed and we were not very well treated, though we got a hot supper. We breakfasted the next morning and set off at about 1/2 past 8 o'clock. It was a cheerful sunny morning.'

Dorothy relives during this journey her first journey with William when they came to Grasmere, their home; she also feels safe and included in William and Mary's love in the post chaise, a healing reassurance for her childhood misery and shock at being excluded from her father's household after the death of her mother.

161

On their return to Dove Cottage, Dorothy records, 'On Friday the 8th we baked bread, and Mary and I walked, first upon the hill side, and then in John's Grove, then in view of Rydale, the first walk that I had taken with my Sister.' Dorothy and Mary were sisters and friends: with all the ardent self-discipline of their loving hearts, they accepted and loved and helped each other all the years they lived together. Never did they quarrel, and they commiserated with each other on working so hard, each wishing the other more ease; Mary was gentle and generous and humble; not greedy and demanding all for herself. True, William once wrote to her saying the deep love between a man and wife being sensual and sexual is more than the love between a sister and brother can be - but he was very careful to blot out anything in most letters to Mary that Dorothy might find obnoxious. On first arriving home at Dove Cottage William and Mary slept downstairs together and Dorothy had her bedroom upstairs. She must have felt excluded and probably overheard their love making as it was a very small house. It was indeed a great delight to her when Sara Hutchinson arrived to stay with them, and probably shared Dorothy's bed. Humourous, intelligent Sara Hutchinson, who was to be Dorothy's greatly loved friend in the household till she died just before the onset of Dorothy's last terrible illness, probably alzheimers.

When William and Mary's first baby, John, was born Dorothy was in the seventh heaven of delight. She loved children and to care for them, and helping Mary to care for baby John, her adored nephew, swept all other sorrows and cares out of her mind.

Dorothy writes on 24th December, 1802, 'William is now sitting beside me at 1/2 past ten o'clock.' She and William, Sara and Molly are all living happily together.

Mrs. Clarkson became a close and dear friend of Dorothy's. Catherine Clarkson, wife of Thomas Clarkson, who from 1785 had worked alongside Wilberforce for the abolition of the slave trade. Clarkson resigned his ministry and travelled about the ports from Liverpool to Portsmouth collecting evidence from ships crews. When his health broke down in 1794 he built a house Eusemere, on Ullswater. William called there with Coleridge during his walking tour of late 1799, but Dorothy did not meet Mrs. Clarkson until September 1800, when she visited her. She wrote to her old friend Jane Marshall, 'Mr. Clarkson is the man who took so much pains about the slave trade, he has a farm at Ullswater and has built a house, Mrs. C is a pleasant woman.'

Catherine Clarkson was the daughter of a rich yam-maker, William Buck of Bury St. Edmonds, and was a year younger than Dorothy. She was not formally educated but very well read and brilliantly amusing. On many a visit to Eusemere, William and Dorothy would walk the steep pass to Pattendale, at the near end of Ullswater, and the Clarksons would send a boat to ferry them the whole length of the lake. Catherine and Thomas Clarkson had one child, Tom; Dorothy took a great interest in him, and advised about planting shrubs in the lakeside garden. Catherine was trusted with the family secrets by the Wordsworths, William's courtship of Mary, and the existence of his little French daughter Caroline and her mother Annette. This was a good friendship for Dorothy, Catherine Clarkson so amusing and kind; Dorothy so ardent, sensitive and emotional, and it became a lifelong and very loving friendship.

Catherine Clarkson, however, had to leave Eusemere for her old home at Bury St. Edmonds in the summer of 1803 for health reasons. Soon afterwards Eusemere was sold to the Earl of Lonsdale, and the Clarksons eventually lived at Playford Hall near Ipswich. Dorothy's letters to Catherine Clarkson tell us much of the daily life of the Wordsworths: 'To Mrs. Thomas Clarkson, 17th July, 1803':

'My dear friend
Mary and I have never ceased to regret that you did not see our own darling child (William and Mary's first son John) before your departure from this country. It would have been very sweet to us to think that you had carried away an image of what we so dearly love. When you see him he will be a different creature and we should have liked that you had known perfectly what he is now; or rather what he was then, for he is much grown since that time, though indeed he does not appear to us to be much altered. He has blue eyes, a fair complexion (which

*is already much sunburnt), a body as fat as a little pig, arms
that are thickening and dimpling and bracelets at his wrists, a
very prominent nose, which will be like his Father's, and a head
shaped upon the very same model. I send you a lock of his hair
sewed to this letter. Today we have all been to church. Mary
was churched and the Babe christened - Coleridge, my Brother
Richard and I were Godfathers and Godmother, old Mr. Sympson
answered for my Brother Richard, and had a hearty enjoyment
of the christening cake, tea and coffee, this afternoon. The
Child sleeps all night, and is a very good sleeper in the day. I
wish you could see him in his basket which is neither more nor
less than a meat basket which costs half a crown. In this basket
he has' ('Not like Moses in his cradle of rushes, but in a boat,
mind that. WW') - added in the margin - 'floated over Grasmere
Water asleep and made one of a dinner party at the island, and
we often carry it to the orchard seat where he drops asleep
beside us ... '*

All her life Dorothy made very good friendships with women,
with Jane Pollard, with Mary and Sara Hutchinson, with her surrogate
mother, Aunt Elizabeth Threlkeld.

We often wonder why Dorothy finished her Grasmere journal
after 16th January - it was in someways because of her devotion to
Mary and helping her in the second half of her pregnancy, and after
the baby was born in caring for her beloved nephew.

'Oh my dear Friend,' she wrote to Mrs. Clarkson,
'how happy we are in this blessed infant!' The nurse was
sent away three days after the birth, *'Mother and child have
gone on so nicely - I have been their sole attendant.'* Dorothy
carried John around in her arms - and all this is probably what
ended her journal writing, even writing a letter was difficult:
*'The darling is sitting on my knee - how I wish you could see
him with his serious face tracing my pen, and how his bonny
eyes are lighted up with a smile, and how the little darling sends
out his voice into every corner of the house!'* She accepted his

'angry squalls' and 'violent passion' when teething and being dressed. She says, 'What peace and pleasure, wakefulness and hope there is in attending upon a healthy infant - one's thoughts are never tired when so employed.'

It seems strange therefore that exactly two months after Johnny's birth Dorothy sets off with William and Coleridge on a tour of Scotland. One of the reasons may have been William's health, for he had chest trouble and the tour did improve this; also Dorothy suffered from bad bilious attacks brought on by intense overwork, and these improved too - though she put this down to taking wine regularly. In fact just as they were setting off she was torn two ways, wanting both to go and to stay, causing one of her bilious attacks. Coleridge put this down to the 'hurry and bustle of packing'. Dorothy often suffered from bouts of illness, headaches, vomiting. She tells Catherine Clarkson, 'I began as usual with sickness followed by a complaint in my bowels with a violent looseness that lasted four days - ' She went to bed and lost weight, alarming William. She was thin already. The headaches improved later, but the trouble in her bowels continued in times of stress (and cold). Dorothy said, 'I have fits of illness occasionally and probably shall have all my life.' She diagnosed these well, saying 'any agitation of mind, either sorrow or joy, will bring it on - if anything puts me past my sleep for instance.'

No other attempt, however, was made to diagnose these attacks and with old age, they became a severe, disabling illness.

Dorothy continues her letter to Mrs. Clarkson, 'C is much better in health and spirits than he has been for some time past. We expect to set off on our Scotch tour in about ten days - William and C talk of it with thorough enjoyment - and I have no doubt that I shall be as happy as they when I am fairly off, but I do not love to think of leaving home, and parting with the dear Babe, who will be no more the same Babe when we return.'

'You will rejoice to hear that the affair with Lord Lowther is entirely settled, except for signing releases and a few law

forms. We are to receive eight thousand five hundred pounds.
The whole of the money is to be paid in a year. I cannot tell you
yet what our shares will be as there will be some deductions. I
will write to you when we are on our Tour - you will like to
know what we see and do. God bless you my ever dear Friend.
May God restore your health and may you come back to us
with a body as fit for enjoyment among these noble and quiet
mountains and vales as your heart is. Best respects to your
Father and Mother. Love to your Brother Robert who is a huge
favourite of mine, little though he be! and to your dear Son,
Yours ever and ever, Dorothy Wordsworth'

Dorothy hopes in her letter that Sara, or if not she, then Joanna
Hutchinson should stay with Mary and the baby while she and
William are away in Scotland. She says, ' ... besides Sara does not
come. This is a sad mortification to us, particularly as she had given
us the strongest reason to expect her, however we still hope for
Joanna ... '

Dorothy and William and Coleridge all started off together to
Scotland but, as with their journey to Germany, Coleridge left William
and Dorothy after a fortnight; he was very uncomfortable in their
jaunting car, and with their nervous horse which William managed
badly. Coleridge wrote, 'A horse and jaunting car is an anxiety -
and almost wish we had adopted our first thought and walked', with
a pony and side-saddle for Dorothy. Coleridge actually proved himself
to be right - he parted from the other two at Loch Lomond, and
achieved in a marathon walk by himself the vast loop of the highland
journey on foot in a mere eight days!

Dorothy and William continued for another month. They went
into the Highlands, to Inverary, the Vale of Glencoe, Killikrankie,
and back via the Trossachs. They finished at Edinburgh, meeting
and making friends with Walter Scott, and then travelled home through
the Vale of Tweed, Teviot and Esk, arriving back at Grasmere on
25th September: 'We had a joyful meeting' with Mary, her sister
Joanna, who had kept her company, and, of course, Johnny.

Dorothy had to do most of the practical hard work for herself

166

and William during their Scottish tour. Every evening she made sure that she and her brother had some food at least, and reasonable beds, and she persuaded their landladies (despite their reluctance) to 'give fire' at the cold inns in which they stayed. On top of this she was continually soaked with rain in the inadequate 'jaunting car' and was often unable to borrow a dry change of clothes. Yet with terrific courage and energy she kept them both going in this very difficult country. William was unhelpful. He could not manage the horse, and once even dropped their whole picnic into a loch.

Dorothy, exhausted, wrote to Mrs. Clarkson on their return: 'I was not as well as I could have wished at my return - but I am now perfectly well, though I had a bad attack on Friday of my old complaint.' And no wonder!

Dorothy, however, immediately began to nurse Joanna Hutchinson, who had found the strain of looking after Mary and baby Johnny too much for her, and had had many symptoms of nervous illness during her stay, ending in a 'hysteric and fainting fit'. Dorothy kept Joanna at the cottage to be looked after for another week until she was well enough to go home.

Also undaunted by all her usual household work and caring for Joanna and helping care for Johnny, Dorothy began her account of their journey in Scotland. This was not from notes, as she had been too worn out to make any during the actual tour; but was an actual remembered account intended for friends, like the Clarksons. It was recollections in the form of a journal. It has sometimes the brilliance and beauty of her early journals; and shows that Dorothy, like William, had an immense power of recall of past events. William could remember in lovely detail his past life, and could recite hundreds of lines of recently-made poetry. Dorothy says, 'I am writing not a journal, for we took no notes, but recollections of our tour in the form of a journal'. Only by her great capacity for recreating in writing other places, people, their speech, and events could Dorothy have written this journal-like account of their tour in Scotland. She began this almost as soon as she reached home and worked at it until 20th December, when she was interrupted by the arrival of Coleridge, ill and demanding attention and care, for a whole month.

She began again on 2nd February 1804, but had to stop again because of Coleridge; he wanted her to copy all William's poems for him to take abroad, where he was going to seek a warmer climate. This really threw her, but she did it. Then, encouraged by William, she continued her recollections of their tour in Scotland the year before (1803) and went on with it in April 1805, finishing it on the last day of May 1805.

CHAPTER 10
RECOLLECTIONS OF A TOUR MADE IN SCOTLAND. A.D. 1803

Now, Dorothy's Recollections of a Tour made in Scotland is written not as a diary, day by day, but recollected as she says totally after her return to Grasmere.

This Dorothy writes giving dates, but it is all from memory: 'William and I parted from Mary on Sunday afternoon, August 14th, 1803; and Wm and Coleridge and I left Keswick on Monday morning, the 15th, at twenty minutes after eleven o'clock.'

There are two really beautiful observations: 'Slept at Mr Young husband's public house, Hesket Newmarket. In the evening walked to Caldbeck's Falls, a delicious spot in which to breath out a summer's day - limestone rocks, hanging trees, pool and waterbreaks-caves and cauldrons which have been honoured with fairy names, and no doubt continue in the fancy of the neighbourhood to resound with fairy revels.'

August 16th, Tuesday, 'Passed Rose Castle upon the Caldew, an ancient building of red stone with sloping gardens, an ivied gateway, velvet lawns, old garden walls, trim flower borders with stately and luxuriant flowers. We walked up to the house and stood some minutes watching the swallows that flew about restlessly, and flung their shadows upon the sunbright walls of the old building; the shadows glanced and twinkled, interchanged and crossed each other, expanded and shrunk up, appeared and disappeared every instant; as I observed to Wm and Coleridge, seeming more like living things than the birds themselves.'

August 17th, Wednesday, 'Afterwards the road treeless, over a peat-moss common - the Solwan Moss - and here and there an earthbuilt hut with its peat stack, a scanty-growing willow hedge round the Kailgarth, perhaps the cow pasturing near - a little lass watching it - the dreary waste cheered by the endless singing of larks.'

'Those houses by the roadside which are built of stone are comfortless and dirty; but we peeped into the clay biggin that was very canny, and I dare say will be as warm as a swallows nest in winter. The town of Annac made me think of France and Germany; many of the houses large and gloomy, the size of them outrunning the comfort. One thing which was like Germany pleased me: the shopkeepers express their calling by some device or painting: bread bakers have biscuits, loaves, cakes painted on their window-shutters; blacksmiths horses shoes, iron tools, etc., etc., and so on thro the trades.'

August 18th, Thursday, 'When our guide had left us we turned again to Burns' house. Mrs. Burns was gone to spend some time by the sea-shore with her children. We spoke to the servant-maid at the door, who invited us forward, and we sate down in the parlour. The walls were covered in blue wash; one side of the fire was a mahogany desk, opposite to the window a clock, and over the desk a print from the Cotter's Saturday Night which Burns mentioned in one of his letters as having received as a present. The house was cleanly and meat in the inside, the stairs of stone, scoured white, the kitchen on the right side of the passage, the parlour on the left. In the room above the parlour the poet died, his son after him in the same room. The servant told us she had lived five years with Mrs. Burns, who was now in great sorrow for the death of 'Wallace'. She said that Mrs. B's youngest son was at Christ's Hospital.

'There is no thought surviving in connection with Burns' daily life that is not heart-depressing.'

'William and I walked out after dinner, C was not well and slept upon the carriage cushions. We made our way to the cottages among the little hills and knots of wood, and then saw what a delightful country this part of Scotland might be made by planting forest trees. The ground all over heaves and swells like the sea; but for miles there are neither trees nor hedgerows, only mound fences and tracts, or slips of corn, potatoes, clover with hay between, and barren land; but near the cottages many hills and hillocks covered with wood. We passed some fine trees, and passed under the shade of one close by an old mansion that seemed from its neglected state to be inhabited by farmers. (But I must say that many of the 'gentlemen's' houses which we have passed in Scotland have an

170

air of neglect, and even of desolation.) It was a beech, in full glory of complete and perfect growth, very tall with one thick stem mounting to a considerable height, which was split into four 'thighs'; as Coleridge afterwards called them, each in size a fir tree. Passed another mansion now tenanted by a schoolmaster; many boys playing upon the lawn. I cannot take leave of the country which we passed through today, without mentioning that we saw the Cumberland mountains within half a mile of Ellisland, Burns' house, the last view we had of them. Drayton has prettily described the connexion which this neighbourhood has with ours when he makes Skiddaw say -

'Sturfell from the sky,
That Anandale doth crown, with a most amourous eye,
Salutes me every day, or at my pride looks grim,
Oft threatening me with clouds, as I oft threatening him.'

These lines recurred to Wm's memory, as we talked of Burns, and of the prospect he must have had, perhaps from his own door, of Skiddaw and his companions, indulging in the fancy that we ourselves might have been personally known to each other, and he looked upon those objects with more pleasure for our sakes. We talked of Coleridge's children and family, there at the foot of Skiddaw, and our own new-born John a few miles behind it, while the grave of Burns' son which we had just seen by the side of his father, and some stories heard at Dumfries respecting the dangers his surviving children were exposed to, filled us with melancholy concern, which had a kind of connexion with ourselves. In recollection of this, William long afterwards wrote the following Address to the sons of the ill-fated poet:

'Ye are panting up life's hill,
'Tis twilight time of good and ill,
And more than common strength and skill
Must ye display,
If ye would give the better will
Its lawful way.

171

Strong-bodied if ye be to bear
Intemperance with less harm, beware,
But if your Father's wit ye share,
Then, then, indeed,
Ye sons of Burns, for watchful care
There will be need.'

For honest men delight will take
To shew you favour for his sake,
Will flatter you, and Fool and Rake
Your steps pursue,
And of your Father's name will make
A snare for you.

Let no mean hope your souls enslave,
Be independent, generous, brave;
Your Father such example gave,
And such revere,
But be admonished by his grave,
And think and fear.'

August 19th, Friday, 'About a mile and a half from Drunlanrigg is a turnpike road. We left our car at the top of a hill. We left our car with the man, and turned aside into a field where we looked down upon the Nith, which runs below in deep and rocky channel; the banks woody. The view was pleasant down the river towards the cornhill, an open country, cornfields, pastures and trees. Returned to the turnpike house, a cold spot upon a common black cattle feeding close to the door. Our road led us down the hill to the side of the Nith, and we travelled along its banks for some miles; here were clay cottages perhaps every half or quarter of a mile, the bed of a stream rough with rocks; banks irregular, now woody, now bare; here a patch of broom, there of corn, there of pasturage; and hills green or heathy, above. We were to have given our horse meal and water at a public house in one of the hamlets we passed through, but missed the house, for as is common in Scotland, it was without a signe-board. Travelled on, still beside the Nith, till we came to a Turnpike house, which stood rather high on the hillside, and from the door we looked a long way up and down the river. The air coldish, the wind strong.

We asked the turnpike man to let us have some meal and water; he had no meal but luckily we had part of a feed of corn brought from Keswick, and he procured some hay at a neighbouring house. In the meantime I went into the house, where was an old man with a grey plaid over his shoulders, reading a newspaper. On the shelf lay a volume of the Scotch Encyclopaedia, a History of England, and some other books. The old man was a caller by the way. The man of the house came back and we began to talk - he was very intelligent, had travelled all over England and Scotland and Ireland as a gentleman's servant, and now lived alone in that lonesome place. He said he was tired of his bargain for he feared he would lose by it; and he had indeed a troublesome office, for coal-carts without number were passing by, and the drivers seemed to do their utmost to cheat him. There is always something peculiar in the house of a man living alone. This was but half-furnished, yet nothing seemed wanting for his comfort, though a female who had travelled half as far would have needed fifty other things. He had no other meat or drink in the house but oat-meal and cheese (the cheese was made with the addition of seeds) and some skimmed milk. He gave us of his bread and cheese, and milk (which proved to be sour).

'We had yet ten or eleven miles to travel, and no food with us. Wm lay under the wind in a cornfield below the house, being not well enough to partake of the milk and bread. C gave our host a pamphlet: the Crisis of the Sugar Colonies; he was well acquainted with Burns' poems. There was a politeness and manly freedom in this man's manners which pleased me very much. He told us he had served a gentleman, a Captain in the Army - he did not know who he was, for none of his relations had ever come to see him, but he used to receive many letters, that he had lived near Dumfries till they would let him stay no longer, he made such havoc with the game ... ' Dorothy then goes on to describe the rather obsessive killer behaviour of this man which is truly horrific - 'One does not wonder he was asked to leave Dumfries - his whole delight from morning till night was in field-sports; he would be on his feet in the worst days of winter, and wade through snow up to his middle after his game. If he had company he was in torture till they were gone, he would then throw off his coat and put on an old jacket not worth half a crown; he drank his bottle of wine every day, and two if he had better sport than usual. Ladies sometimes came to stay with his wife, and he often carried them out in an Irish jaunting car, and if they vexed him he would choose the dirtiest roads possible, and spoil their clothes by jumping in and out of the car, and treading upon them. But for all that (so he ended it all) "he was a good fellow and a clever fellow, and he liked him well". He would have ten or dozen hares in the larder at once, he half maintained his family with game, and he himself was very fond of eating the spoil - unusual with a true heart and soul sportsman.'

'The man gave us an account of his farm where he had lived, which was so cheap and pleasant that we thought we should have liked to have it ourselves. Soon after leaving the turnpike house we turned up a hill to the right, the road for a little way very steep, bare hills, with sheep.

'After ascending a little we heard the murmur of a stream far below us, and saw it flowing downwards on our left, towards the Nith, and before us, between steep green fields, coming along a winding valley. The simplicity of the prospect impressed us very much. There was a single cottage by the brook-side - the dell was not heathy, but it was impossible not to think of Peter Bell's Highland Girl.

'We felt now indeed that we were in Scotland; there was a natural peculiarity in this place. In the scenes of the Nith it had not been the same as England, but yet not simple, naked Scotland. The road led us down the hill, but now there was no room in the vale but for the river and the road; we had sometimes the stream to the right, sometimes to the left. The hills were pastural, but we did not see many sheep. Green smooth turf on the left; no ferns. On the right the heath plant grew in abundance, of the most exquisite colour;

it covered a whole hillside, or it was in streams and patches. We travelled along the vale without appearing to ascend for some miles; all the reaches were beautiful, in exquisite proportion, the hills seeming very high from being so near to us. It might have seemed a valley which nature had kept to herself for pensive thoughts and tender feelings, but that we were reminded at every turning of the road or something beyond by the coal carts which were travelling towards us. Though these carts broke in upon the tranquility of the glen, they added much to the picturesque effect of different views, which indeed wanted nothing, though perfectly bare, houseless, and treeless.

'After some time our road took us upwards towards the end of the valley. Now the steeps were heathy all around. Just as we began to climb the hill, we saw three boys who came down the cleft of a brow on our left, one carried a fishing rod, and the hats of all were braided with honey-suckle; they ran after one another as wanton as the wind. I cannot express what a character of beauty those few honey-suckles in the hats of the three boys gave to the place; what bower could they have come from. We walked up the hill, met two well-dressed travellers, the woman barefoot. Our little lads before they had gone far were joined by some half-dozen of their companions, all without shoes and stockings. They told us they lived at Warlockhead, the village above, pointing to the top of the hill; they went to school and learned Latin (Virgil) and some of them Greek (Homer), but when Coleridge began to inquire further, off they ran, poor things I suppose afraid of being examined.'

This is reminiscent of Dorothy's description of the beggar boys with flowers in their hats, with their tall mother who came to Dorothy's door at Grasmere, and about whom William later wrote the poem The Beggars'.

'When, after a steep ascent, we had reached the top of the hill, we saw a village about half a mile before us on the side of another hill, which rose up above the spot where we were, after a descent, a sort of valley or hollow. Nothing grew upon the ground, or the hills above or below, but heather, yet round about the village (which consisted of a great number of huts, all alike, but all thatched, with a few larger slated houses among them, and a single

175

modern-built one of considerable size) were a hundred patches of cultivated ground, potatoes, oats, hay, and grass. We were struck with the sight of haycocks fastened down with aprons, sheets, pieces of sacking (as we supposed to prevent the wind from blowing them away). We afterwards found that this practice was very general in Scotland. Every cottage seemed to have its little plot of ground. Fenced by a ridge of earth; this plot contained 2 or 3 different divisions, Kail, potatoes, oats, hay, the houses all standing in lines, or never far apart; the cultivated ground was all together also and made a very strange appearance with its many greens among the dark brown hills, neither tree nor shrub growing; yet the grass and the potatoes looked greener than elsewhere, owing to the bareness of the neighbouring hills; it was indeed a wild, singular spot (to use a woman's illustration) like a collection of patchwork, made of pieces as they might have chanced to have been cut by the mantua-maker, only just smoothed to fit each other, the different sorts of produce being in such a multitude of plots, and those so small and of such irregular shapes. Add to the strangeness of the village itself, that we had been climbing upwards, though gently, for many miles, and for the last mile and a half up a steep ascent, and did not know of any village till we saw the boys who had come out to play. The air was very cold, and one could not help thinking what it must be in winter, when those hills now ("red-brown") should have their three walls covered in snow.

'The village, as we guessed, inhabited by miners; the mines belong to the Duke of Queensbury. The road to the village down which the lads scampered away, was straight forward. I must mention that we met, just after we had parted from them, another little fellow, about six years old, carrying a bundle over his shoulder; he seemed poor and half-starved, and was scratching his fingers, which were covered with the itch. He was a miner's son, and lived in Warlockhead; did not go to school, but this was probably on account of his youth. I must mention him because he seemed to be poor, that there was poverty and wretchedness among these people, though we saw no other symptom of it and afterwards we met scores of inhabitants of the same village. Our road turned to the road, and we saw, at the distance of less than a mile, a tall upright building of grey stone, with several men standing on the roof, as if they were looking out over battlements. It stood beyond the village upon higher ground, as if presiding over it, - a kind of enchanter's castle, which it might have been, a place which Don Quixote would have gloried in. When we drew near we saw, coming out of the side of the building, a large machine or lever, in appearance like a great forge-hammer, as we supposed for raising water out of the mines. It heaved upwards once in half a minute with a slow motion, it seemed to rest, to take breath at the bottom, its motion being accompanied with a sound between a groan and a 'jike' (a word used in the dialect of Cumberland for a creaking noise). There would have been something very striking in this object in any place, it was impossible not to invest the machine with some faculty of intellect; it seemed to have made the first step from brute matter to life with a purpose , ...' Here Dorothy followed as so often by William and Coleridge, into surrealism, science fiction, prophecy - 'showing its progress by great power. William made a remark to this effect and Coleridge observed that it was like a giant with one idea. At all events the object produced a striking effect in that place, where everything was in unison with it, particularly the building itself, which was turret-shaped, and with its figures upon it resembling much one of the fortresses in the wooden cuts of Bunyans Holy War.

'After ascending a considerable way we began to descend again; and now we met a team of horses dragging an immense tree to the leadmines (to repair or add to the building), and presently after we came to a cart, with another large tree, and one horse left in it, right in the middle of the highway. We were a little out of humour thinking we must wait till the team came back. There were men and boys without number all staring at us; after a little consultation they set their shoulders to the cart, and with a good heave all at once they moved it, and we passed along. These people were decently dressed, and their manners decent; there was no hooting or impudent laughter. Leadhills, another mining village, was the place of our destination for the night; and soon after we had passed the cart we came in sight of it. This village and the mines

177

belong to Lord Hopetoun; it has more stone houses than Warlockhead, one large old mansion and a considerable number of old trees - beeches I believe. The trees told of the coldness of the climate; they were more brown than green - far browner than the ripe grass of the little hay-garths - Here, as at Warlockhead were hay-cocks, haystacks, potato beds, and Kail garths, in every possible variety of shape, but (I suppose from the irregularity of the ground) it looked far less artificial - indeed I think a painter might make several beautiful pictures of this village. It straggles down both sides of a mountain glen. As I have said, there is a large mansion, there is also a stone building that looks like a school, and the houses are single, or in clusters, or rows as it may chance.

'We passed a decent-looking Inn, the Hopetoun Arms; but the house of Mrs. Otto, a widow, had been recommended to us, with high econiums. We did not understand Scotch Inns, and were not quite satisfied at first with our accommodations, but all things were smoothed over by degrees; we had a fire lighted in our dirty parlour, tea came after a reasonable waiting; and the fire with the gentle aid of twilight, burnished up the room into cheerful comfort. C was weary; but W and I walked out after tea. We talked with one of the miners, who informed us that the building which we had supposed to be a school was a library belonging to the village. He said they had got a book for it a few weeks ago, which had cost thirty pounds; and that they had all sorts of books. "What have you Shakespear?" "Yes we have that," and we found on further inquiry, that we had a large library, of long standing, that Lord Hopetown had subscribed liberally to it, that gentlemen who came with him were in the habit of making larger or smaller donations. Each man who had the benefit of it paid a small amount monthly (I think about fourpence).

The man we talked with spoke much of the comfort and quiet in which they lived, one among another, he made use of a noticeable expression saying:

They were "very peaceable people, considering they lived so much underground," wages were about thirty pounds a year, they had land for potatoes warm houses, plenty of coals and only six hours work each day, so that they had leisure for reading if they chose". He said the place was healthy and that the inhabitants lived to a great age; and indeed we saw no appearance of ill-health in their countenances; but it is not common for people working in lead mines to be healthy and I have since learned that it is *not* a healthy place. However, it may be they are unwilling to allow it, for the landlady the next morning, when I said "You have a cold climate" replied "Aye but it's varra halesome"

'We visited the burying ground, a plot of land not very small, crowded with graves, and upright gravestones, over-looking the village and the dell. It was now the closing of the evening. Women and children were gathering in the linen for the night, which was bleaching by the burn-side. The graves overgrown with grass, such as, by industrious culture had been raised up about the houses, but there were bunches of heather here and there, and with the blue-bells that grew among the grass the small plot of ground had a beautiful wild appearance.

I returned to the inn, William left me and I went to the shop to purchase some thread; the woman had none that suited me; but she would send a 'wee lad' to the other shop. In the meantime I sat with the mother and was much pleased with her manner and conversation. She had an excellent fire and her cottage tho very small looked comfortable and cleanly; but remember I saw it only by firelight. She confirmed what the man had told us of the quiet manner in which they lived; and indeed her house and fireside seemed to need nothing to make it a cheerful happy spot, but health and good humour. There was a bookishness, a certain formality in this woman's language. She had a dark complexion, dark eyes, and wore a very white cap, much over her face, which gave her a look of a French woman, and indeed afterwards the women on the roads frequently reminded me of French women, partly from the extremely white caps of the elder women, and still more perhaps a certain gaiety and party-coloured appearance in their dress in general. White bed-gowns are very common, and you rarely meet a young girl with either hat or cap; they buckle up their hair in a graceful manner.

'I returned to the inn, and went to the kitchen to speak with the landlady; she had made a hundred hesitations when I told her we wanted three beds. At last she confessed she had 3 beds, and showed me into a parlour which looked damp and cold, but she assured me in a tone that showed me she was unwilling to be questioned further, that all the beds were well-aired. I sat a while by the kitchen fire with the landlady, and began to talk to her; but, much as I had heard in her praise (for the shopkeeper told me she was a varra discreet woman) I cannot say that her manners pleased me much; but her servant made amends, for she was as pleasant and cheerful a lass as ever was seen; and when we asked her to do anything she answered "oh yes" with a merry smile, and almost ran to get it for us. She was about sixteen years old; wore shoes and stockings, and had her hair tucked up with a comb. The servant at Brownhall was a coarse-looking wench, bare-foot and bare-legged. I examined the kitchen round-about; it was crowded with furniture drawers, cupboard, dishcover hung in rows. These were very clean, but floors, passages, everything else dirty. There were two beds in recesses in the wall; above them I noticed a shelf with some books; it made me think of Chaucer's Clerk of Oxenford -

'Liever had he at his bed's head
Twenty books clothed in black and red.'

They were baking oat-bread which they cut into quarters, and half-baked over the fire, and half-toasted before it. There was a suspiciousness about Mrs. Otto, almost like ill-nature; she was very jealous of any inquiries that might appear to be made with the faintest idea of a comparison between Leadhills and any other place, except the advantage was evidently on the side of Leadhills. We had nice honey to breakfast. When ready to depart, we learned that we might have seen the library, which we had not thought of till it was too late, and we were very sorry to go away without seeing it.'

Here we have Dorothy making the arrangements for herself and William and Coleridge, writing brilliant portrait sketches of people, communities, noticing that people had books in their houses, which books - recording the library. In the following paragraphs Dorothy unwittingly describes the effects of the 'clearances', the evictions, departures of the Scots people by the English and their traitorous clan chiefs; after the rebellions.

'Our road carried us down the valley, and we soon lost sight of Leadhills, for the valley made us turn almost immediately, and we saw two miles, perhaps, before us, the glen sloped somewhat rapidly - heathy, bare, no hut or house. Passed by a shepherd, who was sitting upon the ground, reading, with the book on his knee, screened from the wind by his plaid, while a flock of sheep were feeding near him among the rushes and coarse grass (for, as we descended we came among lands where the grass grew with the heather).'

This exquisite picture is a poem in itself, as are many of Dorothy's prose descriptions.

'Travelling through several reaches of the glen, which somewhat resembled the valley of Mendock on the other side of Wenlockhead; but it was not near so beautiful; the forms of the mountains did not melt so exquisitely into each other, and there was a coldness, and, if I may so speak, a want of simplicity in the surface of the earth; the heather was poor, not covering a whole hillside; not by luxuriant streams and bed interviened with rich verdure, but patchy and stunted, with here and there coarse grass and rushes. But we soon came in sight of a spot that impressed us very much. At the lower end of this new reach of the vale was a deceased tree, beside a decayed cottage, the vale spreading out into a level area which was one large field, without fence and without division of a dull yellow colour; the vale seemed to partake of the desolation of the cottage, and to participate in its decay; and yet the spot was in its nature so dreary that one would rather have wondered how it ever came to be remembered by man, than lament that it was left to waste and solitude. Yet the encircling hills were so exquisitely formed that it was impossible to conceive anything more lovely than this place would have been if the valley and hillsides had been interspersed with trees, cottages, green fields, and hedgerows; but all was desolate; there one large field which filled up the area of the valley appeared, as I have said, in decay, and some ways alalagous to the ruined building; for it was as much of a field as Mr. King's best pastures scattered over with his fattest cattle.'

William's poetry too is full of such ruined desolate beautiful places, which had a tale to tell filled with the past, of such mysterious, desolate, rural people.

'We went on looking before us - the place losing nothing of its hold upon our minds, when we discovered a woman sitting right in the middle of the field, wrapped up in a grey cloak or plaid. She sat motionless all the time we looked at her, which might be nearly half an hour. We could not conceive why she sat there, for there was neither sheep nor cattle in the field, her appearance was very melancholy. In the meantime our road carried us nearer to the cottage though we were crossing over the hill to the left, leaving the valley below us, and we perceived that a part of the building was inhabited, and that which we had supposed to be one blasted tree was eight trees, four of which were entirely blasted, the other partly so, and round about the place was a little potato and cabbage garth, fenced with earth. No doubt, that woman had been an inhabitant of the cottage; however this might be, there was so much obscurity and uncertainty about her, and her figure agreed so well with the desolation of the place, that we were indebted to the chance of her being there at all for some of the most interesting feelings that we ever had from natural objects connected with man in dreary solitariness.'

This is a truly Wordsworthian and Coleridgian figure, this mysterious woman in the desolate field, the lightening blasting trees, the cottage semi-inhabited garden encircled semi-ruined, with beautiful mountains all round. Dorothy loved these solitudes and Scotland might even have been formed especially for their singular type of imagination. She goes on to say:

'The air was cold and clear - the sky blue, we walked cheerfully along in the sunshine, each of us alone, only William had charge of the horse and car, so he sometimes took a ride, which did but poorly recompense him for the trouble of driving. I have never travelled with more cheerful spirits than this day: our road was along the side of a high moor. I can always walk over a moor with a light foot; I seem to be drawn more closely to nature in such places than anywhere else; or rather I feel more strongly the power of nature over me and am better satisfied with myself for being able to find enjoyment in what unfortunately to many persons is either dismal or insipid.'

This is like Emily Bronte. She too on the moors was in tune with her true self; on the wild moors behind her father's parsonage in tune with the energy of nature. She would always go out of the house and up onto the moors, with the larks and the harebells, rather than the other way into town.

'This moor, however, was more than commonly interesting; we could see a long way, and on every side of us were larger or smaller tracts of cultivated land. Some were extensive farms (yet in so large a waste they did look but small), with farm-houses, barns, etc., others (like little cottages) with enough to feed a cow, and supply the family with vegetables. In looking at these farms I had always one feeling. Why did the plough stop there!? Why might they not as well have carried it twice as far? There were no hedgerows near the farms, and very few trees. As we were passing along, we saw an old man, the first we had seen in a Highland bonnet, walking with a staff at a very slow pace by the edge of one of the moorland cornfields; he wore a grey plaid and a dog was by his side. There was a scriptural solemnity in this man's figure, a sober simplicity which was most impressive. Scotland is the country above all others that I have seen, in which a man's imagination may carve out his own pleasures; there are so many inhabited solitudes; and the employments of the people are so immediately connected with the places where you find them, and their dress so simple, so much alike, yet, from their being folding garments admitting of an endless variety, and falling so often so gracefully.'

These descriptions of people by Dorothy are like figures carved in wood, or vast oil paintings of figures in landscapes.

'After some time we descended towards a broad vale, passed one farm-house, sheltered by fir-trees, with a burn close to it; children playing, linen bleaching. The vale was open pastures and cornfields unfenced, the land poor. The village of Crawford John on the slope of the hill a long way before us to the left - asked about our road of a man who was driving a cart; he told us to go thro the village, then along some fields, and we should come to a herd's house by the burn side. The highway was right through the vale, unfenced on either side; the people of the village who were making hay, all stared at us and our carriage. We inquired the road of a middle-aged man, dressed in a shabby black coat, at work in one of the hay-fields; he looked like the minister of the place, and when he spoke we felt assured that he was so, for he was not sparing of hard words, which however he used with great propriety, and he spoke like one who had been accustomed to dictate. Our car wanted mending in the wheel, and we asked him if there was a blacksmith in the village. "Yes," he replied, but when we showed him the wheel he told Wm that he might mend it himself without a blacksmith, and he would put him in the way; so he fetched hammer and nails and gave him directions which William obeyed, and repaired the damage entirely to his own satisfaction and the priest's, who did not offer to lend any assistance himself; not as if he would not have been willing in case of need; but as if it were more natural for him to dictate, and because he thought it more fit that Wm should do it himself. He spoke much about the propriety of every man's lending all the assistance in his power to travellers, and with some ostentation and self-praise. Here I observed a honey-suckle and some flowers growing in a garden, the first I had seen in Scotland. It is a pretty cheerful-looking village, but must be very cold in winter, standing on a hill-side (and the vale itself is very high-ground) unsheltered by trees.

'Left the village behind us, and our road led through arable ground for a considerable way, on which were growing very good crops of corn and potatoes. Our friend accompanied us to show us the way, and C, and he had a scientific conversation concerning the uses and properties of lime and other manures. He seemed to be a well-informed man, somewhat pedantic in his manner; but this might be only the difference between Scotch and English.' This was probably the Rev. John Aird, the minister of the parish. 'Soon after he had parted from us, we came to a stony rough road over a black moor; and presently to the "herd's house by the burn side"; we could hardly cross the burn dry-shod, over which was the only road to the cottage. In England there would have been stepping stones or

184

a bridge; but the Scotch need not be afraid of wetting their bare feet. The hut had its little kail-garth fenced with earth; there was no other enclosure; the common, heathy with coarse grass. Travelled along the common for some miles, before we joined the great road from Long Town to Glasgow - saw on the bare hill-sides at a distance, sometimes a solitary farm, now and then a plantation, and one very large wood, with an appearance of richer ground above; but it was so very high we could not think it possible. Having descended considerably; the common was no longer of a peat mossy-brown heath colour, but grass with rushes was its chief produce; there was sometimes a solitary hut (no enclosures except for the kail-garth) and sheep pasturing in flocks, with shepherd boys tending them. I remember one boy in particular; he had no hat on, and only a grey plaid wrapped round him. It is nothing to describe, but on a bare moor, alone with his sheep, standing as he did in utter quietness and silence, there was something uncommonly impressive in his appearance, a solemnity which recalled to our minds the old man in the corn-field. We passed many people who were mowing, or raking the grass of the common; it was a little better than rushes, but they did not mow straightforward, only here and there, where it was the best; in such a place hay-cocks have an uncommon appearance to us.'

Dorothy, William and Coleridge saw these strange portentous, brooding figures wherever they went. It seems as if they create their own kind of landscape anywhere.

There was an almost Millet-like description of the woman with the cow, and of William questioning her in his rather leech-gatherer manner: 'We often passed woman and children, who were watching a single cow while it fed upon the slips of grass between the corn. William asked a strong woman of about thirty years of age, who looked like the mistress of the family (I suppose being moved by some sentiment of compassion for her being so employed)- if the cow would eat the corn if it were left to itself - she smiled at his simplicity, this waiting, this waiting, as it were body and soul devoted to the poor beast; yet even this is better than working in a manufactury the day through.'

Dorothy as always was very aware of and affectionately attentive to the children - she had a little girl to guide her through a 'dark, satanic' mill-town. She says of her - 'My guide, a sensible little girl, answered my inquiries very prettily. She was eight years old, read in the 'Collection', a book which all the Scotch children whom I have questioned read in. I found it was a collection of hymns; she could repeat several of Dr. Watts.'

Dorothy arrived too late at the porter lodge at the gate of the gentleman's grounds wherein were the falls of Clyde she wished to see, which could only be viewed by means of a lock and key. 'The girl left me at the porter's lodge. Having asked about Wm I was told that no person had been there, or could enter but by the gate. The night was coming on, therefore I did not venture to go in, as I had no hope of meeting William. I had a delicious walk alone through the wood; the sound of the water was very solemn, and even the cotton mills in the fading light of evening had somewhat of the mystery and stillness of the natural objects. It was nearly dark when I reached the inn. I found C sitting by a good fire, which always makes an inn room look comfortable. In a few minutes Wm arrived; he had heard of me at the gate, and followed me as quickly as he could, shouting after me. He was pale and exceedingly tired. After he had left us he had taken a wrong road, and while looking about to set himself right had met with a barefooted boy, who said he would go with him.'

Both William and Dorothy seemed to turn in trust when they were lost to these wild but wise children to guide them, who appeared in their way like messengers! 'The little fellow carried him by a wild path to the upper of the Falls, the Boniton Linn, and coming down unexpectedly upon it, he was exceedingly affected by the solemn grandeur of the place. The fall is not much admired or spoken of by travellers; you have never a full, breast view of it; it does not make a complete self-satisfying place, an abode of its own, as a perfect waterfall seems to me to do, but the river down which you look, through a long vista of steep and ruin-like rocks, the roaring of the waterfall and the solemn evening lights must have been most impressive. One of the rocks on the near bank, even in broad daylight, as we saw it the next morning, is exactly like the fractured arch of an abbey. With the lights and shadows of evening upon it, the resemblance must have been much more striking.

'Wm's guide was a pretty boy, and he was exceedingly pleased with him. Just as they were quitting the waterfall, Wm's mind being full of the majesty of the scene, the little fellow pointed to the top of a rock. "There's a fine Slae bush there," "Aye," said Wm, "but there are no sloes upon it," which was true enough; but I suppose the child remembered the sloes of another summer, though as he said, he was but "half seven years old," namely six and a half. He conducted Wm to the other fall, and as they were going along a narrow path, they came to a small cavern, where Wm lost him, and looking about, saw his pretty figure in a sort of natural niche fitted for a statue, from which the boy jumped out laughing, delighted with the success of his trick. Wm told us a great deal about him, while he sat by the fire and of the pleasure of his walk, often repeating, "I wish you had been with me." Having no change he gave the boy sixpence, which was certainly, if he had formed any expectations at all, far beyond them, but he received it with the utmost indifference, without any remark of surprise or pleasure; the most likely he did not know how many halfpence he could get for it, and two pence would have pleased him more. My little girl was delighted with the sixpence I gave her, and said she would buy a book with it on Monday morning. What a difference between the manner of living and education of boys and girls among the lower classes of people in towns! She had never seen the falls of the Clyde, nor ever had been further than the porter's lodge. The boy, I daresay, knew every hiding place in every accessible rock, as well as the fine 'Slae Bushes', and the nut trees.'

Dorothy, who could think herself with such easy empathy into the minds of children - to her and William a good education was to see the Falls of Clyde, to know the hiding places in the rocks and the Slae bushes and the nut trees; all freedom of nature; though Dorothy did appreciate the brightness and the booklearning of her little girl guide, who was even going to spend her precious sixpence on a book.

'We left our inn immediately after breakfast. The lanes were full of people going to church; many of the middle-aged women wore long scarlet cardinals, and were without hats; they brought to my mind the women of Goslar as they used to go to church in their silver and gold caps, with their long cloaks, black or coloured.

'The banks of the Clyde from Lanark to the falls rise immediately from the river; they are lofty and steep and covered with wood. The road to the falls is along the top of one of the banks, and to the left you have a prospect of the open country - corn fields and scattered houses. To the right, over the river, the country spreads out, as it were, into a plain covered with hills, no one hill much higher than the other, but hills all over; there were endless pastures overgrown with broom, and scattered trees, without hedges or fences of any kind, and no distinct footpath. It was delightful to see the lasses in gay dresses running like cattle among the broom, making their way straight forward towards the river, here and there, as it may chance. They waded across the stream, and when they had reached the top of the opposite bank, sate down by the roadside (about 1/2 a mile from the town) to put on their shoes and cotton stockings, which they brought tied up in pocket handkerchiefs.

'We walked after we had entered the private grounds. In a minute and a half we were opposite the great waterfall. I was much affected by the first view of it. The majesty and strength of the water (for I had never before seen so large a cataract), struck me with astonishment which died away, giving place to more delightful feelings;

'A lady and gentleman, more expedition tourists than we, came to the spot; they left us at the seat, and we found them again at another station above the falls. C, who is always good-natured enough to enter into conversation with anybody whom he meets in his way, began to talk with the gentleman, who observed that it was a "majestic waterfall". Coleridge was delighted with the accuracy of the epithet, particularly as he had been settling in his own mind the precise meaning of the words grand, majestic, sublime, etc.; and had discussed the subject with Wm at some length the day before. "Yes, Sir," says Coleridge, "it is a majestic waterfall."

"Sublime and beautiful," replied his friend. Poor C could make no answer, and, not very desirous to continue the conversation, came to us and related the story, laughing heartily.'

'After dinner we set off towards Hamilton, but on foot, for we had to turn aside to the Cartland Rocks, and our car was to meet us on the road. A guide attended us, who might almost in size, and certainly in activity, have been compared with Wm's companion who hid himself in the niche in the cavern. His method of walking and a very quick step soon excited our attention: I could hardly keep up with him; he paddled by my side just reaching to my shoulder, like a little dog, with his long snout pushed before him (for he had an enormous nose) and walked with his head foremost. I said to him, "How quick you walk!" He replied, "That was not quick walking," and when I asked him what he called so, he said "Five miles an hour"; and then related in how many hours he had lately returned from Lanark to Edinburgh, done some errands and returned to Lanark, (I have forgotten the particulars, but it was a very short time) and added that he had an old father who could walk at the rate of four miles an hour, for twenty-four miles a day, and had never had an hour's sickening in his life. "Then," said I, "he has not drunk much strong liquor?" "Yes, enough to drown him." From his eager manner of uttering this, I inferred he himself was a drinker; and the man who met us with the car told Wm that he gained a great deal of money as an errand goer, but spent it all on tippling. He had been a shoe-maker, but could not bear the confinement on account of the weakness in his chest.'

When Dorothy returned later, she was in great grief at her friend Mrs. Clarkson's moving away from the Lake District. Dorothy had a constant, desperate belief that her adored friend would return to live amongst them. This shows Dorothy's deep love for her female friend, Mrs. Clarkson, who made her laugh in delight at her wit and imagination; who faithfully kept all Dorothy's letters and who had as well kept a copy of Dorothy's journal, so when part of the original was lost, she could supply it from her own copy - Catherine Clarkson, who loved Dorothy and really knew who she was.

Dorothy also shows her love for her female friends in her delight (by way of her letter to Lady Beaumont) that Sara Hutchinson was coming to live near them. She was moving with her brother Tom to a farm near Penrith. Sara, Dorothy's own close friend and Coleridge's intimate friend and beloved.

CHAPTER 11

Dorothy's Scottish Recollections continue: 'The neighbourhood of Lanark is exceedingly pleasant; we came to a sort of district of glens or little valleys that cleave the hills, leaving a cheerful, open country above them, with no superior hills, but an undulating surface. Our guide pointed to the situation of the Cartland Crags. We were to cross a narrow valley, and walk down on the other side, and then we should be at the spot; but the little fellow made a sharp turn down a footpath to the left, saying "we must have some conversation here!" He paddled with his small pawing feet till we came right opposite the gentleman's house on the other side of the valley, when he halted repeating some words (I have forgotten what) which were taken up by the most distinct echo I ever heard. This is saying little: it was the most distinct echo that it was possible to conceive. It shouted the names of our fireside friends in the very tone in which Wm and Coleridge spoke; but it seemed to make a joke of me, and I could not help laughing at my own voice, it was so shrill and pert, exactly as if someone had been mimicking it very successfully, with an intention of making me ridiculous. I wished Joanna had been there to laugh for the echo is an excellent laugher, and would have almost made her believe it was a true story which Wm and told of her and the mountains!'

This is William's poem to Joanna:

'As it befell,
One summer morning we had walked abroad
At break of day, Joanna and myself.
- 'Twas that delightful season when the broom,
Full-flowered, and visible on every steep,
Along the copses runs in veins of gold.
Our pathways led us on to Rotha's banks;
And when we came in front of that tall rock
That eastward looks, I there stopped short - and stood
Tracing the lofty barrier with my eye

191

From base to summit; such delight I found
To note in shrub and tree, in stone and flower
That intermixture of delicious hues,
Along so vast a surface, all at once
In one impression, by connecting force
Of their own beauty, imaged in the heart.
- When I had gazed perhaps two minutes space,
Joanna, looking in my eyes, beheld
That ravishment of mine, and laughed aloud.
The Rock, like something starting from a sleep
Took up the Lady's voice, and laughed again;
That ancient Woman seated on Helm-crag
Was ready with her cavern; Hammer-scar,
And the tall Steep of Silver-how, sent forth
A noise of laughter; southern Loughrigg heard,
And Fairfield answered with a mountain tone;
Helvellyn far into the clear blue sky
Carried the Lady's voice, - old Skiddaw blew
His speaking-trumpet; - back out of the clouds
Of Glaramara southward came the voice;
And Kirkstone tossed it from his misty head.
- Now whether (said I to our cordial Friend
Who in the hey-day of astonishment
Smiled in my face) this were in simple truth
A work accomplished by the brotherhood
Of ancient mountains, or my ear was touched
With dreams and visionary impulses
To me alone imparted, sure I am
That there was a loud uproar in the hills
And, while we both were listening, to my side
The fair Joanna drew, as if she wished
To shelter from some object of her fear.
- And hence, long afterwards, when eighteen moons
Were wasted, as I chanced to walk alone
Beneath this rock, at sunrise, on a calm
And silent morning, I sat down and there,

In memory of affections old and true,
I chiselled out in those rude characters
Joanna's name deep in the living stone:
And I, and all who dwell by my fireside
Have called the lovely rock, JOANNA'S ROCK.'

'We turned back, crossed the valley, went through the orchard and plantations belonging to the gentleman's house. By the by, we observed to our guide that the echo must bring many troublesome visitors to disturb the quiet of the owner of that house. "Oh no," said he, he 'glories in much company'. He was a native of that neighbourhood, and had made a moderate fortune abroad, purchased an estate, built the house, and raised the plantations; and further had made a convenient walk through the woods to the Cartland Crags. The house was modest and neat, and though not adorned in the best taste, and though the plantations were of fir, we looked at it with great pleasure, there was such true liberality and kind-heartedness in leaving his orchard path open, and his walks unobstructed by gates. I hope this goodness is not often abused by plunderers of the apple trees, which were hung with tempting apples close to the path.'

'At the termination of the little valley, we descended through a wood along a very steep path to a muddy stream running over limestone rocks; turned up to the left along the bed of the stream, and soon we were closed in by rocks on each side. They were very lofty - of limestone, trees starting out of them, high and low overhanging the stream and shooting up towards the sky. No place of the kind could be more beautiful if the stream had been clear, but it was of a muddy yellow colour; had it been a large river, one might have got the better of the unpleasantness of the muddy water in the grandeur of its roaring, the boiling up of the foam over the rocks, or the obscurity of its pools.

'We had been told that the Cartland Crags were better worth going to see than the Falls of the Clyde. I did not think so; but I have seen rocky dells resembling this before, with clear water instead of that muddy stream, and never saw anything like Falls of the Clyde.

It would be a delicious spot to have near one's house; one would linger out many a day in the cool shade of the caverns, and the stream would sooth one by its murmuring; still, being an old friend, one would not love it the less for its homely face. Even we, as we passed along, could not help stopping for a long while to admire the beauty of the lazy foam, for ever in motion, and never moved away, in a still place of the water, covering the whole surface of it in streaks and lines and every-varying circles. Wild marjoram grew upon the rocks in great perfection and beauty; our guide gave me a bunch, and said he should come hither to collect a store for the winter, and that it was 'Varra halesome', he drank none else. We walked perhaps half a mile; but it might seem to be much further than it was, owing to the difficulty of the path, and the sharp and many turnings of the glen. Passed two Wallace's caves. There is scarce a noted glen in Scotland that has not a cave for Wallace or some other hero. Before we left the river the rocks became less lofty, turned into a wood through which there was a convenient path upwards, met the owner of the house and the echo-ground, and thanked him for the pleasure which he had provided for us and other travellers by making such pretty pathways.'

'The general face of the country near Hamilton is much in the ordinary English style; not very hilly, with hedgerows, corn-fields, and stone houses. The Clyde is here an open river with low banks, and the country spreads out so wide that there is no appearance of a regular vale. Barncleugh is in a beautiful deep glen through which runs the River Avon, a stream that falls into the Clyde. The house stands very sweetly in complete retirement; it has gardens and terraces one above another, with flights of steps between, box trees and yew trees cut in fantastic shapes, flower borders and summer trees; and summer-houses; and still below, apples and pears were hanging in abundance on the branches of large old trees, which grew intermingled with the natural woods, elms, beeches, etc., even to the water's edge. The whole place is in perfect harmony with the taste of our ancestors, and the yews and hollies are shaven so nicely, and the gravel-walks and flower-borders kept in exact order, as if the spirit of the first architect of the terraces still presided over them. The opposite bank of the river is left still in its natural wilderness, and nothing to be seen higher up but the deep dell, its steep banks being covered with fine trees, a beautiful relief or contrast to the garden, which is one of the most elaborate old things ever seen, a little hanging garden of Babylon.' This is very appreciative of Dorothy to understand the beauty and art of this very elaborate garden. Her own garden at home was very different.

Dorothy's was a wild garden. She brought in her plants from the hills, so that her garden was a continuation of the wild countryside around her with all her plants and flowers; over and over again she tells us in her journals that she dislikes the unnaturalness of 'modern' gardens with stiff flower borders, and such things as 'adorning' the ruined castle of Bothwell. At Town End she could maker her own garden with William and John. They enclosed the two or three yards between their door and the road with stones 'to make it more our own', and took down the fence which divided the cottage from the steep orchard at the back. Then Dorothy began to bring her wild plants in. Again and again in her journals she tells us: 'I carried a basket for mosses,' she wrote in May 1800, 'and gathered some wild plants' - 'Oh that we had a book of botany.' A week later, 'Brought down Batchelors Buttons (Rock Ranunculus) and other plants'. John joined in and helped, 'we went up the hill to gather sods and plants and went down to the lakeside and took up orchises.' John turfed the well where Dorothy planted London Pride, and many things on the borders. She came back late with some Lemon Thyme, and too impatient to wait, she planted this by moonlight. She also planted wild columbine, fox-gloves, and wild snowdrops.

Gifts from other country gardens delighted her, such as from Jenny Dockeray's farmhouse garden on the Easedale Road. Dorothy went into her garden and got white and yellow lilies, periwinkles, etc. which she watered into her own garden; the Sympsons gave her flowers, sunflowers, mulliens and pansies.

Dorothy planted things not in order to display her garden, but in order to join in the work of nature, joining vegetables with flowers, roses and scarlet beans growing against the cottage walls together, honeysuckle twining round the yew tree. On a day of summer rain she wrote, 'the rain fell so gently and the air is so mild and all living things seem so much to rejoice in it that one can hardly find in one's heart to wish it over.'

'Ark-like island feathered to the edge with wild flowers,' said De Quincy about the Wordsworth's dwelling.

Thomas De Quincy is the writer/author of *Confessions of an English opium eater* and *Recollections of the lakes and the lake poets*, who was an ardent friend and admirer of the Wordsworth's and who lived in Dove cottage after them.

Dorothy wrote to Jane Marshall about their garden - the 'small orchard and smaller garden which as it is the work of our hands we regard with pride and partiality.' The orchard was indeed very small, but a beautiful place in which to sit because of its enchanting view of the Fell and lake.

As we have seen, Dorothy was pleased that her lovely small garden was noticed by the people in the coroneted landau driving by on June 9th 1800; these people of taste would have appreciated her garden, so well-tended was it; although she grew only poor people's plants, beans and honeysuckle, like her poor neighbours did.

'Dined and left Glasgow at about 3 o'clock, in a heavy rain. We were obliged to walk through the street, to keep our feet dry, and, in spite of the rain, every person as we went along stayed his steps to look at us; indeed we had the pleasure of spreading smiles from one end of Glasgow to the other (for we travelled through the whole length of the town). A set of schoolboys (perhaps there might be eight) with satchels over their shoulders, and, except one or two, without shoes or stockings, yet very well dressed in jackets and trousers, like gentlemen's children, followed us in great delight, admiring the car and longing to jump up. At last, though we were seated, they made several attempts to get on behind; and they looked so pretty and wild, and at the same time so modest, that we wished to give them a ride, and there being a little hill near the end of the town, we got off, and four of them who still remained, the rest of them having dropped into their homes by the way, took our places; and indeed I would have walked two miles willingly to have had the pleasure of seeing them so happy. When they were to ride no longer, they scampered away, laughing and rejoicing. New houses are rising up in great numbers round Glasgow, citizen-like houses, and new plantations, chiefly of fir; the fields are frequently enclosed by hedgerows, but there is no richness, nor any particular beauty for some miles.'

'We saw the Clyde, now a stately sea-river, winding away mile after mile, spotted with boats and ships, each side of the river hilly, the right populous with single houses and villages - Douglas Castle was upon a promontory by the rock of Dunbarton, at five or six miles distance, which stands by itself, without any hills near it, like a sea-rock.

'While tea was preparing we lolled at our ease, and though the room-window overlooked the stable yard, and at our entrance there appeared to be nothing but gloom and unloveliness, yet while I lay stretched upon the carriage cushions on three chairs, I discovered a little side peep which was enough to set the mind at work. It was no more than a smoking vessel lying at anchor, with its bare masts, a clay hut and the shelving bank of the river, with a green pasture above. Perhaps you will think there is not much in this, as I describe it. It is true; but the effect produced by these simple objects, as they happened to be combined, together with the gloom of the evening, was exceedingly wild. Our room was parted by a slender partition from a large dining room, in which were a number of officers and their wives, who, after the first hour, never ceased singing, dancing, laughing or loud talking. The ladies sang some pretty songs, a great relief to us. We went early to bed but poor C could not sleep for the noise at the street door; he lay in the parlour below stairs. It is no uncommon thing in the best inns in Scotland to have shutting up beds in the sitting rooms.'

August 24th, Wednesday, 'The rock of Dumbarton is very grand when you are close to it, but, at a little distance under an ordinary sky, and in open day, it is not grand, but curiously wild. The castle and fortifications add little effect to the general view of the rock, especially since the building of a modern house, which is white-washed, and consequently jars, wherever it is seen with the natural construction of the place. There is a path up to the house, but it being low water, we could walk round the rock, which we were resolved to do. On that side next the town green grass grows to a considerable height up the rock, but wherever the river borders upon it, it is naked stone. I never saw rock more noble massey, or more deeply stained by time and weather, nor is this to be wondered at; for it is in the very eye of sea-storms, and land-storms, of mountain-winds, water-winds. It is of all colours, but a rusty yellow predominates. As we walked along, we could not look up continually, and the mass above being on every side so huge, it appeared more wonderful than when we saw the whole together.

'When we reached the bottom of the rock along the same road by which we had ascended; we made our way over the rough stones left bare by the tide, round the bottom of the rock, to the point where we had set off. This is a wild and melancholy walk on a blustering cloudy day - the naked bed of the river, scattered over with seaweed; grey swampy fields on the other shore; sea-birds flying overhead - the high rock perpendicular and bare. We came to two very large fragments, which have fallen from the main rock,' C thought that one of them was as large as a Bowder Stone, William and I did not (here it is to be noticed that Coleridge and William and Dorothy often disagreed during this tour; Coleridge felt deeply that Dorothy and William were wrapped up in each other, to the exclusion of himself, also he was ill and probably taking Laudanum; after he parted from them he got on like one inspired, making a tour of Scotland by himself, for most of the time, with great enjoyment, light-hearted in his own company), 'but it is impossible to judge accurately; we probably, without knowing it, compared them with the whole mass from which they had fallen, which, from its situation, we consider as one rock or stone, and there is no object of the kind for comparison with the Bowder Stone. But soon we came to such a place as we wanted to see. The road was close to the water, and a hill, bare, rocky or with scattered copses rose above it. A deep shade hung over the road, where some little boys were at play; we expected a dwelling house of some sort; and when we came nearer, saw three or four huts under the trees, and at the same moment felt that it was Paradise.' This is magical Scotland, the same now as it was then, real Paul et Virginie country of the simple life, shared by loving brother and sister in idyllic countryside!

'We had before seen the lake only as one wide plain of water; but here the portion of it which we saw was bordered by a high and steep, heathy and woody island opposite, which did not appear like an island, but the main shore; framed out a little oblong lake apparently covered with trees, apparently not so broad as Rydale water, with one small island covered with trees, resembling some of the most beautiful trees of the holms of Windermere, and only a river's breadth from the shore. This was a place where we should have liked to have lived, and the only one we had seen near Loch Lomond - how delightful to have a little shed concealed under the branches of the fairy island! The cottages and the island might have been made for the pleasure of each other. It was like a natural garden, the distance was so small; nay one could not have forgiven anyone living there, not compelled by daily labour, if he did not connect it with his dwelling by some feeling of domestic attachment, like what he has for the orchard where his children play. I thought what a place for Wm! He might row himself over with twenty strokes of the oars, escaping from the business of the house, and as safe from intruders, with his boat anchored beside him, as if he had locked himself up in the strong tower of a castle. We were unwilling to leave this sweet spot; but it was so simple, and therefore so rememberable, that it seemed almost as if we could have carried it away with us. It was nothing more than a small lake enclosed by trees at the ends and by the way-side, and opposite by the island, a steep bank on which the purple heath was seen under a low oak coppice-wood, a group of houses overshadowed by trees, and a bending road. There was one remarkable tree, an old larch with long branches, which bent out its main stem horizontally across the road, an object that seemed to have been singled out for injury where everything else was lovely and thriving, tortured into that shape by storms, which one might have thought could not have reached it in that sheltered place.'

August 25th, Thursday, (this was one celebration of the beauty of the islands of the loch): 'We were glad when we awoke to see it was a fine morning - the sky was bright blue, with quick moving clouds, the hills cheerful, lights and shadows vivid and distinct. The village looked exceedingly beautiful this morning from the garret windows - the stream glittering near it; while it flowed under trees through the level fields to the lake. After breakfast Wm and I went down to the waterside. The roads were dry as if no drop of rain had fallen, which added to the pure cheerfulness of the appearance of the village, and even of the distant prospect, an effect which I always seem to perceive from clearly bright roads (for they are always brightened by rain) after a storm; but as we came among the houses I regretted even more than last night, because the contrast was greater, the slovenliness and dirt near the doors; and could not but remember, with pain from the contrast, the cottages of Somersetshire, covered with roses and myrtle; and their small gardens of herbs and flowers. While lingering by the shore we began to talk to a man who offered to row us to Inch-ta-vannach; but the sky began to darken, and the wind being high, we doubted whether we should venture, therefore made no engagement. He offered to sell me some thread, pointing to his cottage, and added that many English ladies carried thread away from him. Presently, after C joined us, we determined to go to the island.'

Now before Coleridge left Dorothy and William to go off on a Scots walking tour of his own, the three of them seemed to be in perfect accord and harmony as of yore, all appreciating and adoring the beauty they so carefully worshipped and understood. 'I was sorry that the man who had been talking with us was not our boatman; Wm by some chance had engaged another. We had two rowers and a strong boat, so I felt myself bold, though there was a great chance of a high wind. The nearest point to Inch-tu-vannach is not perhaps more than a mile and a quarter from Luss; we did not land there, but rowed round the end, and landed on that side which looks towards our favourite cottages, and their own island, which, wherever seen, is still their own. It rained a little when we landed, and I took up my cloak, which afterwards served us to sit down upon in our road up the hill, when the day grew much finer, with gleams of sunshine. This island belongs to Sir James Colquhoun, who made an ancient road which winds gently to the top of it.

We had not climbed far before we were stopped by a sudden burst of prospect, so singular and beautiful that it was like a flash of images from another world. We stood with our backs to the hill of the island, which we were ascending, and which shut off Ben Lomond entirely, and all the upper part of the lake, and we looked towards the foot of the lake, scattered over with islands without beginning and without end. The sun shone and the distant hills were visible, some through sunny mists, others in gloom with patches of sunshine; the lake was lost under the low and distant hills, and the islands lost in the lake, which was all in motion with travelling fields and light, or dark shadows under rainy clouds. There are many hills, but no commanding eminence at a distance - to confine the prospect, so that the land seemed endless as water.

'What I had heard of Loch Lomond, or any other place in Great Britain, had given me no idea of anything like what we beheld: it was an outlandish scene - we might have believed ourselves in North America. The islands were of every possible variety of shapes and surface - hilly and level, large and small, bare, rocky, pastoral, or covered with wood. Immediately under my eyes lay one large flat island, bare and green, so flat and low that it scarcely appeared to rise above the water, with straggling peat-stacks and a single hut upon one of its outlooking promontaries (for it was of a very irregular shape though perfectly flat). Another, its next neighbour, and still nearer to us, was covered over with heath and coppice wood, the surface undulating, with the flat or sloping banks towards the water, and hollow places, cradle-like valleys behind. These two islands, with Inch-ta-vanna, where we were standing, were intermingled with the water; I might say interbedded inter-veined with it, in a manner that was exquisitely pleasing. There were bays innumerable, straits or passages like calm rivers, landlocked lakes, and, to the main water stormy promontaries - the solitary hut on the flat green island seemed unsheltered and desolate, and yet not wholly so, for it was but a river's breadth from the covert of the wood of the other island. Near to these is a miniature, an islet covered with trees, on which stands a small ruin that looks like the remains of a religious house; it is overgrown with ivy, and were it not that the arch of a window or gateway may be distinctly seen, it would be difficult to believe that it was not a tuft of trees growing in the shape of a ruin, rather than a ruin overshadowed by trees. When we had walked a little further we saw below us, in the nearest large island, where some of the wood had been cut down, a hut, which we conjectured could be a bark hut. It appeared to be on the shore of a little forest lake, enclosed by Inch-ta-vannah (where we were), and the woody island on which this hut stands.

'Beyond we had the same intricate view as before and could discern Dumbarton Rock with its double head. There being a mist over it, it had a ghost-like appearance(as I observed to Wm and C), something like the Tor of Glastonbury from the Dorsetshire hills. Right before us, on the flat island mentioned before, were several small single trees or shrubs, growing at different distances from each other, close to the shore, by some optical delusion had detached them from the land on which they stood, and they had the appearance of many vessels sailing upon the coast of it. I mention the circumstances, because, with the ghostly image of Dumbarton Castle, and the ambiguous ruin on the small island, it was much in the character of the same withall was throughout magical and enchanting - a new world in its great permanent outline and composition, and changing at every moment, in every part of it by the effect of sun and wind, and mist and shower and cloud, and the blending lights and deep shades which took the place of each other, traversing the lake in every direction. The whole way indeed a strange mixture of soothing and restless images, of images inviting to rest, and others hurrying the fancy away into activity still more pleasing than repose; yet intricate and homeless that is, without lasting abiding place for the mind, as the prospect was, there was no perplexity; we still had a guide to lead us forward.

'Wherever we looked, it was a delightful feeling that there was something beyond. Meanwhile, the sense of quiet was never lost sight of; the little peaceful lakes among the islands might make you forget that the great water, Loch Lomond, was so near, and yet are more beautiful, because you know that it is so; they have their own bays and creeks sheltered within a shelter. When we had ascended to the top of the island we had a view up to Ben Lomond, over the long, broad water without spot or rock; and, looking backwards, saw the islands below us as on a map. This view, as may be supposed, was not nearly so interesting as those we had seen before. We hunted out all the houses on the shore, which were very few; there was the village of Luss, the two gentlemen's houses, our favourite cottages, and here and there a hut; but I do not recollect any comfortable looking farmhouses, and on the opposite shore not a single dwelling. The whole scene was a combination of natural wildness, loveliness, beauty and barreness, or rather bareness, yet not comfortless or cold; but the whole was beautiful. We were too far off the more distant shore to distinguish any particular spots which we might have regretted were not better cultivated, and near Luss there was no want of houses.

'After we had left the island, having been so much taken with the beauty of the bark hut and the little lake by which it appeared to stand. We desired the boatman to row us through it, we landed at the hut. Walked upon the island for some time, and found out sheltered places for cottages. There were several woodman's huts, which, with some scattered fir trees, and others in irregular knots, that made a delicious murmuring in the wind, adding greatly to the romantic effect of the scene. They were built in the form of a cone from the ground, like savages hut, the door being just large enough for a man to enter with stooping. Straw beds were raised on logs of wood tools lying about, and a forked bough of a tree was generally suspended from a root in the middle to hang a kettle upon. It was a place that might have been just visited by new settlers. I though of Ruth and her dreams of romantic love:

'And then he said how sweet it were,
A fisher or a hunter there,
A gardener in the shade,
Still wandering with an easy mind
To build a household fine, and find
A home in every glade.'

We found the main lake very stormy when we had left the shelter of the islands, and there was again a threatening of rain, but it did not come on. I wanted much to get to the old ruin, but the boatmen were in a hurry to be at home.'

This is typical of Dorothy wanting to set off into the wind and rain in the boat to see an old ruin. She was totally romantic and loved to be in wind and weather, regardless of her clothes or her comfort, but so loving wild nature and ruined castles and religious houses, and lieux sacrés, the sight and sound and feel of these.

'We had a pleasant journey to Tarbert; more than half of it on foot, for the road was hilly, and after we had climbed one small hill we were not desirous to get into the car again, seeing another before us, and our path was always delightful, near the lake, and frequently through woods. When we were within about half a mile of Tarbert; at a sudden turning, looking to the left, we saw a very craggy-topped mountain amongst the smooth ones; the rocks on the summit, distinct in shape as if they were buildings raised up by man, or uncouth images of some strange creature. We called out with one voice, "That's what we wanted!" alluding to the framelike uniformity of the side-screens of the lake for the last five or six miles. As we conjectured, this singular mountain was the famous Cobbler near Arrocher. Tarbert was before us in the recess of a deep, large bay, under the shelter of a hill. When we came up to the village we had to inquire for the inn, there being no signboard. It was a well-sized white house, the best in the place; we were conducted upstairs into a sitting room that might make any good-humoured travellers happy - a square room, but with windows on each side, looking one way towards the mountains, and across the lake to Ben Lomond the other.

'There was a pretty stone house before (i.e. towards the lake), some huts, scattered trees, two or three green fields with hedgerows, and a little brook making its way towards the lake; the fields were almost flat and screened on that side nearest the head of the lake by a hill, which, pushing itself out, forms the bay of Tarbert, and, towards the foot, by a gentle slope and trees. The lake is narrow, and Ben Lomond shuts up the prospect, rising directly from the water. We could have believed ourselves to be by the side of Ulswater, at Glenridden, or in some other of the inhabited retirements of that lake; we were in a sheltered place among mountains; it was not an open joyous bay, with a cheerful populous village, like Luss; but a pastoral and retired spot, with a few single dwellings. The people of the inn stared at us when we spoke, without giving an answer immediately, which we were at first disposed to attribute to coarseness of manners, but found afterwards that they did not understand us at once, Erse being the language spoken in the family. Nothing but salt meat and eggs for dinner - no potatoes. The house smelt strongly of herrings, which were hung to dry over the kitchen fire.'

August 26, Friday, 'After long waiting, and many preparations, we got ourselves seated in the boat; but we had not floated five yards before we perceived that if any of the party (and there was a little Highland woman who was going over the water with us, the boatman, his helper, and ourselves), should stir but a few inches, leaning to one side or the other, the boat would be full in an instant, and we at the bottom; besides it was very leaky, and the woman was employed to lade out the water continually. It appeared that this crazy vessel was not the man's own, and that his was lying in a bay at a little distance.

'He said he would take us to it as fast as possible, but I was so much frightened that I would gladly have given up the whole day's journey; indeed not one of us would have attempted to cross the lake in that boat for a thousand pounds. We reached the larger boat in safety after coasting a considerable way near the shore, but just as we were landing, Wm dropped the bundle which contained our food into the water: the fowls were no worse, but some sugar, ground coffee and pepper-cake seemed to be entirely spoiled. We gathered together as much of the coffee and sugar as we could and tied it up, and again trusted ourselves to the lake. The sun shone, and the air was calm (luckily it had been so when we were in the crazy boat), we had rocks and woods on each side of us, or bare hills; seldom a single cottage, and there was no rememberable place till we came opposite a waterfall of no inconsiderable size, that appeared to drop directly into the lake; close to it was a hut, which we were told was the ferry house. On the other side of the lake was a pretty farm under the mountains, beside a river, the cultivated grounds lying all together, and sloping towards the lake from the mountain-hollow down which the river came. It was not easy to conceive how beautiful these spots appeared after moving so long between the solitary steeps. We went a considerable way further, and landed at Rob Roy's Caves, which are in fact no caves, but some of the fine rocks on the brink of the lake, in the crevices of which a man might hide himself cunningly enough; the water is very deep below them, and the hills above steep and covered with wood. The little Highland woman who was in size about a match for our guide at Lanerk, accompanied us hither. There was something very gracious in the manner of this woman; she could scarcely speak five English words, yet she gave me, whenever I spoke to her, as many intelligible smiles, as I had needed English words to answer me, and helped me over the rocks in the most obliging manner. She had left the boat out of good-will to us, or for her own amusement. She had never seen these caves before; but no doubt had heard of them, the tales of Rob Roy's exploits being found familiarly round the ingles hereabouts, for this neighbourhood was his home. We landed at Inversneyde, the ferry house by the waterfall, and were not sorry to part with our boatman, who was a coarse hard-featured man, and, speaking of the French, uttered the basest and most cowardly sentiments. His helper, a youth fresh from the Isle of Sky, was innocent of this fault, and though but a bad rower, was a far better companion; he could not speak a word of English, and sang a plaintive Gaelic air in a low tone while he plied his oar.

'We walked about a mile and a half over the moor without seeing any other dwelling,' - what Dorothy liked was the contrast between the vast bareness of the steeps, and the suddenly come upon rare places of cultivation, such as farms and small hamlets, with vegetables and linen bleaching. ' ... but one hut by the burn-side with a peat stack and a ten-yards square enclosure for the potatoes; where we came to several clusters of houses, even hamlets they might be called, but where there is any land belonging

206

to the Highland huts there are so many out-buildings near, which differ in no respect to the dwelling-houses except that they send out no smoke; that one house looks like two or three. Near these houses was a considerable quantity of cultivated ground, potatoes and corn, and the people were busy making hay in the hollow places of the open vale, and all along the sides of the becks. It was a pretty sight altogether - men and women, dogs, little running streams, with linen bleaching near them, and cheerful sunny hills and rocks on every side. We passed by one patch of potatoes that a florist might have been proud of; no carnation bed ever looked more than this square plot of ground on the waste common. The flowers were in very large bunches, and of an extraordinary size, and of every conceivable shade of colouring from snow-white to deep purple. It was pleasing in that place, where perhaps was never yet a flower cultivated by man for his own pleasure, to see these blossoms grow more gladly than elsewhere, making a summer garden near the mountain dwellings.

'After C came up to us, while we were debating whether we should turn back or go forward, we espied a man on horseback at a little distance, with a boy following him on foot, no doubt a welcome sight, and we hailed him. We should have been glad to have seen either man or woman or child at this time, but there was something uncommon and interesting in this man's appearance, which would have fixed our attention wherever we had met him. He was a complete Highlander in dress, figure and face, and a very fine-looking man, hardy and vigorous, though past his prime. While he stood waiting for us in his bonnet and plaid, which never looked more graceful than when on horseback, I forgot our errand, and only felt glad that we were in the Highlands. Wm accosted him with "Sir do you speak English?" He replied, "A little." He spoke, however, sufficiently well for our purpose, and very distinctly, as all the Highlanders do who learn English as a foreign language; but in a long conversation they want words; he informed us that he himself was going beyond the Trossachs, to Callander, that no boats were kept to let; but there were two gentlemen's houses at the end of the lake, one of which we could not yet see, it being hidden from us by a part of the hill on which we stood. The other house was that which we saw opposite us; both the gentlemen kept boats, and probably might be able to spare one of their servants to go with us. After we had asked many questions, which the Highlander answered with patience and courtesy, he parted from us, going along a sort of horse-track, which a foot-passenger, if he once gets onto it, need not lose if he be careful.

'When he was gone again we debated whether we should go back to Tarbert, or throw ourselves upon the mercy of one of the two gentlemen for a night's lodging. What we had seen of the main body of the lake made us little desire to see more of it; the Highlander upon the naked heath, in his highland dress, upon his careful-going horse, with the boy following him, was worth it all; but after a little while we resolved to go on, ashamed to shrink from an adventure. Pursued the horse-track, and soon came in sight of the other gentleman's house, which stood on the opposite side of the vale, a little above the lake. It was a white house; no trees near it except a new plantation of firs; but the fields were green, sprinkled over with hay-cocks, and the brook coming down the valley and falls into the lake ran thro them. It was like a new-made farm in a mountain vale, and very pleasing after the depressing prospect which had been before us.

'Our road was rough, and not easy to be kept. It was between five and six o'clock when we reached the brook-side, where C and I stopped, and Wm went up towards the house, which was in a field, where about half a dozen people were at work - He addressed himself to one who appeared like the master, and all drew near him, staring at Wm, as nobody could have stared but out of sheer rudeness, except in such a lonely place. He told his tale and inquired about boats; there were no boats and no lodging nearer than Callander, ten miles beyond the foot of the lake. A laugh was in every face when Wm said we were come to see the Trossachs; no doubt they thought we had better have stayed at our own homes. Wm endeavoured to make it appear not so very foolish, by informing them that it was a place much celebrated in England, though perhaps little thought of by them, and that we only differed from many of our countrymen in having come the wrong way in consequence of an erroneous direction.

'After a little time the gentleman said we should be accommodated by such beds as they had, and should be welcome to rest in their house if we pleased. Wm came back for C and me; the men all stood at the door to receive us, and now their behaviour was perfectly courteous. We were conducted into the house by the same man who had conducted us hither on the other side of the lake, and afterwards we learned he was the father of our hostess. He showed us into a room upstairs, begged we would sit at our ease, walk out, or do just as we pleased. It was a large square deep wainscoted room, the wainscots black with age, yet had never been painted. It did not look like an English room, and yet I do not know in what it differed, except that in England it is not common to see a large well-built room so ill-furnished; there were two or three large tables, and a few old chairs of different sorts, as if they had been picked up one did not know how, at sales, or had belonged to different rooms of the house ever since it was built. We sate perhaps three quarters of an hour, and I was about to carry down our wet coffee and sugar and ask leave to boil it, when the mistress of the house entered - a tall fine-looking woman, neatly dressed in a dark-coloured gown, with a white handkerchief tied round her head; she spoke to us in a very pleasing manner, begging permission to make tea for us, an offer we thankfully accepted, encouraged by the sweetness of her manners, I went downstairs to dry my feet by the kitchen fire; she lent me a pair of stockings, and behaved to me with the utmost attention and kindness. She carried the tea-things into the room herself, leaving me to make tea, and set before us cheese and butter and barley-cakes. These cakes were as our oat-bread, but, instead of being crisp, are soft and leathery, yet we, being hungry, and the butter delicious, ate them with great pleasure, but when the same bread was set before us afterwards we did not like it.

'After tea Wm and I walked out: we amused ourselves with watching the highlanders at work: they went leisurely about everything, and whatever was to be done all followed, old men, and young, and little children. We were driven into the house by a shower, which came on with the evening darkness, and the people leaving their work paused at the same time. I was pleased to see them a while after sitting round a blazing fire in the kitchen, father and son-in-law, master and man and the mother with her little child on her knee. When I had been there before tea I had observed what a contrast there was between the mistress and her kitchen; she did not differ in appearance from an English country lady; but her kitchen, roof, walls, and floor of mud, were all black alike; yet now, with the light of the bright fire upon so many countenances, the whole room made a pretty sight.

'We heard the company talking and laughing long after we were in bed; indeed I believe they never work till they are tired. The children could not speak a word of English: they were very shy at first, but after I had caressed the eldest, and given her a red leather purse, with which she was delighted, she took hold of my hand and hung about me, changing her sidelong looks for pretty smiles. Her mother lamented they were so far from school, they should be obliged to send the children down to the lowlands to be taught reading and English. Callander, the nearest town, was twenty miles from them, and it was only a small place: they had their groceries from Glasgow. She said that at Callender was their nearest church, but they sometimes "got a preaching at the Garrison." In explaining herself, she informed us that the large building which had puzzled us in the morning had been built by the Government, at the request of one of the dukes of Montrose, for the defence of his domains against the attacks of Rob Roy. I will not answer for the truth of this; perhaps it might have been built for this purpose; and as a check in the Highlands in general; certain it is however that it was a garrison; soldiers used to be continually stationed there, and have only been withdrawn within the last thirteen or fourteen years. Mrs. Mcfarland attended me to my room; she said she hoped I would be able to sleep upon blankets, and said they were fresh from the Fauld.'

August 27th, Saturday, 'Before I rose Mrs. Macfarlande came into my room to see if I wanted anything,' - here we have Dorothy certainly appreciating the beautiful hospitality of the Scots, especially those living in wild and isolated places -'and told me she would send the servant up with a basin of whey, saying "we make very good whey in this country," indeed I thought it the best I had ever tasted; but I cannot tell how this should be, for they only make skimmed milk cheeses. I asked her for a little bread and milk for our breakfast, but she said it would be no trouble to make tea, as she must make it for the family; so we all breakfasted together. The cheese was set out as before, with plenty of butter and barley cakes, and fresh baked oaten cakes, which, no doubt, were made for us: they had been kneaded with cream and were excellent. All the party pressed us to eat and were very jocose about the necessity of helping out their coarse bread and butter, and they themselves ate almost as much butter as bread. In talking of the French and the present times, their language was what most people would call Jacobincial. They spoke much of the oppressions endured by the Highlanders further up, and of the absolute impossibility of their living in any comfort, and of the cruelty of laying so many restraints on emigration. Then they spoke with animation of the attachment of the clans to their lands:- "The Laird of this place, Glengyle, where we live, could have commanded so many men who would have followed him to the death; and now there are none left." It appeared that Mr. Macfarlane, and his wife's brother, Mr. Macalpine, farmed the place, inclusive of the whole vale upwards to the mountains, and the mountains themselves, under the lady of Glengyle, the mother of the young laird, a minor. It was a sheep farm.

'Speaking of another neighbouring Laird, they said he had gone, like the rest of them, to Edinburgh, left his lands and his own people, spending his money where it brought him not any esteem, so that he was of no value either at home or abroad. We mentioned Rob Roy, and the eyes all glistened; even the lady of the house who was very diffident, and no great talker, exclaimed, "He was a good man, Rob Roy!" He had been dead only about eighty years, had lived in the next farm, which belonged to him, and there his bones were laid.' This is mistaken. He is buried about 15 or 20 miles from thence in Balqidder Kirkgard. 'He was a famous swordsman. Having an arm much longer than other men, he had a greater command with his sword. As a proof of the length of his arm, they told me that he could garter his tartan stockings below the knee without stooping, and added a dozen different stories of single combats, which he had fought in perfect good humour, merely to prove his powers. I daresay they had stories of this kind which would hardly have been exhausted in the long evenings of a whole December week, Rob Roy being as famous here as even Robin Hood was in the Forest of Sherewood, he also robbed from the rich, giving to the poor and defending them from oppression. They will tell of his confining the factor of the Duke of Montrose in one of the islands of the Loch Ketterine, after having taken his money from him (the Duke's rents) in open day, while they were sitting at table. He was a formidable enemy of the Duke, but being a small laird against a greater, was overcome at last, and forced to resign all his lands on the Braes of Loch Lomond (including the caves which we visited), on account of the money he had taken from the Duke and could not repay.

'When breakfast was ended the mistress desired the person whom we took to be her husband to "return thanks". He said a short grace, and in a few minutes they all went off to their work. We saw them about the door following each other like a flock of sheep, with the children after, whatever job they were engaged in.

'Mrs. Macfarlane told me she would show me the burying place of the lairds of Glengyle, and took me to a square enclosure like pinfold, with a stone ball at each corner; we noticed it in the evening before, and wondered what it could be. It was in the middle of a 'planting' as they call plantations, which was enclosed for the preservation of the trees, therefore we had to climb over a high wall; it was a dismal spot, containing four or five graves overgrown with long grass, nettles and brambles. Against the wall was a marble monument to the memory of one of the lairds, of whom they spoke with veneration. Some English verses were inscribed upon the marble, purporting that he had been the father of the clan, a brave good man. When we returned to the house she said she would show me what curious feathers they had in their country, and brought out a bunch carefully wrapped in paper. On my asking her what bird they came from, 'Oh' she replied, 'It is a great beast'! We conjectured it was an eagle, and from her description of its ways, and the manner of destroying it, we knew it was so. She begged me to accept some of the feathers, telling me that some ladies wore them in their heads. I was much pleased with the gift, and I shall preserve it in memory of her kindness and simplicity of manners, and the Highland solitude where she lived.' This lady was obviously very taken with Dorothy, as real country people so often were, and could not do enough for her. The gift of the eagle feathers is a marvellous token for 'To give is an act of love'.

'We took leave of the family with regret. They were handsome healthy and happy-looking people. It was ten o'clock when we departed. We had learned that there was a ferry boat kept at three miles distance, and if the man was at home he would row us down the lake to the Trossachs. Our walk was mostly thro coppice woods, along a horse-road, upon which narrow carts might travel. Passed that white house which had looked at us with such a friendly face when we were on the other side; it stood on the slope of a hill; with green pastures below it, plots of corn and coppice-wood, and behind, a rocky steep covered with wood. It was a very pretty place, but that morning being cold and dull the opposite shore appeared dreary. Near to the white house we passed by another of those little pinfold squares, which we knew to be a burying place: it was a sloping green field among woods, within sound of the beating water against the shore, if there were but a gentle breeze to stir it; I thought if I lived in that house, and my ancestors and kindred were buried there, I should sit many an hour under the walls of the plot of earth, where all the household would be gathered together.' Dorothy, who was so much friends with areas of peace, who was even in her mind so much at peace with the idea of death among natural sounds; I think of how she and William and Mary, much, much later, buried Hartley Coleridge, when he, a poet also, died 6th January 1849 in Nab Cottage, just up the road from them; how they buried Hartley amongst those in their family plot in Grasmere Churchyard, knowing he would want to lie amongst them - a child of their community, a child of nature - and he, at peace there.

'We found the ferryman at work in the field above his hut, he

213

was at liberty to go with us, but, being wet and hungry, we begged that he would let us sit by his fire till we had refreshed ourselves. This was the first genuine Highland hut we had been in. We entered by the cow-house, the house-door being within, at right angles to the outer-door. The woman was disturbed that she had a bad fire, but she heaped up some dry peats and heather, and blowing it with her breath, in a short time raised a blaze that scorched us into comfortable feelings. A small part of the smoke found its way out of the hole in the chimney, the rest through the open window places, one of which was within the recess of the fireplace, and made a frame to a little picture of the restless lake and the opposite shore, seen when the outer door was open.' Dorothy loved these framed glimpses of the world outside through windows, of odd places, the doors left ajar from one room to another in the twilight. She came to the Highland hut where the beasts were within the house-place, their byre and tall door being at right angles to the outer door.

'The woman of the house was very kind: whenever we asked for anything it seemed a fresh pleasure to her so that she had it for us. She always answered with a sort of softening down of the Scotch exclamation, 'Hoot!', "Ho! Yes you'll get that," and hied to her cupboard in the spence. We were amused with the phrase 'Ye'll get that' in the Highlands, which appeared to us as if it came from a perpetual feeling of the difficulty with which most things are procured. We 'got' oatmeal, butter, bread and milk, made some porrige, and then departed. It was rainy and cold, with a strong wind.'

Here Dorothy writes beautifully of the especial magic of Scotland, in her fairy tale lakes and rocks, mountains and islands. 'C was afraid of the cold in the boat, so he determined to walk down the lake, pursuing the same road we had come along.' - 'The wind fell, and it began to rain, heavily. On this Wm wrapped himself in the boatman's plaid, and lay at the bottom of the boat till we came to a place where I could not help rousing him. We were rowing down that side of the lake which had little to see, little else than a moorish ridge. After turning a rocky point we came to a bay closed in by rocks and steep woods, chiefly of full grown birch. The lake was elsewhere ruffled, but at the entrance of this bay the breezes sunk, and it was calm; a small island was near, and the opposite shore, covered with wood, looking soft through the misty rain. Wm, rubbing his eyes for he had been asleep, called out that he hoped that I had not let him pass by anything that was as beautiful as this; and I was glad to tell him that it was the beginning of a new land. After we had left this bay we saw before us a long reach of woods and rocks and rocky points, that promised other bays more beautiful than what we had passed. The ferryman was a good-natured fellow, and rowed very industriously following the ins and outs of the shore; he was delighted with the pleasure we expressed continually repeating how pleasant it would have been on a fine day. I believe he was attached to the lake by some sentiment of pride, as his own domain (his being almost the only boat upon it), which made him (seeing we were willing gazers) take far more pains than the ordinary boatman; he would often say, after he had compassed the turning point, "This is a bonny part," and he always chose the bonniest, with greater skill, that our prospect-hunters and picturesque travellers' places screened from the winds - that was the first point; the rest followed of course - richer growing trees, rocks and banks and curves which the eye delights in.

'The second bay we came to differed from the rest; the hills retired a short space from the lake, leaving a few level fields between, on which was a cottage embosomed in the trees: The bay was defended by rocks at each end, and the hills behind made a shelter for the cottage, the only dwelling, I believe, except one, on this side of Loch Ketterine. We now came to steeps that rose directly from the lake, and passed by a place called in Gaelic, The Den of the Ghosts, which reminded us of Lodore: it is a rock, or man of rock, with a stream of large black stones like the naked or dried-up bed of a torrent down the side of it; birch trees start out of the rock in every direction, and cover the hill above, further than we can see. The water of the lake below was very deep, black, and calm. Our delight increased as we advanced, till we came in view of the termination of the lake, seeing where the river issues out of it through a narrow chasm between the hills.

'Here I ought to rest, as we rested, and attempt to give utterance to our pleasure; but indeed I can impart but little of what we felt, we were still on the same side of the water, and, being immediately under the hill, within a considerable bending of the shore, we were enclosed by hills all round, as if we had been on a smaller lake of which the whole was visible. It was an entire solitude; and all that we beheld was the perfection of loveliness and beauty; we had been through many solitary places since we came to Scotland, but this place differed as much from any we had seen before, as if there had been nothing in common between them; no thought of dreariness or desolation found entrance here; yet nothing was to be seen but water, wood, rocks, and heather, and bare mountains above. We saw the mountains by glimpses as the clouds passed by them, - and were not disposed to forget, with our boatman that it was not a fine day, for the near objects were not concealed from us, but suffered from being seen through the mists. The lake was not very wide here, but appeared to be much narrower than it really is, owing to the many promontaries, which are pushed so far into it that they are much more like islands than promontaries. We had a longing desire to row to the outlet and look up into the narrow passage through which the river went; but the point where we were to land was on the other side, so we bent our course right across, and just as we came in sight of two huts, which have been built by Lady Perth as a shelter for those who visit the Trossachs C hailed us with a shout of triumph from the door of one of them, exulting in the glory of Scotland. The huts stand at a small distance from each other, on a high and perpendicular rock, that rises from the bed of the lake. A road, which has a very wild appearance, has been cut through the rock; yet even here, among these bold precipices, the feeling of excessive beautifulness overcomes every other. While we were upon the lake, on every side of us were bays within bays, often more like tiny lakes or pools than bays, and these not in long succession only, some almost on the broad breast of the water, the promontaries shot out so far.

'After we had landed we walked along the road to the uppermost of the huts, where C was standing. From the door of this hut

216

we saw Benvenue opposite to us - a high mountain, but clouds concealed its top; its side, rising directly from the lake, is covered with birch trees to a great height, and seamed with innumerable channels of torrents; but now there was no water in them, nothing to break in upon the stillness and repose of the scene; nor do I recollect hearing the sound of water from any side, the wind being fallen and the lake perfectly still; the place all eye, and completely satisfied the sense and heart. Above and below us, to the right and to the left, were rocks, knolls and hills, which, wherever anything could grow (and that was everywhere between the rocks) were covered with trees and heather; the trees did not in any place grow so thick as an ordinary wood; and yet I think there was never a bare space of twenty yards; it was more like a natural forest where the trees grow in groups or singly, not hiding from the surface of the ground which, instead of being green and mossy, was of the richest purple. The heather was indeed the most luxuriant I ever saw; it was so tall that a child of ten years old struggling through it would often have been buried head and shoulders, and the exquisite beauty of the colour, near or at a distance, seen under the trees, is not be conceived. But if I were to go on describing thus for evermore, I should give but a faint, and very often a false, idea of the different objects and the various combinations of them in the most intricate and delicious places; besides I tired myself out with describing at Loch Lomond, so I will hasten to the end of my tale. This reminds me of a sentence in a little pamphlet written by the minister of Callander, descriptive of the environs of that place. After having taken up at least six closely written pages with the Trossachs, he concludes thus, "In a word the Trossachs beggar all description," a conclusion in which everybody who has been there will agree with him. I believe the word 'Trossach' signifies many hills; it is a name given to all the eminences at the foot of Loch Ketterine, and about a half a mile beyond.

'We left the hut, retracing a few lines of the road which we had climbed; our boat lay at anchor under the rock in the last of all the compartments of the lake, a small oblong pool, almost shut up within itself, as several others had appeared to be, by jutting points of rock. It was the termination of a long outshooting of water, pushed up between the steeps of the main shore (where the huts stand) and a broad promontory which, with its hillocks and points and lesser promontaries, occupies the centre of the foot of the lake. A person sailing through the lake up the middle of it, would just as naturally suppose that the outlet was here as on the other side; and so it might have been, with the most trifling change in the disposition of the ground, for at the end of this strip of water the lake is confined only by a gentle rising of a few yards towards an opening between the hills, a narrow pass or valley through which the river might have flowed. The road is carried through this valley, which only differs from the lower part of the vale of the lake in being excessively narrow, and without water; it is enclosed by mountains, rocky mounds, hills and hillocks scattered over with birch trees, and covered with Dutch myrtle and heather, even surpassed what we had seen before. Our Mother Eve had made no fairer, though a more diversified garden to tend, than we found within this little close valley. It rained all the time, but the mists and calm air made us ample amends for the wetting.

'At the opening of the pass we climbed up a low eminence, and had an unexpected prospect suddenly before us - another lake, small compared with Ketterine, though perhaps four miles long, but the misty air concealed the end of it. The transition from the solitary wildness of Loch Ketterine and the narrow valley or pass to this scene was very delightful: it was a gentle place with lovely open bays, one small island, corn fields, woods, and a group of cottages. This vale seemed to have been made to be a tributary to the comforts of man, Loch Ketterine too for the lonely delight of Nature, and kind spirits delighting in beauty. The sky was grey and heavy, - and floating mists on the hillsides, which softened the objects, and where we lost sight of the lake it appeared so near to the sky that they almost touched one another giving a visionary beauty to the prospect. While we were overlooking this quiet scene we could hear the stream rumbling along the rocks between the lakes, but the mists concealed any glimpse of it which we might have had. This small lake is called Loch Achray.

'We returned of course by the same road. Our guide repeated over and over again his lamentation that the day was so bad, though we had often told him (not indeed with much hope that he would believe us) that we were glad of it. As we walked along he pulled a leafy twig from a birch tree, and, after smelling it, gave it to me saying, how sweet and halesome it was, and that it was pleasant and very halesome on a fine summer's morning to sail under the banks where the birks are growing. This reminded me of the old Scotch songs, in which you continually hear of the "pu'ing the birks". Common as birches are in the north of England, I believe their sweet smell is a thing unnoticed among the peasants. We returned again to the huts to take a farewell look. We had shared out food with the ferryman and a traveller whom we had met here, who was going up the lake, and wished to lodge at the ferryhouse, so we offered him a place in the boat. C chose to walk. We took the same side of the lake as before, and had much delight in visiting the bays over again; but the evening began to darken, and it rained so heavily before we had gone two miles that we were completely wet. It was dark when we landed, and on entering the house I was sick with cold.

'The good woman had provided, according to her promise, a better fire than we had found in the morning; and indeed when I sat down in the chimney corner of her smoking 'biggin' I thought I had never been more comfortable in my life. C had been long enough to have a pan of coffee boiling for us, and having put our clothes in the way of drying, we all sate down, thankful for the shelter. We could not prevail upon the man of the house to draw near the fire, though he was cold and wet, or to suffer his wife to get him dry clothes till she had served us, which she did, though most willingly, not very expeditiously.

'A Cumberland man of the same rank would not have had such a notion of what was fit and right in his own house, or if he had, one would have accused him of servility; but in the Highlander it only seemed like politeness (however erroneous and painful to us) naturally growing out of the dependence of the inferiors of the Clan upon their laird: he did not, however, refuse to let his wife bring out the whiskey-bottle at our request: "she keeps my dram" as the phrase is; indeed I believe there is scarcely a lonely house by the wayside in Scotland where travellers may not be accommodated with a dram. We asked for sugar, butter, barley bread, and milk, and with a smile and a stare more of kindness than wonder, she replied, "Ye'll get that", bringing each article separately. We caroused our cups of coffee, laughing like children at the strange atmosphere in which we were; the smoke came in gusts, and spread along the walls and above our heads in the chimney, where the hens were rousting like light clouds in the sky; we laughed and laughed again, in spite of the smarting of our eyes, yet had a quieter pleasure in observing the beauty of the beams and rafters, gleaming between clouds of smoke. They had been crusted over and varnished by many winters, till, where the firelight fell upon them, they were as glossy as black rocks on a sunny day cased in ice. When we had eaten our supper we sate about half an hour, and I think I had never felt so deeply the blessing of a hospitable welcome and a warm fire. The man of the house repeated from time to time that we should often tell of this night when we got to our homes, and interposed praises of his own lake, which he had more than once, when we were returning to the hut, ventured to say was "bonnier than Loch Lomond".' This was very much Dorothy's scene, in the wilds of Scotland, with these very simple, hospitable people, and having come in from their day on the beautiful wild lake worshipping nature with William and Coleridge; her love for and lovely descriptions of the scene: the rafters, the smoke where the hens roosted like 'light clouds in the sky'. She was hidden in the heart of her own wild sort of reality.

CHAPTER 12

Dorothy carries on with her 'Recollections', describing the house and their sleeping there very beautifully: 'Our companion from the Trossachs, who it appeared was an Edinburgh drawing-master going during the vacation on a pedestrian tour to John-o-Groat' house, was to sleep in the barn with Wm and Coleridge, where the man said he had plenty of dry hay. I do not believe that the hay of the Highlands is often very dry, but this year it had a better chance than usual: wet or dry, however, the next morning they said they had slept comfortably. When I went to bed, the mistress, desiring me to 'go ben' attended me with a candle, and assuring me that the bed was dry, though not "sic as I had been used to". It was of Chaff: there were two others in the room, a cupboard and two chests, on one of which stood the milk in wooden vessels covered over; I should have thought that milk so kept could not have been very sweet, but the cheese and butter were good. The walls of the whole house were of stone unplaistered. It consisted of three apartments, - the cow-house at one end, the kitchen or house in the middle, and the spence at the other end. The rooms were divided, not up to the rigging, but only to the beginning of the roof, so that there was a free passage for light and smoke from one end of the house to the other.

'I went to bed some time before the family. The door was shut between us, and they had a bright fire, which I could not see; but the light it sent up amongst the varnished rafters and beams which crossed each other in almost as intricate and fantastic a manner as I have seen the underboughs of a large beech-tree withered by the depths of the shade above, produced the most beautiful effect that can be conceived. It was like what I should suppose an underground cave or temple to be, with a dripping moist roof, and the moonlight entering in upon it by some means or other, and yet the colours were more like the colours of melted gems. I lay looking up till the light of the fire faded away, and the man and his wife and child had crept into their bed at the other end of the room.

I did not sleep much, but passed a comfortable night, for my bed, though hard, was warm and clean: the unusualness of my situation prevented me from sleeping. I could hear the waves beat against the shore of the lake; a little Syke close to the door made a much louder noise; and when I sate up in my bed I could see the lake through an open window-place at the bed's head. Add to this, it rained all night. I was less occupied by the remembrance of the Trossachs, beautiful as they were, than the vision of the Highland hut, which I could not get out of my head. I thought of the Fairyland of Spenser, and what I had read in romance at other times, and then, what feast it would be for a London Pantomime maker, could he but transplant it to Drury Lane with all its beautiful colours.' This is indeed a jewel among Dorothy's many very beautiful descriptions.

August 28th, Sunday, 'We were desirous to have crossed the mountains above Glengyle to Glenfalloch at the head of Loch Lomond, but it rained so heavily that it was impossible, so the ferryman engaged to row us to a point where C and I had rested, while Wm was going our doubtful adventure. The hostess provided us with tea and sugar for breakfast; the water was boiling in an iron pan, and dealt out to us in a jug, a proof that she does not often drink tea, though she said she had always tea and sugar in the house. She and the rest of the family breakfasted on curds and whey, as taken out of the pot in which she was making cheese; she insisted on my taking some also; and her husband joined in with the old story that it was "Varra halesome". I thought it exceedingly good, and said to myself that they lived nicely with their cow: She was meat and drink and company. Before breakfast the housewife was milking behind the chimney, and I thought I had seldom heard a sweeter fire-side sound; in an evening, sitting over a sleepy low-burnt fire, it would lull one like the purring of a cat.

'When we departed the good woman shook me cordially by the hand, saying she hoped that if ever we came into Scotland again, we would come and see her. The lake was calm, but it rained so heavily that we could see little.

'When beginning to descend the hill towards Loch Lomond, we overtook two girls, who told us we could not cross the ferry till evening, for the boat was gone with a number of people to church. One of the girls was exceedingly beautiful; and the figures of both of them, in grey plaids falling to their feet, their faces being uncovered, excited our attention before we spoke to them; but they answered us so sweetly that we were quite delighted, at the same time that they stared at us with an innocent look of wonder. I think I never heard the English language sound more sweetly than from the mouth of the elder of these girls, while she stood at the gate answering our inquiries, her face flushed with rain; her pronunciation was clear and distinct; without difficulty, yet slow, like that of foreign speech. They told us we might sit in the ferry-house till the return of the boat, went in with us, and made a good fire as fast as possible to dry our wet clothes. We learnt that the taller was the sister of our ferryman, and had been left in charge with the house for the day, that the other was his wife's sister, and was come with her mother on a visit, - an old woman, who sate in a corner beside the cradle, nursing her little grandchild. We were glad to be housed, with our feet upon a warm hearth-stone; and our attendants were so active and good-humoured that it was pleasant to have to desire them to do anything. The younger was delicate and unhealthy-looking girl; but there was an uncommon meekness in her countenance, with an air of premature intelligence, which is often seen in sickly young persons. The other made me think of Peter Bell's Highland Girl:

'As light and beauteous as a squirrel
As beauteous and as wild!'

She moved with unusual activity, which was chastened very delicately by a certain hesitation in her looks. When she spoke, being able to understand us but imperfectly. They were both exceedingly desirous to get me what I wanted to make me comfortable. I was to have a gown, a petticoat of the mistress's; so they turned out the whole wardrobe upon the parlour floor, talking Erse to one another, and laughing all the time. It was long before they could decide which of the gowns I was to have; they chose at last, no doubt thinking that it was the best, a light-coloured sprigged cotton, with long sleeves, and they both laughed while I was putting it on, with the blue lindsey petticoat, and one or the other, or both together, helped me to dress, repeating at least half a dozen times, "You never had on the like of that before". They had a consultation of several minutes over a pair of coarse woollen stockings, gabbling Erse as fast as their tongues would move, and looked as if uncertain what to do: at last, with great diffidence, they offered them to me, adding as before, that I had never worn "the like of them". When we entered the house we had been not a little glad to see a fowl stewing in barley-broth; and now when the wettest of our clothes were stripped off, began again to recollect that we were hungry, and asked if we could have dinner. "Oh yes, ye may get that", the elder replied, pointing to the pan on the fire.

'Conceive what a busy house it was - all our wet clothes to be dried, dinner prepared and set out for us four strangers, and a second cooking for the family; add to this, two rough Callans, as they called them, about eight years old, were playing beside us; the poor baby was fretful all the while, the old woman sang doleful Erse songs, rocking it in its cradle the more violently the more it cried; then there were a dozen cookings of porridge, and it could never be fed without the assistance of all three. The hut was after the Highland fashion, but without anything beautiful except its situation; the floor was rough, and wet with the rain that came in at the door, so that the lasses bare feet were as wet as if they had been walking through street puddles, in passing from one room to another; the windows were open, as at the other hut; but the kitchen had a bed in it, and was much smaller, and the shape of the house was like that of a common English cottage, without its comfort; yet there was no appearance of poverty - indeed, quite the contrary. The peep out at the open door place across the lake made some amends for the want of the long roof and elegant rafters of our Boatman's cottage, and all the while the waterfall, which we could not see, was roaring at the end of the hut, which seemed to serve as a sounding-board for its noise, so that it was not unlike sitting in a house where a mill is going. The dashing of the waves against the shore could not be distinguished; yet in spite of my knowledge of this I could not help fancying that the tumult and storm came from the lake, and went out several times to see if it was possible to row over safely.'

One is reminded of Katleen Rain's lines about Gavin Maxwell's house, 'Camusfeàrna':

'In my love's house
There is a waterfall that flows all night'.

'After long waiting we grew impatient for our dinner: at last the pan was taken off and carried into the other room; but we had to wait at least another half hour before the ceremony of dishing up was completed; and yet with all this bustle and difficulty, the manner in which they (particularly the elder of the girls) performed everything was prefectly graceful; we ate a hearty dinner, and had time to get our clothes quite dry before the arrival of the boat. The girls could not say at what time it would be at home; on our asking if the churches were far off they replied "not very far"; and when we asked how far, they said "Perhaps about four or five miles". I believe a Church of England congregation would hold themselves excused for non-attendance three parts of the year, having but half as far to go; but in the lonely parts of Scotland they made little of a journey of nine or ten miles to a preaching. They have not perhaps an opportunity of going more than once in a quarter of a year, and, setting piety aside, have other motives to attend: they hear the news public and private, and see their friends and neighbours; for though the people who meet at these times may be gathered together from a circle of 20 miles diameter, a sort of neighbourly connection must be so brought about. There is something extraordinarily pleasing to my imagination in this gathering together or the inhabitants of these secluded districts - for instance the borders of these two large lakes meeting at the deserted garrison which I have described. The manner of their travelling is on foot, on horseback, and in boats across the waters - young and old, rich and poor, all in their best dress.'

Dorothy here has intuited something very old, in the remote country district as far back as the Neolithic times people have come for distances of ten - thirty miles to meet, at borders of lakes and lands, at sacred places, standing stones, stone-circles, to hear the news, the trade, to arrange marriages, to see remote friends and neighbours, to make peace treaties even and to arrange territorial boundaries, to dance in the harvest-time, to pray for the sun to return in midwinter, to arrange for burials and funeral ceremonies - all that is communal and to do with the crossing over of boundaries between tribes, and to do with the friendly rituals like those of animals that keep peace amongst them.

'If it were not for these Sabbath-day meetings one summer month would be like another - detached from the goings on of the world, and solitary throughout; from the time of earliest childhood they will be like landing-places in the memory of a person who has passed his life in these thinly peopled regions; they must generally leave distinct impressions, differing so from each other so much as they do in circumstances, in time and place, etc., - some in open fields, upon hills, in houses, under large rocks, in storms, in fine weather.

'But I have forgotten the fireside of our hut. After long waiting, the girls, who had been on the look-out, informed us that the boat was coming. I went to the water-side, and saw a cluster of people on the opposite shore; but being yet at a distance, they looked more like soldiers surrounding a carriage than a group of men or women; red and green were the distinguishable colours. We hastened to get ourselves ready as soon as we saw the party approach, but had longer to wait than we expected, the lake being wider than it appears to be. As they drew near we could distinguish men in tartan plaids, women in scarlet cloaks, and green umberellas by the half dozen. The landing was as pretty a sight as ever I saw. The bay which had been so quiet two days before, was all in motion with small waves while the swollen waterfall roared in our ears. The boat came steadily up, being pressed almost to the water's edge by the weight of her cargo; perhaps twenty people landed, one after another. It did not rain much, but the women held up their umberellas; they were dressed in all the colours of the rainbow, and, with their scarlet cardinals, the tartan plaids of the men, or Scotch bonnets, made a gay appearance. There was a joyous bustle surrounding the boat, which even imparted something of the same character to the waterfall in its tumult, and the restless grey waves; the young men laughed and shouted, the lasses laughed, and the

226

elder folks seemed to be in a bustle to be away. I remember well with what haste the mistress of the house where we were ran up to seek after her child, and seeing us, how anxiously and kindly she inquired how we had fared, if we had had a good fire, and been well waited upon, etc., etc. All this in three minutes - for the boatman had another party to bring from the other side and hurried us off.

'The hospitality we met with at the two cottages and Mr. Macfarlane's gave us very favourable impressions on this our first entrance into the Highlands, and at this day the innocent merriment of the girls, with their kindness to us, and the beautiful figure and face of the elder, come to my mind whenever I think of the ferry-house and water-fall of Loch Lomond, and I never think of the two girls but the whole image of that romantic spot is before me, a living image as it will be to my dying day. The following poem was written by Wm not long after our return from Scotland:

'Sweet Highland Girl, a very shower
Of beauty is thy earthly dower!
Twice seven consenting years have shed
Their utmost beauty on thy head,
And these grey rocks, this household lawn
These trees, a veil just half withdrawn,
This fall of water that doth make
A murmur near the silent lake;
This little Bay, a quiet road
That holds in shelter thy abode;
In truth together you do seem
Like something fashioned in a dream;
Such forms as from their covert peep
When earthly cares are laid asleep,
Yet dream and vision as thou art
I bless thee with a human heart:
God shield thee to thy latest years!
I neither know thee nor thy peers,
And yet my eyes are filled with tears.

With earnest feeling I shall pray
For thee when I am far away:
For never saw I mien or face
In which more plainly I could trace
Benignity and home-bred sense
Ripening in perfect innocence;
Here, scattered like a random seed
Remote from men, thou dost not need
Th'embarrassed look of shy distress
And maidenly shamefacedness;
Thou wear'st upon thy forehead clear
The freedom of a mountaineer.
A face with gladness overspread!
Sweet looks by human-kindness bred.
And seemliness complete that sways
Thy courtesies about thee plays;
With no restraint but such as springs
From quick and eager visitings
Of thoughts that lie beyond the reach
Of thy few words of English speech:
A bondage sweetly brooked, a strife
That gives thy gestures grace and life!
So have I not unmoved in mind
Seen birds of tempest-loving kind,
Thus beating up against the wind.

What hand but would a garland cull
For thee who art so beautiful?
O happy pleasure! Here to dwell
Beside thee in some heathy dell
Adopt your homely ways and dress,
A shepherd, thou a Sherperdess!
But I could frame a wish for thee
More like a grave reality
Thou art to me but as a wave
Of the wild sea: and I would have

Some claim upon thee if I could,
Though but of common neighbourhood.
What joy to hear thee and to see!
Thy elder brother I would be,
Thy father, anything to thee.

Now thanks to Heaven that of its grace
Hath led me to this lonely place!
Joy have I had, and going hence
I bear away my recompense.
In spots like this it is we prize
Our memory, feel that she hath eyes,
Then why should I be loth to stir?
I feel the place is made for her;
To give new pleasure like the past
Continued long as life shall last.
Nor am I loth, tho pleased at heart,
Sweet highland Girl, from thee to part;
For I methinks as I grow old
As fair before me shall behold
As I do now; the cabin small,
The lake, the Bay, the waterfall,
And thee, the spirit of them all.'

Dorothy's prose and William's poem are both very beautiful
about this episode and the girl. Here we see their equality as great
writers, who deeply loved and inspired each other.
    'We were rowed over speedily by the assistance of two youths,
who went backwards and forwards for their own amusement, helping
at the oars, and pulled as if they had strength and spirit to spare for
a year to come; we noticed that they had uncommonly fine teeth,
and that they and the boatman were very handsome people. Another
merry crew took our place in the boat.
    'We had then three miles walk to Tarbet. It rained but not
heavily; the mountains were not concealed from us by the mists,
but appeared larger and more grand; twilight was coming on, and

the obscurity under which we saw the objects, with the sounding of the torrents, kept our minds alive and wakeful; all was solitary and huge - sky, water, and mountains mingled together. While we were walking forward, the road leading us over the top of the brow, we stopped suddenly at the sound of a half articulated Gaelic hooting from the field close to us; it came from a little boy, whom we could see on the hill between us and the lake, wrapped up in a grey plaid; he was probably calling home the cattle for the night. His appearance in the highest degree moving to the imagination - mists on the hillsides, darkness shutting in upon the huge avenue of mountains, torrents roaring, no house in sight to which the child might belong; his dress, cry and appearance all different from anything we had been accustomed to. It was a text as Wm has since observed to me, containing in itself the whole history of the highlander's life - his melancholy, his simplicity, his poverty, his superstition, and above all, that visionariness which results from communion with the unworldliness of nature. Coleridge also describes this and their note and poem as so often echo each other "Never never let me forget that small herdboy in his tartan plaid, dim-seen on the hilly field, and long heard ere seen, a melancholy voice calling to his cattle! - nor the beautiful harmony of the heath, the dancing fern and ever moving birches". This also may have inspired Wordsworth's 'The Solitary Reaper' among other lovely sights.

'When we reached Tarbet the people of the house were anxious to know how we had fared, particularly the girl who had waited upon us. Our praises of Loch Ketterine made her exceedingly happy, and she ventured to say (of which we had not heard a word before) that it was "bonnier to her fancy than Loch Lomond". The landlord who was not at home when we had set off, told us that if he had known of our going he would have recommended us to Mr. Macfarlane's or the other farmhouse, adding that they were hospitable people in that vale. C and I got tea; and Wm and the drawing master chose supper; they asked to have a broiled fowl, a dish very common in Scotland, to which the mistress replied, "Would not a 'boiled' one do as well?" They consented, supposing that it would be more easily cooked, but when the fowl made its appearance, to their great disappointment it proved a cold one that had been stewed in the broth at dinner.'

August 29th, Monday, 'It rained heavily this morning, and having heard so much of the long rains since we came into Scotland, as well as before, we had no hope that it would be over in less than three weeks at the least; so poor C being very unwell, determined to send his clothes to Edinburgh and make the best of his way thither, being afraid to face much wet weather in an open carriage. Wm and I were unwilling to be confined at Tarbet, so we resolved to go to Arrochar, a mile and a half on the road to Inverary, where there is an inn celebrated as a place of good accommodation for travellers. C and I set off on foot, and Wm was to follow with the car, but a heavy shower coming on, C left me to shelter in a hut and wait for Wm, while he went on before. This hut was unplastered, and without windows, crowded with beds, uncomfortable, and not in the simplicity of the ferryman's house. A number of good clothes were hanging against the walls, and a green silk umberella was set up in a corner. I should have been surprised to see an umberella in such a place before we came to the Highlands; but umberellas are not so common anywhere as there, a plain proof of the wetness of the climate; even five minutes after this a girl passed us without shoes and stockings; whose gown and petticoat were not worth half a crown, holding an umberella over her bare head!

''Left Arrochar at about four o'clock in the afternoon. C accompanied us a little way; we portioned out the contents of our purse before our parting; (Coleridge kindly only took 6 guineas from their communal 35) and, after we had lost sight of him, drove heavily along, crossed the bridge, and looked to the right, up the vale, which is soon terminated by mountains; it was of a yellow-green, with but a few trees and few houses; sea-gulls were flying above it. Our road (the same along which the carriages had come) was directly under the mountains on our right hand, and the lake was close to us on our left, the waves breaking among stones overgrown with yellow sea-weed, fishermen's boats and other larger vessels than are seen on freshwater lakes were lying at anchor near the opposite shore; sea-birds flying overhead; the noise of the torrents mingling with the beating of the waves, and misty mountains enclosed the vale; a melancholy but not a dreary scene. Often have I, in looking over a map of Scotland, followed the intricate windings of one of these sea-lochs, till, pleasing myself with my own imaginings, I felt a longing, almost painful, to travel among them by land or by water.

'This was the first sea-loch we had seen. We came prepared for a new and great delight, and the first impression which Wm and I received, as we drove rapidly through the rain down the lawn of Loch Arrochar, the objects dancing before us; was even more delightful than we had expected; but, as I have said, when we looked through the window, as the mists disappeared and the objects were seen more distinctly, there was less of sheltered valley-comfort than we had fancied to ourselves, and the mountains were not so grand; and now that we were near to the shore of the lake, and could see that it was not of fresh water, the wrack, the broken sea-shells, and scattered sea-weed gave somewhat of a dull uncleanly look to the whole lake, and yet the water was clear, and might have appeared as beautiful as that of Loch Lomond, if with the same pure pebbly shore. Perhaps had we been in a more cheerful mood of mind we might have seen everything with a different eye; the stillness of the mountains, the motion of the waves, the streaming torrents, the sea-birds, the fishing boats were all melancholy; yet still, occupied as my mind was with other things, I thought of the long windings through which the waters of the sea had come to this island retreat, visiting the inner solitudes of the mountains, and I could have wished to have mused out a summers day on the shores of the lake. From the foot of these mountains whither might not a little barque carry one away? Though so far inland, it is but a slip of the great ocean: seamen, fishermen and shepherds here find a natural home.'

These thoughts of Dorothy's about the inner solitude of the mountains and about the travels in the little barque are very much of a piece with her thoughts about Coleridge, of him voyaging alone; and the inner solitudes of the mountains being like the caverns in Kubla Kahn.

'We did not travel far down the lake, but turning to the right through an opening of the mountains entered a glen called Glen Croe.

'Our thoughts were full of Coleridge, and when we were enclosed in the narrow dale, with a length of winding road before us, a road that seemed to have insinuated itself into the very heart of the mountains (the brook, the road, bare hills, floating mists, scattered stones, rocks and heads of black cattle being all we could see) I shivered at the thought of his being sickly and alone, travelling from place to place.' Coleridge on the contrary when he got away from William and Dorothy, and their absorption in each other, which he felt was rather to the exclusion of himself, actually made a very good walking tour of Scotland on his own marred by an illness at Fort William due to opium withdrawal. The highlanders looked after him kindly. At Perth he recovered his sense of reality at the news of the death of Southeys daughter Margaret, and that Southey was coming to Greta Hall to be comforted. 'The Cobbler, on our right, was pre-eminent above the other hills; the singular rocks on its summit, seen so near, were like ruins, castles or watchtowers. After we had passed one reach of the glen, another opened out, long, narrow, deep, and homeless, with herds of cattle and large stones; but the third reach was larger and more beautiful, as if the mountains had there made a warmer shelter, and there were a more gentle climate; the rocks by the river-side had dwindled away, the mountains were smooth and green, and towards the end, where the glen sloped upwards, it was a cradle-like hollow, and at that point where the slope became a hill, at the very bottom of the curve of the cradle, stood one cottage; with a few fields and beds of potatoes. There was also another house near the roadside, which appeared to be a herdsman's hut, being the only one in the vale, had a melancholy face; not being attached to any particular plot of land, one could not help considering it as just kept alive and above ground by some dreary connection with the long barren tract we had travelled through. The afternoon had been exceedingly pleasant after we had left the vale of Arrochar; the sky was often threatening, but rain blew off, and the evening was uncommonly fine. The sun had set a short time before we had dismounted from the car to walk up the hill at the end of the glen; the clouds were moving all over the sky, some of a brilliant yellow hue, which shed a light like bright moonlight upon the mountains. We could not have seen the head of the valley under more favourable circumstances; and the passing away of a storm is always a time of life and cheerfulness, especially in the mountainous country; but the afternoon and evening sky was in an extraordinary degree vivid and beautiful. We often stopped in ascending the hill to look down the long reach of the glen. The road following the course of the river as far as we could see, the farm and cottage, hills smooth towards the bare and rocky higher up, were the sole objects before us. This part of Glen Croe reminded us of some of the dales of the north of England - Grisdale above Ulswater for instance; but the length of it, and the broad highway, which is always to be seen at a great distance, a sort of centre of the vale, a point of reference, gives the whole of the glen and each division of it, a very different character.

'Soon after we had climbed the hill we began to descend into another glen, called Glen Kinglas. We now saw the Western sky, which had hitherto been hidden from us by the hill - a glorious mass of clouds uprising from a sea of distant mountains, stretching out its length before us, towards the west, and close by was a small lake or tarn. From the reflection of the crimson clouds the water appeared of a deep red, like melted rubies, yet with a mixture of grey or blackish hue; the gorgeous light of the sky, with the singular colour of the lake, made the scene exceedingly romantic; yet it was more melancholy than cheerful. With all the power of light from the clouds, there was an overcasting of the gloom of evening, a twilight upon the hills.

'We descended rapidly into the glen, which resembles the lower part of Glen Croe, though it seemed to be inferior in beauty; but before we had passed through one reach it was quite dark and I only know that the steeps were high, and that we had the company of a foaming stream; and many a vagrant torrent crossed us, dashing down the hills. The road was bad, and, uncertain how we should fare, we were eager and somewhat uneasy to get forward, but when we were out of the close glen, and near Cairndow, (as a traveller had told us), the moon showed her clear face in the sky, revealing a spacious vale, with a broad loch and sloping cornfields; the hills were not very high. This cheerful sight put us into spirits, and we thought it was at least no dismal place to sit up all night in, if they had no beds, and they could not refuse us a shelter. We were, however, well received, and sate down in a neat parlour with a good fire.'

'August 30th, Tuesday, 'Breakfasted before our departure, and ate a herring, fresh from the water, at our landlord's earnest recommendation - much superior to the herring we get in the north of England. Though we rose at seven, could not set off before nine o'clock; the servants were in bed; the kettle did not boil - indeed we were completely out of patience; and it had always been so, and we resolved to go off in future without breakfast. Cairndow is a single house by the side of the loch, I believe resorted to by gentlemen in the fishing season; it is a pleasant place for such a purpose; but the vale did not look so beautiful as by moonlight - it had a sort of sea-coldness without mountain grandeur. There is a ferry for foot-passengers from Cairndow to the other side of the water, and the road along which all carriages go is carried round the head of the lake, perhaps a distance of three miles.

'After we had passed the landing place of the ferry opposite to Cairndow we saw the lake spread out to a great width, more like an arm of the sea or a great river than one of our lakes; it reminded me of the Severn at the Chepstow passage; but the shores were less rich and the hills higher. The sun shone, which made the mornings cheerful, though there was a cold wind; our road never carried us far from the lake, and with the beating of the waves, the sparkling sunshiny water, boats, the opposite hills, and on the side on which we travelled, the chance cottages, the coppice woods, and common business of the fields, the ride could not be but amusing. But what most excited our attention was, at one particular place, a cluster of fishing boats at anchor in a still corner of the lake, a still bay or harbour by the wayside; they were overshadowed by fishermen's nets hung out to dry, which formed a dark awning, that covered them like a tent, overhanging the water on each side, and falling in the most exquisite graceful folds. There was a monastic pensiveness, a funereal gloom in the appearance of this little company of vessels, which was the more interesting from the general liveliness and glancing motion of the water, they being perfectly still and silent in their sheltered nook.

'We had travelled about seven miles from Cairndow, winding round the bottom of a hill, we came in view of a great basin or elbow of the lake. Completely out of sight of the long track of water we had coasted; we seemed now to be on the edge of a very large, almost circular, lake, the town of Inverary before us, a line of white buildings on a low promontory right opposite, close to the water's edge; the whole landscape a showy scene, and bursting upon us at once. A traveller who was riding by our side called out, "Can that be the castle?" Recollecting the prints which we had seen, we knew it could not; but the mistake was a natural one at that distance; it is so little like an ordinary town, from the mixture of regularity and irregularity in the buildings with the expanse of water and pleasant mountains and scattered boats and sloops, and those gathered together, it had a truly festive appearance. A few more steps brought us in view of the castle, a stately turreted mansion, but with a modern air, standing on a lawn, retired from the water, and screened behind by woods covering the sides of high hills to the top, and still beyond, by bare mountains. Our road wound round the semi-circular shore, crossing two bridges of lordly architecture. The town looked pretty when we drew near to it in connexion with the situation, different from any place I have ever seen, yet exceedingly like what I imagine to myself from representations in raree-shows, or pictures of foreign places (Venice for example) painted on the scenery of a play-house, which one is apt to fancy are as cleanly and gay as they look through the magnifying glass of the raree-show or in the candle-lit dazzle of the theatre. At the door of the Inn, though certainly the buildings had not that delightful outside which they appeared to have at a distance, yet they looked very pleasant.'

'Returning through the town, we went towards the castle, and entered the Duke's grounds by a porter lodge, following the carriage road through the park, which is prettily scattered over with trees, and slopes gently towards the lake. A great number of lime trees were growing singly, not beautiful in their shape, but I mention them for resemblance to one of the same kind we had seen in the morning, which formed a shade as impenetrable as the roof of any house. The branches did not spread far, nor any branch much further than another; on the outside it was like a green bush shorn with shears, but when we sate upon a bench under it, looking upwards, in the middle of the tree we could not perceive any green at all; it was like a hundred thousand magpie's nests clustered and matted together, the twigs and boughs being so intertwined that neither the light of a midday sun nor showers of hail or rain could pierce them through. The lime-trees on the lawn resembled the trees both in shape and in the manner of intertwisting their twigs, but they were much smaller, and had not an impenetrable shade.

'The views from the castle are delightful. Opposite is the lake, girt with mountains, or rather small high hills; to the left appears a very steep rocky hill, called Duniquoich Hill, at the top of which is a building like a watchtower; it rises boldly and almost perpendicular from the plain, at a little distance from the River Avey, that runs through the grounds. To the right is the town, overtopped by a sort of spire or pinnacle of the church, a thing universal in Scotland, except in the large towns, and which would often give an elegant appearance to the villages, which, from the uniformity of the huts, and the frequent want of tall trees, they seldom exhibit.'

'Sate in the park till the moonlight was perceived more than the light of day. We then walked near the town by the waterside. I observed that the children who were playing did not speak Erse, but a much worse English than is spoken by those Highlanders whose common language is Erse. I went into the town to purchase tea and sugar to carry with us on our journey. We were tired when we returned to the inn, and went to bed directly after tea. My room was at the very top of the house - one flight of steps after another! - but when I drew back the curtains of my window I was repaid for the trouble by panting upstairs by one of the most splendid moonlight prospects that can be conceived; the whole circuit of the hills, the castle, the bridges, the tower on Duniquoich Hill, and the lake with many boats - fit scene for summer midnight festivities! I should have liked to have seen a bevy of Scottish ladies sailing, with music, in a gay barge. William, to whom I read this, tells me that I have used the very words of Brown of Ottery, Coleridge's fellow-townsman.'

> 'As I have seen on the breast of the Thames
> A heavenly bevy of sweet English dames,
> In some calm evening of delightful May,
> With music give a farewell to the day,
> Or as they would (with an admired tune)
> Greet night's Ascension to her ebony throne.'

Brown's Brittania Pastoral.

August 31st, Wednesday, 'We had a long day's journey before us, without a regular baiting place on the road, so we had breakfast at Inverary, and did not set off till nine o'clock having, as usual, to complain of the laziness of the servants - Our road was up the valley behind the castle, the same as we had gone along the evening before. Further up, through the plantations on the hills are noble, the valley was cold and naked, wanting hedgerows and comfortable houses. We travelled several miles under the plantation, the vale all along seemed to belong almost exclusively to the castle. It might have been better distinguished and adorned, as we thought, by neater farm-houses and cottages than are common in Scotland, and snugger fields with warm hedgerows, at the same time testifying its adherence to the chief.

'At that point of the valley where the pleasure grounds appear to end, we left our horse at a cottage door and turned a few steps out of the road to see a waterfall, which roared so loud that we could not have gone by without looking about for it, even if we had not known that there was one near Inverary. The waterfall is not remarkable for anything but the good taste with which it has been left to itself, though there is a pleasure-road from the castle to it. As we went further up the valley the woods died away, and it became an ordinary Scotch glen, the poor pasturage of the hills creeping down into the valley, where it was little better for the shelter, I mean little greener on the hill-sides, but a man must be of churlish nature if, with a mind free to look about, he should not find such a glen a pleasing place to travel through, seeing nothing but the busy brook, with here and there a bush or tree, and cattle pastured near the thinly scattered dwellings. But we came to one spot which I cannot forget, a single green field at the junction of another brook with the Avey, a peninsular surrounded by a close row of trees, which overhung the streams, and under their branches we could just see a neat white house that stood in the middle of the field enclosed by fields. Before us nothing but bare hills, and the road through the bare glen. A person who has not travelled in Scotland can scarcely imagine the pleasure we have had from a stone house, though fresh from the workmen's hands, square and sharp; there is generally such an appearance of equality in poverty through the long glens of Scotland, giving the notion of savage ignorance - no house better than another, and barns and houses all alike. This house had, however, other recommendations of its own; even in the fertile parts of Somerset it would have been a delicious spot; here, "Midmountain wild set like a little nest", it was a resting place for the fancy, and to this day I often think of it, the cottage in its green covert, as an image of romance, a place of which I have the same sort of knowledge as some of the retirements, the little valleys, described so vividly by Spenser in his "Fairy Queen".

'After walking down the hill a long way we came to a bridge, under which the water dashed through a dark channel of rocks among trees, the lake being at a considerable distance below, with cultivated lands between. Close upon the bridge was a small hamlet, a few houses near together, and huddled up in trees - a very sweet spot - the only retired village we had yet seen which was characterised by beautiful wilderness with sheltering warmth. We had been told at Inverary that we should come to a place where we might give our horse a feed of corn, and found on inquiry that there was a little publick-house here, or rather a hut "where they kept a dram". It was a cottage like all the rest, without a signboard - The woman of the house helped to take the horse out of harness, and,

239

being hungry, we asked her if she could make us some porrige, to which she replied, "we should get that" and I followed her into the house, and sate over her hearth while she was making it; as to fire, there was little sign of it, save the smoke, for a long time, she having no fuel but green wood, and no bellows but her breath - My eyes smarted exceedingly, but the woman so kind and cheerful that I was willing to endure it for the sake of warming my feet in the ashes and talking to her. The fire was in the middle of the room, a crook being suspended from a crossbeam, and a hole left at the top for the smoke to find its way out by; it was a rude Highland hut, unadulterated by Lowland fashions, but it had not the elegant shape of the ferry-house at Loch Ketterine, and the fire, being in the middle of the room, could not be such a snug place to draw to on a winters night.'

This is typical of Dorothy, that even if the Highland hut was not fine, she so liked and appreciated the character of the woman of the house that she came into and sat warming her feet in the ashes, and talked with this kind and cheerful woman. It seems to have been close to a 'round house' of the Iron Age, with the fire in the centre of the room, and a hole in the roof for the smoke to find its way out. A primitive dwelling, but illuminated by the kindness and cheerfulness of the woman of the house who readily talked and gave them a meal.

'We had a long afternoon before us, with only eight miles to travel to Dalmally, and, having been told that a ferryboat was kept at one of the islands, we resolved to call for it, and row to the island, so we went to the top of an eminence, and the man who was with us set some children to work to gather sticks and withered leaves to make a smokey fire, a signal for the boatman, whose hut is on a flat green island, like a sheep pasture, without trees, and of a considerable size: the man told us it was a rabbit warren. There were other small islands, on one of which was a ruined house fortification, or small castle; we could not learn anything of the history, only a girl told us that formerly gentlemen lived in such places. Immediately from the water's edge rose the mountain Cruachan on the opposite side of the lake; It is woody near the water and craggy above, with deep hollows on the surface. We thought it was the grandest mountain we had seen, and on saying to the man who was with us that it was a fine mountain, "Yes", he replied, "It is an excellent Mountain", adding that it was higher than Ben Lomond, and then told us some wild stories of the enormous profits it brought to Lord Breadalbane, its lawful owner. The shape of Loch Awe is very remarkable, its outlet being at one side, and only about eight miles from the head, and the whole lake twenty-four miles in length. We looked with longing after that branch of it opposite to us out of which water issues: it seemed almost like a river gliding under the steep precipices. What we saw of the larger branch, of what might be called the body of the lake, was less promising, the banks being merely gentle slopes, with not very high mountains behind, and the ground moorish and cold.

'The children, after having collected fuel for our fire, began to play on the green hill where we stood, as heedless as if we had been trees or stones, and amused us exceedingly with their activity; they wrestled, rolled down the hill, pushed one another over and over again, laughing and screaming, and chattering Erse! They were all without shoes and stockings, which making them fearless of hurting or being hurt, gave a freedom to the action of their limbs which I never saw in English children; they stood upon one another, body, breast or face, or any other part; sometimes one was uppermost, sometimes another, and sometimes they rolled all together, so that we could not know to which body this leg or that arm belonged. We waited, watching them,' A marvellous memorable description by Dorothy of these Highland children, 'till we were assured that the boatman had noticed our signal. By the by if we had received proper directions at Loch Lomond, on our journey to Loch Ketterine, we should have made our way down the lake till we had come opposite the ferryman's house, where there is a hut, and the people who live there are accustomed to call him by the same signal as here. Luckily for us we were not so well instructed, for we should have missed the pleasure of receiving the kindness of Mr. and Mrs. Macfarlane and their family!

'When we had gone a little way we saw before us a young man with a bundle over his shoulder, hung on a stick, bearing a great boy on his back; seeing that they were travellers, we offered to take the boy on the car, to which the man replied that he should be more than thankful, and set him up beside me. They had walked from Glasgow, and that morning from Inverary; the boy was only six years old. "But," said his father, "he is a stout walker", and a fine fellow he was, smartly dressed in light clean clothes and a nice round hat; he was going to stay with his grandmother at Dalmally. I found him good company; though I could not draw a single word out of him, it was a pleasure to see his happiness gleaming through the shy glances of his healthy countenance. Passed a pretty chapel by the lakeside, and an island with a farmhouse upon it, and corn and pasture fields; but, as we went along, we had to regret the want of English hedgerows and English culture; for the ground was often swampy or moorish near the lake where comfortable dwellings among green fields might have been. When we came near to the end of the lake we had a steep hill to climb, so Wm and I walked; and we had such confidence in our horse that we were not afraid to leave the car to his guidance with the child in it; we were soon, however, alarmed at seeing him trot up the hill a long way before us; the child having raised himself up upon the seat, was beating him as hard as he could with a little stick which he carried in his hand; and when he saw our eyes were on him he sate down, I believe very sorry to resign his office, the horse slackened his pace and no accident happened.'

* * * * * * *

These recollections of a tour made in Scotland of Dorothy's was written out by her in order to be read by such friends of hers as Mrs. Cookson, Sara Hutchinson, Coleridge (when he returned), who all loved and appreciated it. Dorothy also gave a private reading to the Clarksons.

The poet Samuel Rogers read one of Dorothy's copies and said that it should be published. Samuel Rogers met the Wordsworths early in the tour, when Coleridge was yet with them, and he said, "Wordsworth and Coleridge were entirely occupied in talking about poetry; and the whole care of looking out for cottages where they might get refreshment and pass the night, as well as seeing their poor horse fed and littered, devolved upon Miss Wordsworth. She is a most delightful person, so full of talent, so simple-minded and so modest." However, the Recollections of a Tour made in Scotland were not published till nearly 20 years after Dorothy's death. It was maybe a good thing, as Dorothy had 'tidied up' William's clumsiness, like dropping all their supplies into the lake!

Dorothy had to interrupt her writing out of her memories in December 1803 when Coleridge came to stay, very ill and querulous. She began again in February 1804, but was again interrupted to make a copy of all William's poems for Coleridge to take abroad. This really disturbed her and she tried hopelessly to continue until William really urged and encouraged her on. Dorothy continued writing out her memories in April 1805 and finally finished them at the end of May that year.

These journals of Dorothy's are all the time mentioning her deep relationship with her brother William, true and spiritual lovers who inspired each other; 'on a wander by ourselves' as Dorothy said when they found Alfoxden Park.

Dorothy's love and poetry extended to her nephews and nieces, William and Mary's children, whom she looked after so much. Dorothy later left alone at home nursing little John and Dora while Mary, pregnant again, was staying with Sara at Park House, where William joined her.

Dorothy wrote poems for her little nephew and niece:

'What way does the wind come, where does he go?
He rides over water and over snow,
Through wood and through vale; o'er rock height
Which the goat cannot climb, takes his sounding flight;
He tosses about in every bare tree
As, if you look up, you plainly may see,
But how he will come, and whither he goes,
There's never a scholar in England knows.'

Dorothy's songs to the children of the house. Dorothy too was a child in the house.

BIBLIOGRAPHY

Journals of Dorothy Wordsworth. Ed. Mary Moorman (1971).
Dorothy Wordsworth, the Grasmere Journals. Ed. Pamela Woof (1995).
Journals of Dorothy Wordsworth Vol. 1. Ed. E. de Selincourt (1952).
Home at Grasmere. Ed. Colette Clark (1960) Extracts from the journals of Dorothy Wordsworth and from the poems of William Wordsworth.
Letters of Dorothy Wordsworth, A selection. Ed. Alan G. Hill (1981).
Dorothy Wordsworth. Robert Gittings and Jo Manton (1985).
William Wordsworth Selected Poems. Ed. Walford Davies (1975).
The Works of William Wordsworth. The Wordsworth poetry library (1994).
William Wordsworth, A Life. Stephen Gill (1989).
William Wordsworth, The Prelude. Ed. T. Maxwell (1971).
The Borders of Vision. Jonathan Wordsworth (1982).
Samuel Taylor Coleridge. A critical edition of the major works Ed. H. Jackson (1985).
Coleridge, Early Visions. Richard Holmes (1989).
Coleridge at Nether Stowey. The National Trust, compiled by Ursula Codrington (1972).
Unruly Times, Wordsworth and Coleridge and Their Time. A. S. Byatt (1989).
Recollections of the Lakes and the Lake Poets. Thomas De Quincy Ed. David Wright (1970).

William Wordsworth Guide to the Lakes. Ed. Ernest de Selincourt (1906).
Letters of William Wordsworth. Ed. Alan G. Hill. A selection (1984).
Lakeland Poets. Illustrated collection compiled by Jenny Wilson, photographs by Rob Talbot (1991).
William Wordsworth Poems. Ed. John O. Hayden English Poetry Penguin (1997).
The Prelude, William Wordsworth. A parallel text. Ed. J. C. Maxwell (1971).